McCall's big book of
QUILTS
and OTHER TREASURES

Also available

McCall's New Book of Needlecrafts
McCall's New Book of Country Needlecrafts

McCall's big book of
QUILTS
and OTHER TREASURES

The Editors of
McCall's Needlework & Crafts Magazine

W.H. ALLEN · LONDON
1985

First published in the United States of America
by Chilton Book Company
First British edition 1985

Printed and bound in Great Britain by
Mackays of Chatham Ltd, Kent
for the Publishers, W.H. Allen & Co. PLC
44 Hill Street, London W1X 8LB

ISBN 0 491 3690 6

Contents

Bold figure is picture page, roman figure is instruction page

General Directions

Quilting

The History of Quilting

The origins of quilting, like those of most needlework, are vague and indistinct, obscured by the veil of centuries of time. The basic construction of layers of fabric, with or without some form of padding between them, has been used as protection and insulation for the human body, and as covering for both beds and floors, for thousands of years. The oldest example known to exist is a carpet found on the floor of a tomb, probably made during the first century B.C. Curiously enough, the quilted pattern in the center of that carpet consists of rows of spirals joined by smaller scrolls between the large circles—a very familiar type of pattern still in extensive use today.

From there the record skips to the early Middle Ages, when two heavy outer fabrics, quilted with layers of soft padding between them, were worn as body armor by the armies of William the Conqueror and the Crusaders. Even when armor of chain or plate was introduced, quilted armor was still worn underneath it, as protection against cold weather and chafing.

Quilted armor probably inspired the use of quilted bedcovers, which are mentioned in inventories and household accounts of the eleventh, twelfth, and thirteenth centuries. And when, in the fourteenth century, a drastic change in the climate of western Europe resulted in winters of unprecedented, lacerating coldness, the quilted bedcover became, quite literally, a necessity of life. The first quilting frames were invented, and anything that would add warmth to the bedcovers made on them served as padding; moss, feathers, and even grass were used

as well as lambs' wool. Quilted clothing for everyday wear, also inspired by the armor, must have appeared about this time; evidence exists that quilted garments were worn at least as early as the beginning of the fifteenth century.

The outer layers of sturdy linen or canvas and the various materials used as padding for quilted armor were simply stitched together with strong thread in straight lines. Protection was the prime concern, and there was no need or desire for any kind of decorative stitching. But as quilting came to be used for clothing and household articles, it was seen that the stitching made a kind of surface decoration, and quilting stitches were soon designed to be more decorative. Scrolls and ornamental motifs were stitched on caps, gloves, and shoes as well as on bedcovers, and by the end of the fourteenth century, bedcovers—or quilts—were being decorated with elaborate stitched designs depicting knights, kings, and castles as well as horses, ships, and flowers.

In southern Europe, where winters were less rigorous, quilting was regarded solely as a means of embellishment. Here trapunto, or corded quilting, came into use because the added warmth of padding wasn't needed. A cord inserted in a channel between two stitched layers of fabric served to outline or emphasize part of a design. In another version, the second layer of fabric was dispensed with, and the cord was simply stitched to the wrong side of a single layer of fabric, giving the same raised effect.

This was all very well for the sunny south of Europe, but in the north quilting was serious business, depended upon as vital protection against the inclement weather. In Britain and Holland it became a kind of business, developing into something akin to a cottage industry. The quilting became more intricate, and as the level of craftsmanship rose, quilts—or "bed furniture," as they were called—became the most-prized possessions of many families. As such, they were passed down from generation to generation, gaining status with every change of ownership. Many were embroidered with pious mottoes and some were decorated with appliqués, but they all differed from later American versions in that the top was always a single piece of fabric—and so, usually, was the backing.

Thus, born of necessity but gradually developing into a folk art, quilts became so important that a kind of mystique grew up around them. The female members of a family started quiltmaking at an early age and thereafter spent a major portion of their time at the quilting frame. Every young girl was intent on having a full quota of intricate quilts in her dowry. When she became formally engaged, her Bridal Quilt was begun, with appropriate ceremony. This would be the most elaborate quilt in her collection, and friends and relatives would be invited to help her finish it.

Like so many other customs, this one crossed the ocean with the pilgrim families who emigrated to America. They often could bring very little, but bed furniture was always included in anticipation of the hard winters ahead. The hard winters came and were—somehow—survived; the unwelcoming land was eventually conquered. But the settlers were poor and had no way of replacing even essential possessions when they wore out. Everything was repaired as completely as possible and used again and again—"recycled," as we say today. This was certainly true of the family quilts, which were patched up with scraps of fabric from old clothing as long as they held together. After many repairs, the quilt top looked more like patchwork than solid

fabric. So again, necessity was the mother of handsome invention, because these worn-out and patched-up quilts were the forerunners of the beautiful and inventive patchwork patterns of the eighteenth and nineteenth centuries.

More and more settlers arrived, and the bitter struggle for survival in the New World gradually gave way to economic prosperity. Commerce between Europe and America was brisk, and trade routes to the Near East and the Orient were established. Imported fabrics became available, at least on the Atlantic seaboard, but the thrifty Colonial housewife still made use of every scrap of fabric. The idea of making bedcovers of patchwork instead of solid pieces of fabric took hold, and now, having at least a little more choice, the industrious quiltmakers began to aspire to attractive color combinations and arrangements.

As the New England colonies and parts of the South became more populated, the more adventurous souls of the day continued their pioneering push westward. Once again, the family quilts went with them and in barren new homes became even more firmly entrenched as basic furnishing. Exposure to new lands, new experiences, and new emotions gave the women new ideas, which found expression in their continued quiltmaking. A patchwork quilt became a kind of chronicle, reflecting what was happening to a family. And since these hard-working pioneer women had to spin and weave their own fabrics, old garments became the major source of patchwork materials. Cut up and used for patches only after years of service and being "handed down," the well-used fabrics were also a kind of history of family life.

In addition to recording family history, quilts became an important part of social life. The custom of friends and relatives gathering to help make a marriage quilt developed into the quilting bee, which was a major social event in the life of the small communities. They were often engagement parties, but no special occasion was needed for friends and relatives to

A typical Bridal Quilt, always the showpiece of
a betrothed girl's dower chest. Here, printed cotton
fabrics are appliquéd on white blocks. No two prints are
identical, but all have a similar soft red background.
A block in the bottom row is embroidered with
the words "Priscilla Halton's Work, 1849."

gather for a day of stitching and gossip followed by an evening of eating and socializing after the men joined the party.

As imported fabrics became more plentiful back in the Colonies, they also became more expensive, and a textile industry began to evolve. Before long, cloth was being produced in a wide selection of colors at lower prices than the bolts that came by sailing ship commanded. Coincidentally or not, appliqué work became popular about this time, and the practice of applying decorative pieces of one fabric over another gave a new dimension to quilts. True, it was considered an extravagant waste of fabric by many still-thrifty settlers, but it gained in popularity none the less. The appli-

Distinctive Hawaiian quilts were created when the wives of New England missionaries taught Hawaiian women how to sew. Since their attire had consisted of grass skirts and flower leis, they had no stockpile of patches and cut large, single-color designs from new fabric.

quéd quilts were kept for "best" and were brought out for display and limited use only on special occasions. Thus, many beautiful examples still exist, whereas antique patchwork quilts, which were used day after day for generations, are rare.

Quiltmaking remained a household art as well as a popular pastime until fabrics manufactured by machine became widely available. Except for a few brief spurts of popularity after that, quiltmaking was largely forgotten until the renaissance of interest in all needlework and crafts swept the country in the 1960s. Since then, some crafts have risen and fallen in favor, but the challenge and satisfaction of quilting—and, by association, of patchwork and appliqué—continue to increase. As more and more people feel compelled to create something of lasting value with their own hands, quiltmaking seems more and more the answer.

Quilting Equipment

Since quilting is simply the stitching that holds two or more layers of material together, it can be done with a few very basic tools. The necessities are pins, needles, thread, and scissors. The other tools and aids listed here are necessary or useful for making patterns and templates, for preparing and finishing fabric, and for the sewing involved in quiltmaking.

PINS

Pins must be fine and sharp for accurate pinning of seams and small pieces of fabric. Some quilters prefer glass-headed pins for anchoring layers of fabric and padding together because they're easy to see and don't get "lost" in puffy quilting. T-pins, upholstery pins, or safety pins are also useful for this purpose.

NEEDLES

Needles for hand quilting should be short, strong, and sharp, between No. 7 and No. 10. A No. 8 or No. 9 needle, specifically, is often recommended for beginners; experienced quilters may prefer a longer one. Have a good supply of the size you prefer on hand so several can be threaded at one time and waiting; this avoids interrupting your work at frequent intervals to rethread a single needle. Fine needles can also be used to pin delicate fabrics that may be marred or damaged by regular pins. When quilting by machine, use a new, medium-sized needle, such as No. 14; needles that have been used for any length of time may be blunted.

THREAD

Thread coated with silicone, specifically made for quilting, is best because it's strong and rather stiff; however, it is not available everywhere and comes in a comparatively limited range of colors. Heavy-duty threads are easy to work with because they're strong and durable. No. 5 mercerized cotton thread has traditionally been used for quilting, but many people now prefer cotton-wrapped polyester-core thread because of its strength and stretchability, although it sometimes has a tendency to knot.

SCISSORS

Scissors should be sharp and should have slender points for accurate cutting. In addition to cutting shears, it is convenient to have a pair of small embroidery scissors handy for fine work and clipping into seam allowances around curves.

LEAD PENCILS

Pencils must be sharply pointed and hard enough to trace cleanly and accurately. When marking dark fabrics for appliqués, use a light-colored pencil. Soft lead pencils should not be used; they'll smudge your fabric, and the lead will come off on hands and paper.

DRY BALL-POINT PEN

Dry ball-point pens are preferred by some people for tracing patterns. The rounded point will not break or tear dressmaker's tracing paper.

TRACING WHEEL

Tracing wheels are useful and fast for tracing large-scale patterns and marking seam lines or long quilting patterns.

PAPER FOR PATTERNS

Paper for patterns should be kept on hand. Any plain paper is suitable for patterns that will be used only once or a few times. Thin, stiff cardboard should be used if the pattern will be traced repeatedly. Edges can be coated with clear nail polish to prevent fraying. Rolls of newsprint (not newspaper) and shelf paper are good for planning, laying out, or copying long quilting patterns. If these are not readily available, tape sheets of plain paper together to obtain the necessary length.

TRACING PAPER

Tracing paper is the thin, transparent paper used by commercial artists; it is needed for copying and transferring patterns.

DRESSMAKER'S TRACING PAPER

Dressmaker's tracing paper is actually carbon paper that comes in a range of colors; it is used with a tracing wheel or other marker for transferring patterns to fabric. It is usually sold in packs that include a selection of colors suitable for use on both light and dark fabrics.

LARGE-GRID GRAPH PAPER

Large-grid graph paper is ideal for copying patterns that must be enlarged. The alternative is to rule plain paper in 1" or 2" squares, whichever is specified in the directions.

PLASTIC OR SANDPAPER SHEETS

Plastic or sandpaper sheets are also used for making patterns and templates. Sandpaper won't slide around on fabric, as cardboard sometimes does. Templates cut from plastic sheets are firm and durable; the transparent type is especially easy to use.

RULER, YARDSTICK, AND TAPE MEASURE

Ruler, yardstick, and tape measure are all useful (and at least one is necessary) for measuring patterns and fabrics, tracing or making patterns, and laying them out.

BEESWAX

Beeswax is useful for the quilter. Running thread across a cake of beeswax or paraffin will both strengthen it and make it easier to pull through thick layers of material.

IRONING BOARD AND IRON

Ironing board and iron should be set up and ready to use to make all the steps involved in quilting and quiltmaking go faster. Fabrics to be quilted should be ironed thoroughly before the layers are tacked together; removing wrinkles and creases is difficult after they have been stitched. Fabric should also be ironed before being marked for cutting so that both marking and cutting will be accurate. The turning allowance on pieces to be appliquéd by hand must be turned and pressed with an iron to ensure a smooth, even edge. Seam allowances should be pressed open or flat.

QUILTING FRAMES AND HOOPS

Quilting frames and hoops not only make quilting easier and better but also save time, because without a frame the layers must be basted together much more closely. A quilting frame was once considered indispensable for keeping the layers of material stretched evenly together and fairly taut while the quilting stitches were being taken through them. Frames large enough for full-size quilts traditionally rested on the backs of four low-backed "quilting chairs," which were standard equipment in Early American kitchens. Such frames went the way of rooms large enough to accomodate them easily for long periods, and adjustable embroidery frames small enough to be used on a table and even smaller double-ring frames known as quilting hoops took their place. The back of a smoothly finished picture frame can also be used for smaller pieces. Today quilting is often done a section at a time with the work resting in one's lap. If using a hoop, start in the center of the piece, pulling it taut between the rings. As you work toward the edges, you can use smaller embroidery hoops to keep the layers taut.

Fabrics Used for Quilting

Linen was originally used more than any other fabric for quilted bedcovers as well as for quilted clothing. Later, silk fabrics, including satin, and various types of woolen material were used for bed quilts until they were largely replaced by cotton prints around the end of the eighteenth century. Sturdy, economical cottons have been used ever since for everyday quilts of the padded variety, with silks and satins being reserved for "best.'

Fabrics used for either quilting or patchwork should be smooth, soft, and firmly woven. For making serviceable, everyday quilts, they should also be washable, wrinkle-resistant, and colorfast. Many expert quilters feel that only fabrics made of natural fibers, notably cotton, meet all these specifications. Broadcloth, calico, medium-weight gingham, percale, and poplin are just a few of the cotton weaves that are suitable for quilting. All-synthetic fabrics are generally considered hard to quilt, especially by hand, but cotton-and-polyester blends, which combine cotton's softness with polyester's easy-care characteristics, are a good solution. Fabrics made of rayon are also considered unsuitable for quilting, as is heavy satin or any stiff, thick fabric that is difficult to pierce with a needle.

The top and backing of padded quilts, which are often reversible, are frequently of the same fabric, or at least of similar quality. If economy is an important factor, inexpensive muslin sheeting, challis, or flannel makes a sturdy backing. Sheer or loosely woven fabric is not a good choice for the quilt top, but a loosely woven fabric that has a little "give" is sometimes best for the backing of corded or stuffed quilts. Silk fabrics in soft, smooth weaves, if affordable, make luxurious tops for padded or stuffed quilts but should not be used for corded quilting; the cord tends to make the silk wear poorly.

An amazing variety of materials has been used for padding down through the centuries, including paper. Wool in many forms, including old blankets, was used when warmth was still the major consideration. Layers of thin flannel were a popular choice until comparatively recently, because they lie flat and are easy to stitch through. Cotton batting came next and was the traditional choice for American quilts until polyester batting appeared. Considered by most contemporary quilters to be the best material available for padding, polyester batting is inexpensive to buy by the yard, is easy to quilt, and washes and dries quickly without bunching up or wadding. It's light and fluffy (although surprisingly warm) and gives quilts a desirable puffiness without the weight of former fillers. The layers can also be pulled and stretched to a thinner consistency if less puffiness is desired.

Preparing to Quilt

LINING AND BATTING

Cut or piece lining and batting as directed. If they are to be same size as the quilt top, you may want to make them a little larger to start with, such as 1″ all around, and trim after basting or quilting.

For comfortable hand quilting, the lining fabric should be soft; sheets, for example, are too densely woven for the needle to pass through easily.

In planning the batting, consider the style of the quilt and its intended use. Antique quilts with their close, ornate quilting designs usually were made with only a very thin filler. If you wish to duplicate the effect, use a split layer of polyester batting. The thinner the layer of batting, the easier and finer the quilting will be. For simpler quilting designs, or where more loft or warmth is desirable, use one or two full layers of polyester batting. Polyester is generally preferable to cotton batting, because it holds together, does not lump, and will dry quickly if the quilt is washed. If using cotton batting, be sure your lines of quilting are no more than 2″ apart.

BASTING

After the quilting design has been marked on the quilt top, assemble top, batting, and lining: Place lining, wrong side up, on large, flat surface. Place batting on top of lining and smooth out any bumps or wrinkles. Before adding quilt top, baste batting to lining by taking two long stitches in a cross. Place quilt top on batting, right side up. Pin all layers together to hold temporarily, using large safety pins. Baste generously through all thicknesses, using a sturdy thread and a large needle. To prevent shifting, first baste on the lengthwise and crosswise grain of fabric, then baste diagonally across in two directions and around sides, top, and bottom. If quilting is to be done with a quilting hoop or on the machine, extra care must be taken to keep basting stitches close, so they will hold in place as you work.

Quilting by Hand

The two basic hand quilting stitches are a short running stitch and the backstitch; the running stitch is the one most frequently used, especially for anything quilted with a fairly thick layer of padding. The running stitch is always used if the work is reversible or will be seen from the wrong side. Each stitch, as well as the space between it and the next, should be the same on both sides, so the pattern will be identical on both sides. Using a No. 9 quilting needle threaded with an 18″ length of quilting or heavy-duty thread, knotted at one end, start in the center of the piece or section to be worked. Bring the needle up from the backing through the padding and the quilt top; tug on the thread gently so the knot passes through the backing and lies buried in the padding. Stitching along the marked line, push the needle straight down through all layers with one hand; take the needle in the other hand, which is held beneath the work, pull the thread through the layers, and push the needle back up through the top close to the point where it was first inserted, thus taking a

small stitch. This is called a "stab" stitch and is the method of stitching recommended for beginners. An experienced quilter may be able to take two, three, or four stitches before pulling the needle all the way through by holding the needle at a slant in one hand while holding the work in place with the thumb of the other hand. This usually can be done successfully only if the work is held taut in a frame.

The backstitch is practical only when a thin layer of padding is used between the top and the backing and the back of the work isn't likely to be seen. The stitches should be short and very even. Starting with a single running stitch, insert the needle where the thread was brought through for the preceding stitch and bring it out again two stitch lengths ahead.

Whichever stitch is used make sure the needle goes completely through to the back of the quilt at every stitch and that the thread is pulled tight. Make the stitches as small as possible, between 8 and 12 to an inch; remember, the longer the stitch, the less durable the quilting. Using heavy or stiff fabrics will make it harder to take small stitches; if this is the case, take only one stitch at a time, with the needle going through the layers in a vertical position. To fasten an end of thread, backstitch for several stitches through all layers, then take a long stitch through the top and padding only; take another backstitch and clip the thread off at the surface. The end of the thread will sink back into the padding.

Quilting by Machine

Machine quilting has come to be considered quite acceptable, especially for utilitarian household articles, and can be quite charming in spite of its regularity. One definite advantage is that it is possible to use thicker batting when quilting by machine than when quilting by hand. Polyester batting as thick as 1″ can be used, resulting in a deeper, more sculptured effect, which is often desirable. It is very important that the top, batting, and backing be tacked together securely during quilting so the layers will not move or shift while being quilted. If they do, bubbling and wrinkling will be the result. Starting at the center and taking stitches 2″ to 3″ long, baste the layers together horizontally and vertically, diagonally from corner to corner in both directions, and around the edges. On a very large piece of work, tacking in horizontal and vertical rows across the entire piece is recommended. If cotton batting is used, it's advisable to tack more closely than is necessary when polyester batting is used.

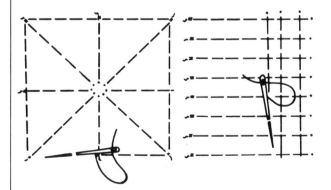

Most machine quilting is done with a straight stitch, with the machine set for a stitch length of 8 to 12 stitches per inch.

If your machine does not have a numbered dial setting, count the number of stitches in an inch. Release the pressure on the presser foot slightly so the layers of fabric being quilted will pass under it easily. Upper and lower tensions must be balanced so the stitching locks in the center of the thickness of the layers. Be sure to use the throat plate with the smaller hole if your machine is equipped with more than one. The smaller opening will help keep the work from pulling against the needle.

To guide the work under the presser foot, spread the fingers of the left hand flat on the work in front of the foot; hold the work behind the presser foot with the right hand to maintain a steady tension, without pulling the fabric. Keep your eye on the edge of the pressor foot, using it as a guide. Don't look at the needle; concentrate on the work about half an inch ahead as it feeds under the presser foot. When pivoting the work, do so with the needle fully inserted; release the presser foot, move the work into position, and replace the presser foot to stitch in the new direction.

If the piece you are working on is large, such as a quilt, the weight of it should not be allowed to pull on the part being stitched as it feeds under the presser foot. Place a small table, a lowered ironing board, or several chairs close to the machine to support the rest of the piece. Whenever possible, try to keep the bulk of the piece to the left of the presser foot. When this is not possible, roll the work tightly from one end toward the center and pin the roll securely so you can work with the roll to the right of the presser foot. You may find it easier to work with the piece rolled from both sides, leaving about 18″ of flat surface to work on in the center.

Patterns that are stitched on the bias in diagonal lines are the easiest to quilt on a machine. It is not necessary to use a quilting foot, and the fabric "gives" a little when on the bias, so it's easier to keep the work flat. In addition, regularly spaced straight lines do not have to be marked; the gauge or edge marker on the machine can be used after the first line is stitched. If cotton batting is used as padding, stitching lines should be no farther than 2″ apart; the spacing between lines can be increased to 3″ when polyester batting is used.

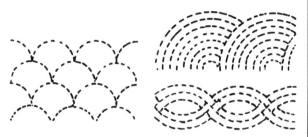

It is possible, of course, to quilt other types of patterns on a machine. If the pattern is scrolled or cursive, use the short, open toe of a quilting foot, which makes it easy to follow curved lines easily and accurately.

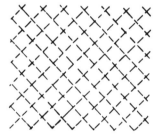

Diagonal quilting does not have to be done only in straight lines across the entire piece. In addition to the simple diamond pattern thus produced, many geometric designs can be worked out. Two easy variations, which can be used for blocks or borders, are shown here.

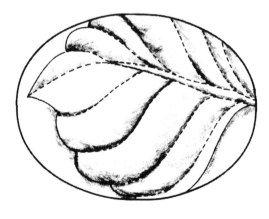

With experience, an entire quilt can be successfully quilted on a sewing machine in about 12 to 15 hours. It's easier, of course, to quilt blocks or sections that are joined after the quilting is completed. If making a quilt in one piece, be sure to remove it from the machine occasionally and place it on a bed as it will eventually be used. It's far easier to judge how the work is progressing when you stand a few feet away from it and see it as a whole.

Types of Quilting

FLAT QUILTING

In this technique, two layers of fabric are quilted together without any padding between them. Used primarily for decoration, flat quilting also adds substance to lightweight fabrics and increases the wearing qualities of articles that will be handled extensively. Small household furnishings, such as pot holders and place mats, are often quilted in this manner. Flat quilting is also used for pillow covers, bedcovers, upholstery, wall hangings, and apparel—both for trimming and for complete garments, particularly vests, skirts, and jackets.

PADDED QUILTING

This is the oldest form of quilting, in which two outer layers of fabric are quilted together with one or more layers of padding between them. Originally devised as protective body armor, padded quilting was a "natural" for adding warmth to bedcovers and clothing during the inclement winters of the Middle Ages in northern Europe. Batting is now commonly used for padding, and the three layers are referred to as the top, the batting, and the backing. Most widely used when warmth combined with a decorative surface treatment is desired, as in bedcovers, housecoats, bedjackets, children's snowsuits, and other cold-weather apparel, it is also employed solely to enhance the design of such things as pillow covers and headboards by giving the design depth and definition. Padded quilting is equally effective in all-over geometric patterns and for outlining individual motifs. Called "wadded" quilting in England, it is sometimes referred to as "American" quilting.

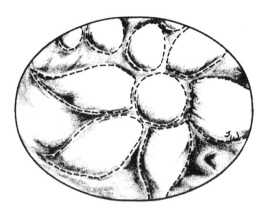

stuffed quilting must be made up of small, separated sections, such as the petals and center of a flower.

Two fabrics are used, the top one preferably smooth and closely woven, the backing a loosely woven muslin or similar material. The design is marked on the backing; then the two layers must be tacked together thoroughly, but over the background areas only, not over the design. After marking and tacking, the design is stitched through both fabrics, by hand or by machine, using a running stitch or a backstitch.

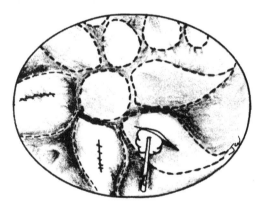

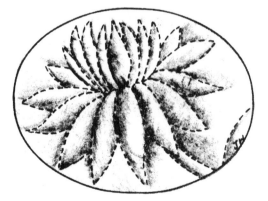

STUFFED QUILTING

This is an interesting variation of quilting in which only certain areas or motifs are padded—or "stuffed"—to make them stand out from the background in bas-relief. This technique is very much in vogue right now because of the sculptural quality it gives to pillows and other decorative furnishings. A design for

Then comes the fun part. Working from the backing side, stuff the sections or motifs individually with fiberfill or pulled-apart pieces of batting, using a knitting needle or a crochet hook and being careful to stuff every corner or point. If the areas are small, a few threads of the backing can be pulled to one side so the motif can be stuffed. Then the parted threads are drawn back together and held with a few lacing stitches so the stuffing can't escape. For larger areas, a slit is made in the backing at the center of the motif. After stuffing, the slit can be closed with a few overcasting stitches. Stuffed quilting should be lined.

CORDED QUILTING

Believed to have originated in Italy, and also known as "trapunto" quilting, corded quilting is used primarily for decoration. Two layers of fabric are stitched together in parallel lines that form a channel. The lines are spaced slightly farther apart than the width of the cord that is inserted between them and between the two fabrics. The cording adds weight and "body" to the fabrics and is sometimes used around necklines, sleeves, and hemlines of women's clothing.

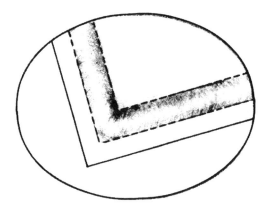

Appreciable warmth is added only when an article is solidly corded, but solid cording is sometimes used as a decorative background for other types of quilting, giving an effect of deeply textured stripes. It is important to space the distance between the two lines accurately for the cord being used. If they're too close, the cord will be too tight and will pull the design out of shape; if they're too far apart, the raised effect will be lost.

The cord is usually cotton, inserted by threading in a rug or tapestry needle that is pushed along between the lines of stitching without piercing either fabric. When a sharp angle or bend occurs in the quilting pattern, the needle is brought out on the backing side and reinserted at the same point, leaving a small amount of cord projecting; this prevents puckering and distortion of the top fabric.

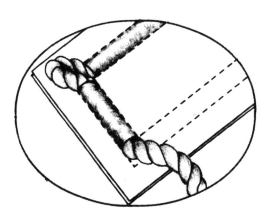

The same effect can be achieved using only one fabric by attaching the cord to the wrong side of the single layer. Two rows of backstitch, one on each side of the cord, are worked simultaneously, with the thread criss-crossing over the cord on the wrong side to hold it in place. Only the two rows of backstitching appear on the right side of the fabric. Corded quilting must be lined unless used for something such as a pillow cover, in which the backing is not exposed.

PILLOW QUILTING

The four traditional types of quilting described earlier are likely to take considerable time and patience, especially if the quilting is done by hand. "Pillow quilting" is one of several techniques that simulate quilting but can be done at a much faster clip. It actually is more like patchwork than quilting, but whatever you choose to call it, it has a certain bouncy, spontaneous charm that blends well with the decorating mood of today. It's used almost exclusively for quilts and throws and is especially well suited to crib or carriage quilts.

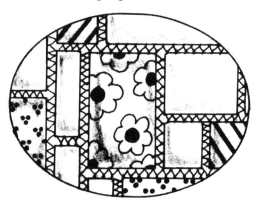

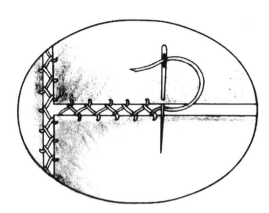

Pillow quilting consists of stuffed geometric patches joined together in one of several ways. Each patch—or miniature pillow—is made just like a real pillow, by cutting top and backing the same size and machine stitching them together with right sides facing around three sides. After the seam allowances are trimmed at the corners, the patch is turned right side out and stuffed with fiberfill or batting. The raw edges of fabric along the fourth side are turned in, and the opening is slipstitched closed. It's a good idea to make the patches square and rectangular in a few modular sizes so they'll fit together evenly, even though the arrangement is random.

Use fabrics of the same weight in related solid colors or in a harmonious mixture of small patterns interspersed with solid colors. When you've made enough miniature pillows, lay them out in a pleasing arrangement and join them together with plain or fancy faggoting. Or place adjoining pillows with right sides facing and overcast the edges on the wrong side.

TIED QUILTING

This is a variation of padded quilting in which the three basic layers of top, batting, and backing are held together by separate stitches that are tied and knotted instead of by continuous stitching that forms a design. The three layers must be tacked securely together, and this type of quilting is difficult to do unless the layers are held taut in a frame.

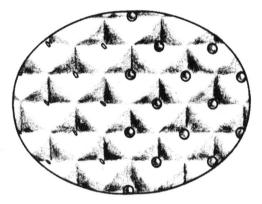

The knots are usually lined up in a simple geometric pattern, but they could follow a cursive course just as well, provided they are spaced at regular intervals and cover the area evenly. Starting at the back and leaving an end of thread about 2″ long, bring the needle through to the top and take two small stitches in the same place, ending at the back just one small stitch away from the end left hanging. Then tie the two ends securely with two or three firm knots and trim the excess thread away. A small bead, such as a make-believe pearl, or a button can be added for decoration while the second small stitch is taken. In any case, a strong

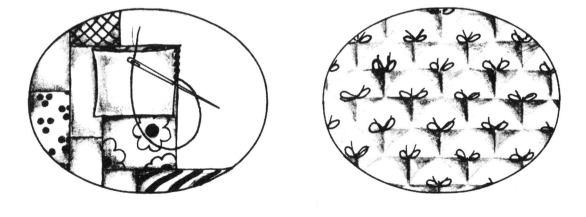

thread, such as buttonhole twist or pearl cotton, should be used.

For a different effect, the stitching can be reversed and the ends tied in little bows on the right side of the quilt. This is often done in contrasting color, using a thick, fluffy yarn.

CABLE QUILTING

This is a method of machine stitching that can be used for flat or padded quilting. It gives either one a distinctive look because the stitching is bolder and more emphatic than the usual running stitch.

First, fill the bobbin of your machine with unstranded embroidery thread, such as pearl cotton. Loosen the tension screw on the bobbin case so the thread is released evenly and smoothly. Thread the top of the machine with regular sewing thread, preferably of the polyester-wrapped cotton variety, and tighten the upper tension slightly. Work with the

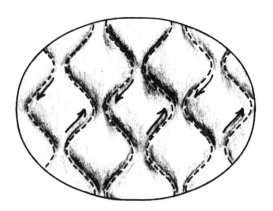

backing of the piece uppermost, so the pearl cotton will be on the right side of the top fabric. The resulting stitching will have the look of a neatly couched line.

The stitch is even more outstanding when used for a cable pattern. Try varying the length of the stitch for different effects. When stitching a cable pattern in this manner, stitch alternate rows in opposite directions.

Quilting Patterns

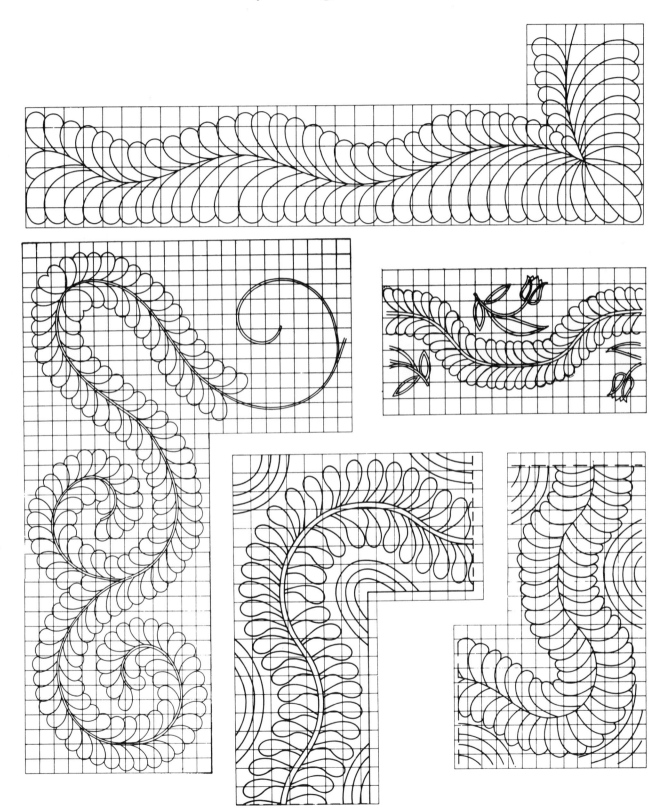

Feather and cable patterns make stunning borders
and are extremely versatile. Here are some variations
you can easily enlarge to any size desired.

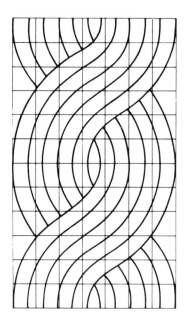

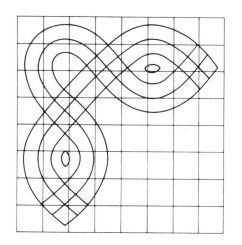

Patchwork

The History of Patchwork

"Patchwork," as we use the term, is another word for piecing—that is, the joining of two or more bits of fabric along their edges to make a larger fabric. It's impossible to say when the craft first began—certainly it is not an American invention, as is sometimes claimed. There are references in French and English literature to pieced coverings as far back as the twelfth or thirteenth century. Few of the earliest American pieced quilts survive; those that remain are the little-used "best" quilts, which are very like their English counterparts: A central medallion, usually of printed fabric, is surrounded by appliquéd or pieced borders. Gradually the style in America changed; the central figure tended to disappear, and the patchwork border sections grew in importance until they became the whole design.

The early quilts that have not survived were the everyday bed coverings made for warmth rather than for show. Many were simply two plain pieces of fabric enclosing a filling. Others might have a top layer pieced with randomly shaped scraps for a "crazy quilt." More often the scraps were probably trimmed into a regular shape, such as a square or a triangle, that could be fitted together in an overall pattern. Hexagons made especially beautiful one-patch quilts, as we see from the early honeycomb Mosaics; a later version was Grandma's Garden, in which the hexagons fell into flower blocks.

Another one-patch was Tumbler, whose name reflects the homey nature of these quilts. The lovely Clamshell pattern, still a one-patch, was nonetheless difficult to piece because of its curving shape. The same effect can be obtained by overlap-

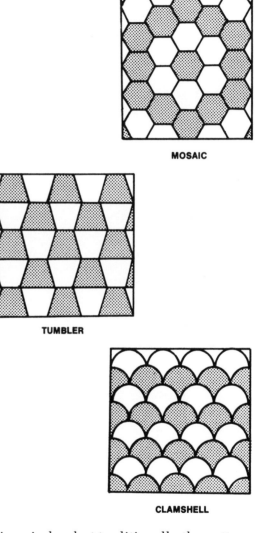

MOSAIC

TUMBLER

CLAMSHELL

ping circles, but traditionally the pattern was made with shell-shaped patches in light and dark rows.

As the bordered "best" quilt and the everyday one-patch evolved, they tended to influence each other's style. Eventually there developed a distinctly American idiom of piecework. This was the block-style quilt, in which geometric patches were sewn into identical square blocks; the blocks were then joined together to make up the entire surface of the quilt. Thus, the first one-patch designs were succeeded by two-patch blocks and then by four-patch and nine-patch blocks. (Some of the patterns discussed are shown here and on the next two pages.) The simplest two-patch, two triangles joined for a square, has a number of variations. One popular block is Birds in the Air, which combines two triangles to make a square, one triangle being already pieced with nine smaller triangles. Appliqué a handle to the plain triangle and you have another pattern, Basket. Flock of Geese is a four-patch version of Birds in the Air. Broken Dishes is all small triangles arranged in four four-patch blocks, which are four-patched again for the final block.

The fundamental Nine-Patch is simply one block divided into nine equal squares. For variety, the dark and light squares can be arranged in a number of different schemes, or they can be divided into smaller squares or triangles. The old Shoofly pattern is a good illustration, and even more intricate variations can be seen in Duck and Ducklings (also known as Hen and Chicks).

Squares and diamonds are combined for an interesting stepped effect in Pandora's Box; another version of this pattern, Baby Blocks, is pieced entirely with diamonds.

One of the most fascinating patchwork patterns is the Log Cabin block, wherein strips of fabric, half light and half dark, are arranged around a central square. The blocks can then be joined in different ways to create several overall quilt designs, such as Courthouse Steps, Barn Raising, and Straight Furrow.

Another popular group of patterns uses variations on the lend-and-borrow theme, in which light and dark curving pieces seem to change places in alternate squares. This group includes Rob Peter to Pay Paul, Drunkard's Path, and Steeplechase. Like Clamshell, these are all difficult to piece

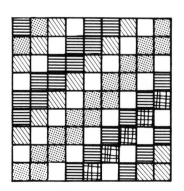

DIAGONAL STRIPES

TRIP AROUND THE WORLD

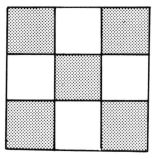

NINE-PATCH

because of the curves. Perhaps the most intricate of all curving blocks is Double Wedding Ring, which nevertheless achieved great popularity in the 1920s; here, tiny wedge-shaped patches are pieced together to make up the curving ring segments.

Today, patchwork continues to fascinate us with its endless variety of geometric forms. We love to copy the old patterns, and some of us are inspired to design new ones. Whichever you prefer, please continue reading for some ideas on how to go about it.

Patchwork Patterns

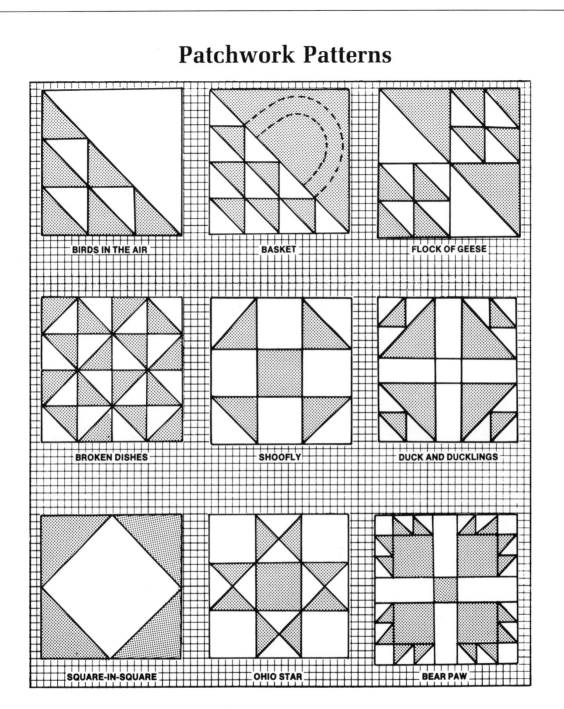

BIRDS IN THE AIR

BASKET

FLOCK OF GEESE

BROKEN DISHES

SHOOFLY

DUCK AND DUCKLINGS

SQUARE-IN-SQUARE

OHIO STAR

BEAR PAW

Making Patterns for Patchwork

Anyone at all can make patch patterns, whether by copying a traditional motif or by designing a new one. A good way to begin is to do as our pioneer ancestors did: Experiment by folding a square of paper in a variety of ways. For a two-patch block of triangles, fold the paper in half diagonally. Fold it again the other way for a block of four triangles. Fold it in half on its side, then in half again, for a simple four-patch of squares. For the basic nine-patch, fold it twice one way, then twice the other way. And so on! These are the simplest shapes, but possibilities exist for five- and seven-patch blocks as well. Early patch quilters sim-

AUNT SUKEY'S CHOICE

LOG CABIN

PINEAPPLE

PANDORA'S BOX

ROB PETER AND PAY PAUL

DRUNKARD'S PATH

SCHOOLHOUSE

STEEPLECHASE

DOUBLE WEDDING RING

ply cut along the folds for their individual patch patterns or used them to make heavier patterns (or templates), perhaps of metal. Although the paper-folding method is useful for an understanding of how to divide a square (and it's doubtful whether many of our ancestors had formal training in geometry), the modern method described in the following paragraphs will give you more accurate patterns.

To start, you will need a few good tools: sharp pencils, a ruler with a perfect edge, a compass if you plan curves in your design, and graph paper. Available at art supply stores, graph paper is printed all over with a grid design of 1″ squares, which are subdivided into smaller squares of 8, 10, or 12 to the inch. It won't matter which size you buy.

Using your tools, draw a square of any size on the graph paper, then experiment

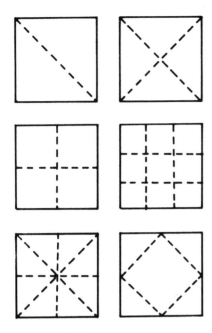

FOLDING A SQUARE OF PAPER

by dividing the square into components until you are pleased with your design. The printed lines will help you make perfect rectangles and triangles. Then shade in some areas for a light-dark contrast. Better yet, fill in the sections with colored pencils. Draw identical squares all around the first one drawn and color them in to get an idea of how the blocks will interact. You will probably want to start by coloring each block the same. Then as an experiment you may want to reverse the colors in alternate blocks. If you've already chosen your fabrics, you could even cut out patches to fit and paste them down on your drawing.

The final step is to decide on scale. Your blocks can be any size you choose; the larger the block, the fewer blocks you will need; the smaller the block, the more intricate and textured your design will appear. Will you be piecing by hand or by machine? If the edges in your design are all straight, you may safely decide on machine sewing, provided that none of the patches within the block are smaller than 2″ square. If your block contains curving patches, you are advised to stick to hand piecing, so the blocks can be smaller.

When you have arrived at a convenient size for your block, draw the final version carefully on graph paper. Letter each separate piece of the design in sequence and write in the number of patches you will need for the quilt. (Multiply the patch by the total number of blocks needed, allowing for identical patches in one block.) Paste the graph paper design to a thin but firm cardboard, such as shirt lining; let dry. Or trace it onto a transparent plastic sheet, using your rulers to draw the lines. Carefully cut the design along the lines with sharp scissors to make templates for individual patch pieces. If each template will be used for many patches, make duplicates and discard each as the edges become frayed from repeated use.

Before cutting any patches from fabric, test the accuracy of your templates by reassembling them into the original design. The edges should meet each other neatly, without any gaps or overlapping. If they don't, your patches will be equally imperfect, making it difficult to join them.

The method described here for making templates will give you a pattern the size of the finished patch; that is, what shows when the patchwork is assembled. The seam allowance is not included in the

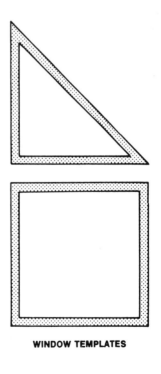

WINDOW TEMPLATES

pattern but is added when patches are cut (see below). If you wish to cut your seam allowance with perfectly even edges, you may want to make a window template. Make template as described earlier. Draw around it on cardboard; then draw another line exactly $\frac{1}{4}$'' away. Cut on both lines, creating a frame. The window is more difficult and time-consuming to make, but it will make patches easier to cut. It is also advisable for using with certain prints, when placement of motifs is important.

Cutting and Sewing Patches

CUTTING PATCH PIECES

Use fabrics that are closely woven, so seams will hold and edges will not fray. Cotton is best, if you can find it. The fabric should be fairly soft but should not be so thin that seam allowances will show through. Before cutting patches, wash new fabrics to preshrink and remove sizing. Wash scraps in a net bag. Press all fabrics smooth. Lay fabric out flat, wrong side up and one layer at a time. Lay template (pattern) wrong side up on fabric, placing it so as many straight sides of template as possible are with the crosswise and lengthwise grain of fabric. If necessary, pull threads in both directions to determine grain. Using a sharp, hard pencil (light-colored for dark fabrics, dark-colored for light fabrics), draw around template; hold pencil at an outward angle, so that point is firmly against edge of template. Reposition pattern $\frac{1}{2}$'' away and draw around as before. Continue marking patches $\frac{1}{2}$'' apart; do not cut fabric until all the patches of one color are marked. (Note: If large border pieces for quilts are to be cut later from the same fabric, be sure to consider their approximate di-mensions when marking smaller pieces; you may wish to mark your patches in vertical rows. Do not, however, cut out the border pieces before cutting and piecing patches.)

When all patches of one color have been marked, cut out each patch, $\frac{1}{4}$'' away from the marked line, which will be the stitching line. Cut the $\frac{1}{4}$'' seam allowance as accurately as you can, to make piecing easier. To keep patches of the same shape and color together; put them in a pile and run a thread through the center with a knot in one end; lift off each patch as needed.

STACK IDENTICAL PATCHES TOGETHER

PIECING

Several patch pieces will be joined to create a new unit, such as a larger patch or a block. Before sewing, lay out all pieces needed for the block. Begin by joining the smallest pieces first, then join the larger pieces you have made into rows, then join the rows for a completed block.

By Hand: If your patch pieces are small, if they have curves or sharp angles, or if

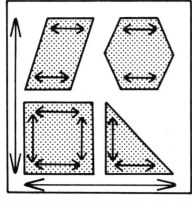

PLACING TEMPLATES ON FABRIC

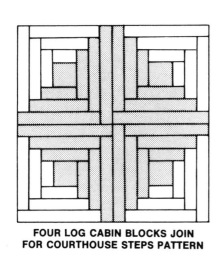

FOUR LOG CABIN BLOCKS JOIN FOR COURTHOUSE STEPS PATTERN

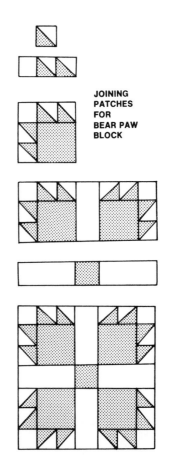

JOINING PATCHES FOR BEAR PAW BLOCK

your fabrics are delicate, you will find it easier to join pieces by hand.

To join two patch pieces, place them together, right sides facing. If pieces are very small, hold firmly to sew. Larger pieces can be pin-basted, matching angles first, then the marked lines between. Pin curved pieces together from center out to each corner. For piecing, use a No. 7 to No. 10 sharp needle, threaded with an 18″ length of mercerized cotton or cotton-wrapped polyester thread. Begin with a small knot, then stitch along the marked seam line with tiny running stitches, ending with a few backstitches; if the seam is long, take a tiny backstitch every few stitches. Try to make 8 to 10 running stitches per inch, evenly spaced. If the thread tends to knot or fray as you sew, run it over a cake of beeswax. If sewing two bias edges together, keep the thread just taut enough to prevent the fabric from stretching. As you join pieces, press seams to one side, unless otherwise indicated; open seams tend to weaken construction. Try to press seams all in the same direction, although darker fabrics should not fall under lighter ones, lest they show through. As you piece and press, clip into seams of curves and other pieces where necessary, so they will lie flat. Clip away

excess fabric to avoid bunching. Be sure that a seam is pressed flat before you cross it with another; take a small backstitch over the crossing.

By Machine: If your patchwork will have large pieces and simple shapes, you might wish to piece by machine. Set the machine for 10 stitches to the inch, unless you are working with very heavy fabrics, and use a No. 14 needle. Use mercerized cotton thread No. 50 or cotton-wrapped polyester. Follow the same procedure as for hand piecing: Pin-baste, stitch, clip seams, and press. You need not, however, begin and end your thread with each patch; let thread run on for a continuous chain of patches. Patches will be snipped apart and their seams anchored by cross-seams.

Clamshells, Diamonds, Hexagons

Clamshells, diamonds, and hexagons are favorite shapes for one-patch patterns; nevertheless, they are not easy to piece.

Unlike most patchwork, the shapes have no right angles, so the templates must be made with extreme care if the patches

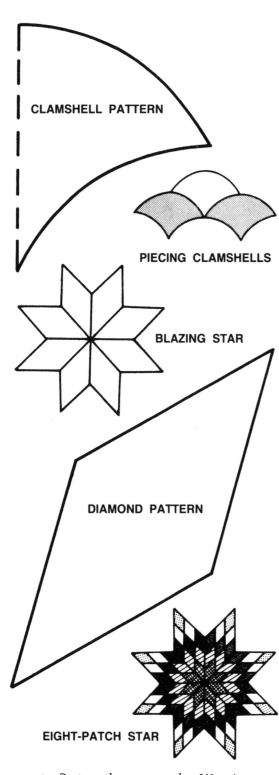

CLAMSHELL PATTERN

PIECING CLAMSHELLS

BLAZING STAR

DIAMOND PATTERN

EIGHT-PATCH STAR

are to fit together properly. We give actual-size patterns for all three. To use in size given, just trace. To enlarge or reduce either the diamond or the hexagon pattern, trace angles only, then lengthen

or shorten the edges between. After making the template and before cutting patches from fabric, test the pattern's accuracy, following individual directions. Cut patches. Since you will be sewing some edges (or, in the case of Clamshell, all edges) on the bias, you will probably find it easier to join the patches by hand, unless they are very large.

PAPER LINER

When doing diamond or hexagon patchwork, you may find that paper liners will help to keep angles sharp and seams precise. Prepare a liner for each patch as follows, referring to details shown for piecing Hexagons: Cut a firm paper pattern from wrapping paper the exact size of your cardboard template. Fit paper liner within pencil outline on wrong side of patch (Fig. 1). Fold seam allowance over edges and finger-press; tack to paper with one stitch on each side, allowing thread to cross corners (Fig. 2); finish by taking an extra stitch on first side. Cut thread, leaving about $\frac{1}{4}$''. To make removal of tacking easier, do not knot thread or make backstitches. Press lightly. Hold prepared patches with right sides together, matching edges to be seamed. Whip together with fine, even stitches (about 16 to the inch), avoiding paper as much as possible (Fig. 3); backstitch when crossing one seam with another. Liners may stay in place until patchwork is completed; to remove, snip tacking thread once on each patch and withdraw thread.

CLAMSHELLS

Trace shell pattern; complete half-pattern indicated by dash lines. Make cardboard template. Test pattern's accuracy as follows: Draw a horizontal line on paper; marking around pattern, draw a row of clamshells across paper, with lower points touching line and upper points of adjacent shells touching at sides. Draw a second row above first, as in piecing detail; curves should match perfectly. Cut patches, marking template on right side of fabric but otherwise following directions on page 30, place template in same position for each patch. On each shell,

(*Continued on page 41*)

Four wide-winged eagles are impressive on a field of bright yellow. The eagle motif, popular since the Revolution, became bolder and more stylized in the nineteenth century. Eagle quilts were also known as Union quilts. Ours was made in Pennsylvania, ca. 1890. For Eagle Quilt directions, see Contents.

(*Quilt courtesy of George E. Schoellkopf.*)

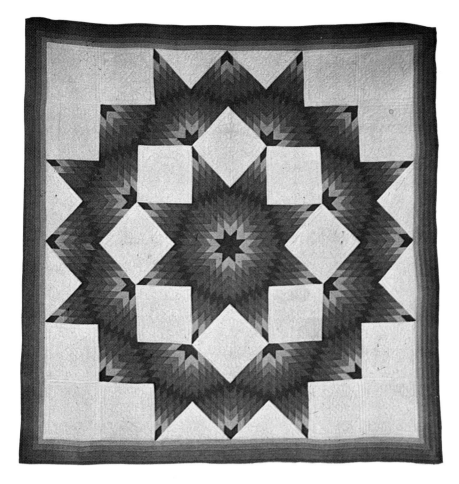

A double star,
radiant in
flaming golds,
is a magnificent variation on the star theme.
The quilt is entirely pieced, with diamonds
for the inner and outer stars, squares
and triangles for the background, and
stripes for the border. This quilt was
made in Missouri, ca. 1930. For Broken Star
Quilt directions, see Contents.

(Quilt courtesy of
Bryce and Donna Hamilton,
Tipton, Iowa.)

A delicate balance of colors, with golds shading into roses shading into lavenders, is the key to the beauty of this Amish quilt. Small diamonds are pieced to make eight sections, then joined for the eight-pointed star. Satellite stars, pieced and appliquéd, decorate the background. For Star of Bethlehem Quilt directions, see Contents. *(Quilt courtesy of George E. Schoellkopf.)*

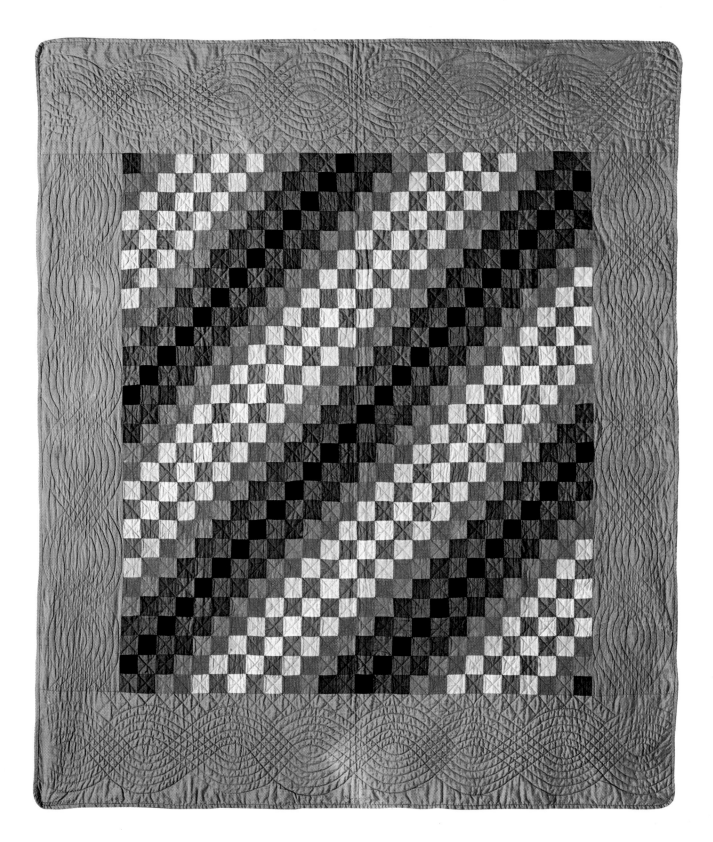

This softly colored quilt is a diagonal variation on the "sunshine-and-shadow" theme. More than 700 patches create the design, but the very easy piecing makes this project a perfect choice for beginners. The border is quilted with a wide cable. This quilt was made ca. 1910. For Amish Diagonal Quilt directions, see Contents. *(Quilt courtesy of Phyllis Haders, American Quilts.)*

A patchwork of triangles and squares creates a pattern so full of
movement, we call it "Wild Goose Chase." In this example,
the fabrics are particularly well chosen, with colors and patterns
blending in a subtle harmony. The quilt was made in Connecticut,
ca. 1860–1870. For Wild Goose Chase Quilt directions, see Contents.

(Quilt courtesy of Thomas K. Woodard, American Antiques and Quilts.)

37

Wheels of brilliant color pattern the Mariner's Compass Quilt.
The design is sometimes worked in appliqué, but ours is
entirely pieced. It takes careful cutting and stitching of the
sharp-angled patches to achieve a smooth effect. This quilt was made
ca. 1865. For Mariner's Compass Quilt directions, see Contents.

(Quilt courtesy of Phyllis Haders, American Quilts.)

In this Whig Rose Quilt, flower appliqués
in red and green are carefully placed
to form a second pattern of
overlapping circles. The quilt was
made in Ohio, ca. 1860. For Whig Rose Quilt
directions, see Contents.

(Quilt courtesy of Phyllis Haders,
American Quilts.)

This pretty quilt is one version of the
"Rose of Sharon" pattern, popular since the eighteenth century.
The bright, cheerful color scheme suggests it was made
in Pennsylvania. For Rose of Sharon Quilt directions,
see Contents.

(Quilt courtesy of Nonesuch Ltd.)

(Continued from page 32)

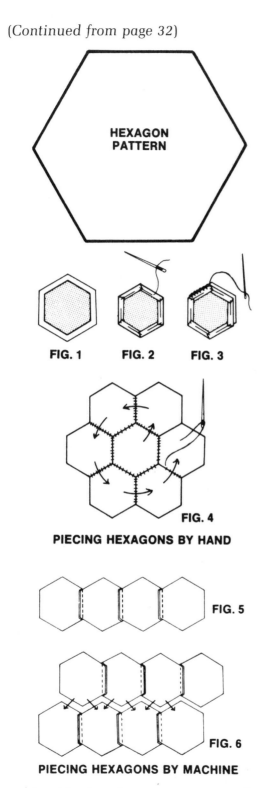

HEXAGON PATTERN

FIG. 1   FIG. 2   FIG. 3

FIG. 4

PIECING HEXAGONS BY HAND

FIG. 5

FIG. 6

PIECING HEXAGONS BY MACHINE

mark midpoint of top curve on seam line. Starting at midpoint and working out to both sides, clip top curve just to seam line every $\frac{3}{8}''$. Fold clipped edge on seam

line to wrong side of piece; press fold carefully without stretching fabric. With right sides up, join two dark shells and one light shell, placing half of upper folded edge of each dark shell on a lower seam line of light shell; at each side point of light shell, seam line should match midpoint of a dark shell; see piecing detail. Pin shells in place. Continue pinning shells until two rows have been joined; add a half shell to ends of rows. Slip stitch pieces together on folded seam line of dark shells. Using first two rows as top of work, continue to add shells a row at a time, alternating light and dark.

DIAMONDS

Make diamond template. Pattern may be used for a simple star of eight patches or for a multi-patch blazing star. For either, test template's accuracy: Draw eight diamonds together with points meeting in center, to create an eight-pointed star; there should be no gaps between or overlapping of diamond segments. Cut patches as directed on page 30, placing template on fabric with two opposite sides parallel with straight of goods. When joining patches for an eight-patch star, stitch from the wide-angled corner to center. For a multi-patch star, stitch diamonds together in rows, using staggered color sequence for each; then stitch rows together, matching corners carefully, for eight diamond-shaped sections; stitch sections together for completed star. When joining diamonds, always try to stitch a bias edge to a straight-of-goods edge.

HEXAGONS

Make hexagon template. Test accuracy of pattern by drawing design in Figure 4, with no gaps or overlaps. Cut patches as directed on page 30, placing template on fabric with two opposite sides parallel with straight of goods. For hand piecing, follow sequence shown in Figures 1 to 4: Make paper liner, baste, and slip-stitch patches together; join in clusters as shown. For machine piecing, see Figures 5 and 6: Omitting paper liners, join patches in rows as for regular piecing, then join rows as shown.

Eagle Quilt

shown on page 33

SIZE: 76'' square.

EQUIPMENT: Scissors. Ruler, Thin, stiff cardboard. Tailor's chalk. Light- and dark-colored pencils. Paper for patterns. Tracing paper. All-purpose glue. Dressmaker's tracing (carbon) paper. Tracing wheel or dry ball-point pen. Sewing and quilting needles. Quilting frame (optional).

MATERIALS: Closely woven cotton fabric 44''–45'' wide: yellow, $4\frac{1}{4}$ yds.; red, $2\frac{1}{2}$ yds.; gray-green, $1\frac{1}{4}$ yds.; orange, $\frac{1}{4}$ yd. Fabric for lining, $4\frac{1}{4}$ yds. Polyester batting. White sewing thread.

DIRECTIONS

Read General Directions for Quilting and How to Appliqué (see contents). Quilt is made up of four appliquéd blocks, plus pieced and plain borders.

Appliqués: Enlarge pattern for eagle appliqué on paper ruled in 2'' squares; complete right wing and leg. Trace pattern made, excluding one leg and wing. Trace actual-size patterns on the following pages for center and corner appliqués; complete half and quarter-patterns indicated by dash lines. Glue all tracings to cardboard and cut out, making a separate pattern for each separate piece of appliqué designs.

Following directions in How to Appliqué, cut and prepare appliqué pieces: From red fabric, cut four eagle's heads (two facing left and, reversing pattern, two facing right), four tails, four olives, eight feet, one inner piece of center appliqué, and four bases of corner appliqués. Cut out a small circle in each eagle's head for eye. From gray-green fabric, cut eight eagle's wings (four pointing left and, reversing pattern, four pointing right), one outer piece of center appliqué, and four leaves of

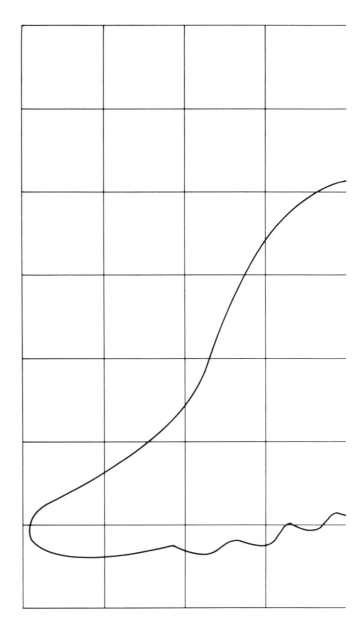

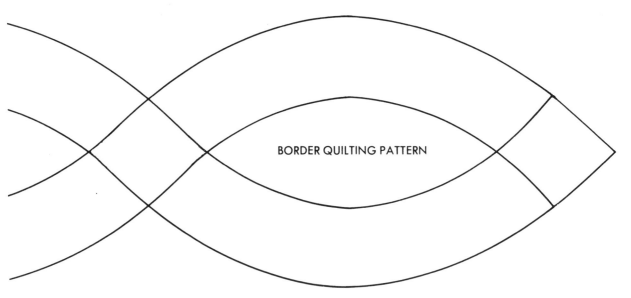

BORDER QUILTING PATTERN

42

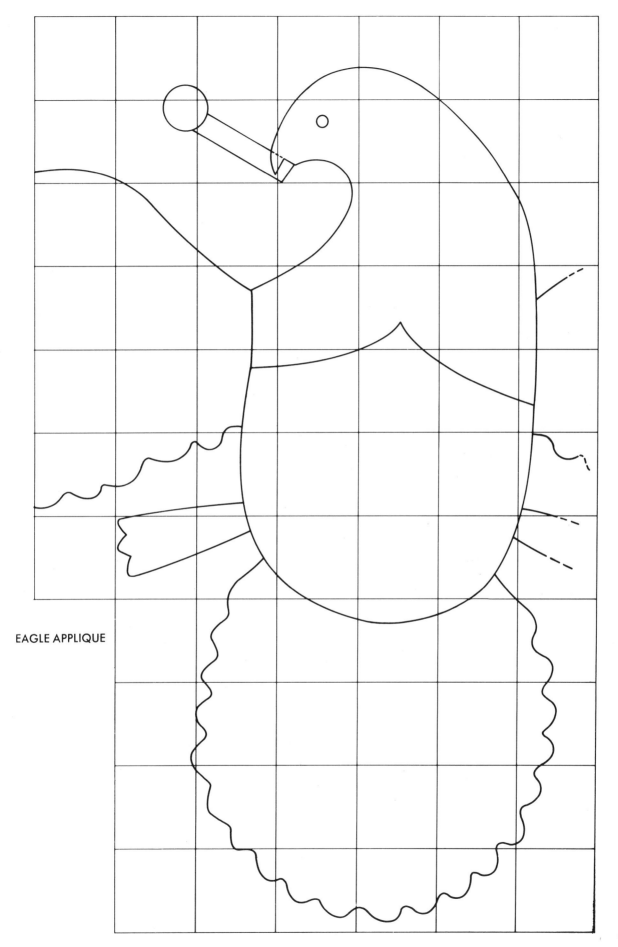

EAGLE APPLIQUE

43

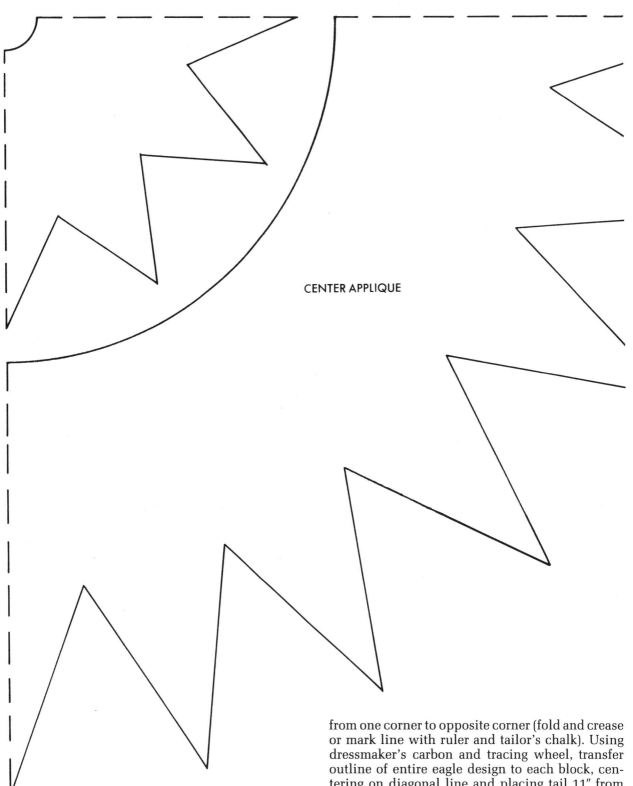

CENTER APPLIQUE

corner appliqués. From orange fabric, cut four eagle's bodies.

Blocks: Cut four pieces 28″ square from yellow fabric, adding $\frac{1}{4}$″ seam allowance all around. To aid in placing eagle appliqués, indicate diagonal center of each yellow square by marking a line from one corner to opposite corner (fold and crease or mark line with ruler and tailor's chalk). Using dressmaker's carbon and tracing wheel, transfer outline of entire eagle design to each block, centering on diagonal line and placing tail 11″ from one corner. Pin, baste, and slip-stitch eagle appliqués in place, starting with wings, feet, and tail, then head, and finally, the orange body. Pin and stitch corner appliqués in place, placing red appliqué against marked seam line of yellow background.

Join blocks, first in pairs to make two strips, then join strips; see color illustration for placement.

CORNER APPLIQUE

Appliqué center motif in place, where the four blocks join. Quilt center should measure 56½″ square, including outside seam allowance.

Borders: To make pattern for pieced first border, draw a 1¾″ square on cardboard; bisect with a corner-to-corner diagonal line; cut on marked lines for triangle patterns. Marking a pattern on wrong side of fabric and adding ¼″ seam allowance all around, cut 136 triangles each from red and yellow fabrics. Sew yellow triangles to red triangles on long sides to make 136 pieced squares. Join squares into four strips of 34 squares each, with red triangles on one side of each strip. Sew strips to quilt center, with red triangles inside; strip will be flush with quilt center at one end and will extend one square beyond quilt center at other end. Piece should measure 60″ square, including outside seam allowance.

For red second border, cut four pieces 4¼″ × 68″ (measurements include ¼″ seam allowance all around). Sew a piece to each side of quilt top, centering so that an equal amount extends at each corner. Miter corners (see Contents for directions).

For yellow third border, cut four pieces 4½″ × 75½″. Sew on in same manner as for red border, mitering corners. Quilt top should measure 76″ square.

Lining: Cut two pieces 38½″ × 76″. Join pieces on long sides, right sides together and with ½″ seams. Press seam open. Cut batting same size as lining and quilt top.

Quilting: With ruler and tailor's chalk, mark diagonal lines 1¼″ apart in both directions over center of quilt top. Trace border quilting pattern. Using dressmaker's carbon and tracing wheel, transfer pattern to both yellow and red solid-color borders, repeating the length of each strip.

Pin and baste quilt top, batting, and lining together, following General Directions. Starting in center and working around and outward, quilt on all marked lines; quilt around all appliqués and along both sides of border seams.

Edges: Cut four strips from red fabric $1\frac{1}{2}'' \times 76\frac{1}{2}''$ (piece to get lengths). Right sides together, sew strips to front of quilt, $\frac{1}{2}''$ from each edge of quilt and $\frac{1}{4}''$ from edge of each strip. Turn strips to back of quilt, turning in raw edges $\frac{1}{4}''$, and slipstitch to back, making $\frac{1}{2}''$ edging on front and back of quilt. Press edges.   ☆

Broken Star Quilt

shown on page 34

SIZE: 92″ square

EQUIPMENT: Ruler. Scissors. Pencil. Thin, stiff cardboard. Tracing paper. Paper for pattern. All-purpose glue. Dressmaker's tracing (carbon) paper. Tracing wheel or dry ball-point pen. Sewing and quilting needles. Quilting frame (optional).

MATERIALS: Closely woven cotton fabric 45″ wide: $2\frac{5}{8}''*$ yds. each of dark orange (A), light yellow (B), gold (C), light orange (D), and medium orange (E); 3 yds. white. Fabric for lining 50″ wide, $5\frac{1}{4}$ yds. Polyester batting. White sewing thread. (*Note: Less fabric will be required if you wish to piece border strips.)

DIRECTIONS:

Read General Directions for Quilting (see Contents). Quilt is made up of a "Broken" star pieced from diamond patches and set in a white background, bordered with stripes.

Diamond Pattern: Trace actual-size diamond pattern for star of Bethlehem Quilt. Glue tracing to cardboard and cut out, for pattern. Make several patterns and replace when edges begin to fray. (*Note:* Before cutting fabric patches, test accuracy of your pattern by drawing around it eight times, to create an eight-pointed star; there should be no gaps or overlapping of diamond segments.)

Diamond Patches: Marking patterns on wrong side of fabric and adding $\frac{1}{4}''$ seam allowance all around, cut diamond patches as follows: Cut 256 diamonds from dark orange (A), 128 from light yellow (B), 192 from gold (C), 256 from light orange (D), and 320 from medium orange (E).

Joining Diamonds: Center star of quilt is made up of eight identical pieced diamond-shaped sections meeting at center point. Each section is made up of six rows of six diamond patches each. See Piecing Diagram for one section. Outer portion of large star is made up of 24 more of the same diamond-shaped sections, joined for a circular design. Make 32 diamond-shaped sections as follows:

For one section, make six rows, following Piercing Diagram and Color Key; start first row with a dark orange patch (A), second row with light yellow (B), etc. Use one of the two methods for joining diamonds described in the General Directions. Matching corners, join the six rows together to make one diamond-shaped section.

Assembling: For center star, join four pieced sections for each half, with dark orange (A) points meeting in center; join halves for star. Each point of star should measure 12″ (plus outside seam allowance) along side edges.

For background blocks, cut cardboard pattern 12″ square. Marking pattern on wrong side of fabric and adding $\frac{1}{4}''$ seam allowance all around, cut 20 blocks from white fabric. Cut cardboard pattern in half diagonally for triangle pattern and cut eight triangles from white fabric in same manner.

Sew eight square background blocks to the center star, fitting two sides of a block between two points of star. Sew remaining diamond-shaped pieced sections together in eight groups of three sections each, as if assembling three points of a star. Sew three-pointed sections in the wide angle formed by the square background blocks; sew adjacent sections to each other to complete larger star. Sew remaining 12 square blocks into four corner sections of three blocks each. Sew corner sections and triangle background blocks to star; see color illustration. Piece should measure 82″ square, plus outside seam allowance.

Border: Cut four strips 1″ × 84″ from light yellow fabric, adding $\frac{1}{4}''$ seam allowance all around. Sew a strip to each side of quilt top, with an equal amount extending at each end. Miter corners; see Contents for directions. Cut four 1″-wide strips from remaining colors as follows, adding $\frac{1}{4}''$ seam allowance all around and sewing on in same manner; gold 86″, light orange 88″, medium orange 90″, and dark orange 92″. Quilt top should measure $92\frac{1}{2}''$ square, including outside seam allowance.

Lining: Cut two pieces 47″ × 93″. Sew together on long sides with $\frac{1}{2}''$ seams; press seam open. Lining measures 93″ square. Cut batting 92″ square.

Quilting: With ruler and tailor's chalk, mark lines

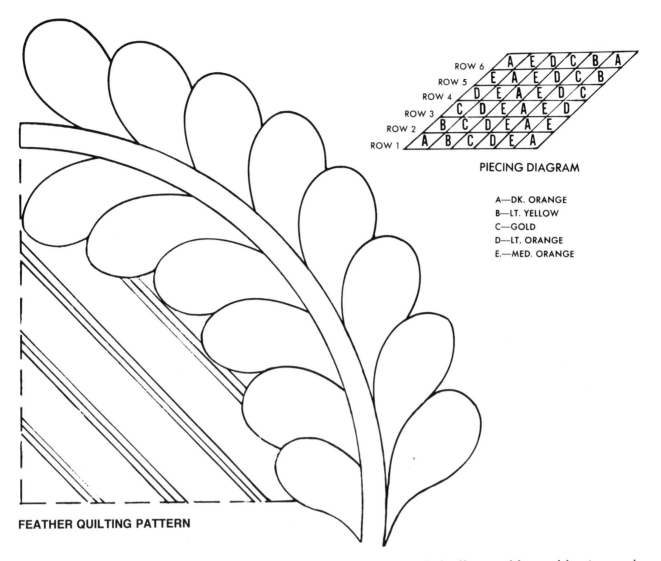

ROW 6 — A E D C B A
ROW 5 — E A E D C B
ROW 4 — D E A E D C
ROW 3 — C D E A E D
ROW 2 — B C D E A E
ROW 1 — A B C D E A

PIECING DIAGRAM

A—DK. ORANGE
B—LT. YELLOW
C—GOLD
D—LT. ORANGE
E.—MED. ORANGE

FEATHER QUILTING PATTERN

$\frac{1}{4}''$ and $\frac{3}{4}''$ in from seams around square blocks, two sides of triangle blocks. Trace actual-size Feather Pattern; complete quarter-pattern indicated by dash lines. Using carbon and a tracing wheel (or dry ball-point pen), transfer pattern to center of square background blocks. Transfer half of pattern to triangle blocks, with half-line of pattern on seam.

Following General Directions, pin and baste quilt top, batting, and lining together, centering layers.

Lining extends $\frac{1}{2}''$ all around beyond batting, and quilt top extends $\frac{1}{4}''$. Starting in center and working around and outward, quilt on all marked lines and $\frac{1}{4}''$ in from all seams of diamond patches and border strips.

Edges: Turn excess $\frac{1}{2}''$ of lining over edge of batting and baste in place. Turn in $\frac{1}{4}''$ seam allowance of quilt top. Slip-stitch folded edges of lining and quilt top together. Press edges. ☆

Star of Bethlehem Quilt

shown on page 35

SIZE: $79\frac{1}{2}''$ square.

EQUIPMENT: Ruler. Light- and dark-colored pencils. Thin, stiff cardboard. Tracing paper. Scissors. All-purpose glue. Dressmaker's tracing (carbon) paper. Tracing wheel or dry ball-point pen. Tailor's chalk. Sewing and quilting needles. Quilting frame (optional).

MATERIALS: Closely woven cotton fabric 45" wide:

½ yd. each dark gold (A), medium gold (B), light gold (C), heather (D), dusty rose (E), muted pink (F), grayish lavender (G), lavender (H), pale gray (I); 3½ yds. blue; 4¾ yds. deep pink (includes lining). Matching sewing thread. Polyester batting.

DIRECTIONS

Read General Directions for Quilting (see Contents). Main design of quilt is made up of a large eight-pointed star pieced from diamond patches; small background stars are pieced and appliquéd.

Diamond Patterns: To piece all stars, trace the actual-size diamond pattern given here. Glue the tracing to cardboard and cut out, for pattern. Cut several patterns and replace as edges begin to fray. (*Note:* Before cutting fabric patches, test accuracy of your pattern by drawing around it eight times, to create an eight-pointed star; there should be no gaps or overlapping of diamond segments.)

Diamond Patches: Marking pattern on wrong side of fabric and adding ¼" seam allowance all around, cut 78 diamond patches each of all colors except blue and deep pink.

Joining Diamonds: Large star is made up of eight identical pieced diamond-shaped sections meeting at center point. Each section is made up of nine rows of nine diamond patches each. Referring to color illustration and to the Piecing Diagram (which shows first three rows of section joined) for color placement, make each section as follows: Piece patches together in rows of nine, starting first row with dark gold (A); start second row with medium gold (B), third row with light gold (C); fourth row with heather (D), fifth row with dusty rose (E);

sixth row with muted pink (F); seventh row with grayish lavender (G); eighth row with lavender (H); ninth row with gray (I). Use one of the two methods for joining diamonds described in the General Directions.

Matching corners carefully, join the nine rows to form a diamond-shaped section. Make seven more sections in same manner.

Large Star: Join four sections for each half of star, having all dark gold points meeting in center; then join halves for complete star. The points of assembled star should measure 18" (plus outside seam allowance) on each side. Check measurements before cutting background pieces.

Background: For blue background of quilt top, make cardboard pattern 18" square. Marking pattern on wrong side of fabric and adding ¼" seam allowance all around, cut four squares from blue fabric. Cut cardboard pattern in half diagonally for triangle pattern. Cut four triangles from blue fabric in same manner as for squares.

Small Stars: Join remaining diamond patches into four stars of eight diamonds each and four half-stars of four diamonds each. (You will have one color left over; discard patches.) Prepare edges of stars and half-stars for appliqué (see Contents); leave the straight edges of half-stars flat. Appliqué stars to center of blue background squares and half-stars to triangles, with raw edges even. Sew the squares and triangles alternately between the star points, to complete center of quilt top. Piece should measure about 62" square, including outside seam allowance.

Borders: For pink border, cut two strips 2½" × 62" (measurements include ¼" seam allowance all around). Sew to top and bottom of quilt center. Cut two more pink strips 2½" × 66" and sew to sides.

For blue border, cut two strips 7¾" × 66". Sew to top and bottom of quilt top, with ¼" seams. Cut two more blue strips 7¾" × 80½" and sew to sides of quilt top: Piece should now measure 80½" square.

Lining: Cut two pieces from deep pink fabric 40¾" × 80½". Sew together on long sides with ½" seams to make lining 80½" square. Cut batting same size as lining and quilt top.

Quilting: With ruler and tailor's chalk, draw diagonal lines 1" apart in both directions on the blue squares and triangles, skipping over stars; on triangles, make lines parallel to short sides of pieces. Mark a line down centers of pink border strips.

Enlarge cable quilting pattern on paper ruled in 1" squares. Trace the medallion pattern; complete quarter-pattern indicated by dash lines. Using dressmaker's carbon and tracing wheel, transfer patterns to blue border. Place a medallion in each corner and repeat cable motif around border, joining corners; place cable design against pink border strips, leaving outer edges of blue border strips unmarked.

Pin and baste quilt top, batting, and lining to-

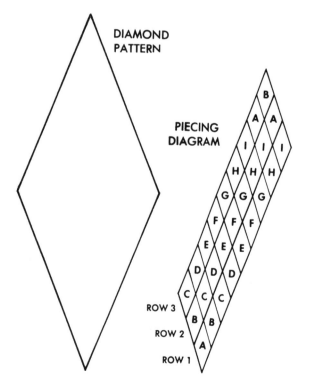

DIAMOND PATTERN

PIECING DIAGRAM

ROW 3

ROW 2

ROW 1

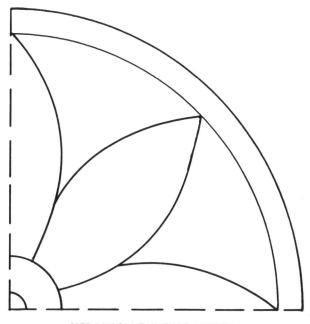

MEDALLION QUILTING PATTERN

gether, following General Directions. Starting in center and working around and outward, quilt inside of each diamond patch and along edges of pink border, close to seams; quilt on all marked lines.

Edges: When quilting is completed, trim edges of batting and lining almost to edge of cable quilting. Turn excess fabric of quilt top to back of quilt; turn in edges $\frac{1}{4}''$ and slip-stitch to lining. Press edges of quilt. ☆

Amish Diagonal Quilt

shown on page 36

SIZE: $75'' \times 67\frac{1}{4}''$

EQUIPMENT: Thin, stiff cardboard. Light- and dark-colored pencils. Ruler. Scissors. Paper for pattern. Dressmaker's tracing (carbon) paper. Tracing wheel or dry ball-point pen. Quilting and sewing needles. Quilting frame (optional).

MATERIALS: Closely woven cotton fabric 44''–45'' wide: $\frac{1}{2}$ yd. each dark blue-green, dusty pink, rose pink, light pink, golden brown, and olive drab; $\frac{1}{4}$ yd. each black and white; $2\frac{1}{8}$ yds. tan. Fabric for lining 36'' wide, $4\frac{1}{4}$ yds. Polyester batting. White sewing thread.

DIRECTIONS

Read General Directions for Quilting (see Contents). Any combination of colors may be used, as

long as a contrast is kept between light and dark colors for the shadowed effect. Quilt is made up of 728 squares sewn together, plus a solid-color border quilted in a cable pattern.

Patches: Make patch pattern by cutting a $1\frac{7}{8}''$ square from cardboard. Make several patterns and replace when edges begin to fray. Cut square patches as indicated in General Directions, marking pattern on wrong side of fabric and adding $\frac{1}{4}''$ seam allowance all around. Cut 104 patches each of blue-green, dusty pink, rose pink, light pink, golden brown, and olive drab; cut 52 patches each of black and white.

Blocks: Following color illustration, sew patches together in diagonal rows to make a square block (one-quarter of pieced top), starting in corner

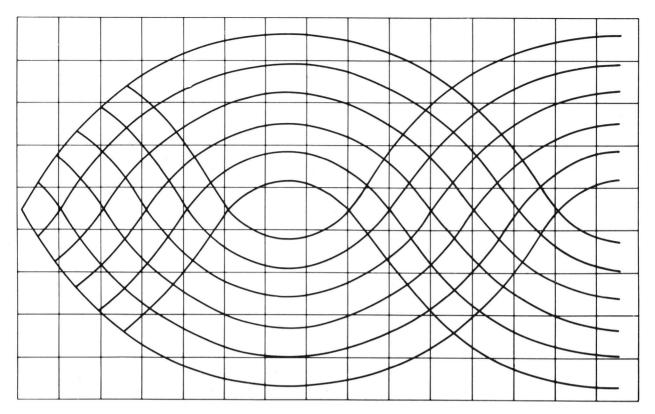

BORDER QUILTING PATTERN

with one blue-green patch. Add 2 dusty pink patches for second row, joined to adjacent sides of blue-green patch. Continue with 3 rose pink; then 4 light pink; 5 golden brown; 6 white; 7 golden brown; 8 light pink; 9 rose pink; 10 dusty pink; 11 blue-green; 12 olive drab; 13 black; 13 olive drab; 12 blue-green; 11 dusty pink; 10 rose pink; 9 light pink; 8 golden brown; 7 white; 6 golden brown; 5 light pink; 4 rose pink; 3 dusty pink; 2 blue-green; 1 olive drab. Make three more pieced blocks in same manner.

Assembling: Join the four blocks into an overall design, turning two blocks halfway around to match colors and to form diagonal rows as shown in illustration; each of the four corner patches will match its diagonal opposite. Piece should measure $49\frac{1}{4}'' \times 53''$, including outside seam allowances.

Border: Cut two pieces $9\frac{1}{2}'' \times 53''$ and two pieces $11\frac{1}{2}'' \times 67\frac{1}{4}''$, all from tan fabric; measurements include $\frac{1}{4}''$ seam allowance. Right sides together, sew shorter pieces to sides of pieced center; sew longer pieces to top and bottom. Quilt top should measure $67\frac{1}{4}'' \times 75''$.

Lining: Cut two pieces $34\frac{1}{8}'' \times 75''$. Sew together along long edges, right sides together and making $\frac{1}{2}''$ seams for piece $67\frac{1}{4}'' \times 75''$. Press seam open. Cut batting same size as quilt top.

Quilting: Enlarge Border Quilting Pattern on paper ruled in 1″ squares. Using dressmaker's carbon and tracing wheel, transfer pattern to top and bottom borders of quilt top, $1\frac{1}{4}''$ from patchwork center; start at midpoint of borders with part of design where quilting lines intersect, and repeat design all the way across to each side. Repeat on side borders, leaving no space between quilting design and patchwork center; start at midpoint with intersecting lines and work out to seam lines between side and end borders.

For patchwork center, mark intersecting diagonal lines over every row of squares, going through corners of squares; use ruler and tailor's chalk. Extend marked lines onto top and bottom borders, up to edges of marked border design.

Pin and baste quilt top, batting, and lining together, and quilt along marked lines as instructed in General Directions, starting in center and working outward.

Edges: Trim corners of quilt for a slightly rounded shape. To bind edges, cut strips $1\frac{1}{2}''$ wide from tan fabric; sew together to make one strip 286″ long. Fold under long edges of strip $\frac{1}{4}''$ and press. Fold strip in half lengthwise. Enclose raw edges of quilt inside strip; slip-stitch strip to quilt top and lining (gathering slightly at corners) to make $\frac{1}{2}''$ edging on both sides. ☆

Wild Goose Chase Quilt

shown on page 37

SIZE: 93½" square.

EQUIPMENT: Ruler. Scissors. Light- and dark-colored pencils. Thin, stiff cardboard. Tailor's chalk. Sewing and quilting needles. Straight pins. Quilting frame (optional).

MATERIALS: Closely woven cotton fabric 36" wide: assorted prints (with one color predominating) totaling about 5½ yds.; white, 5 yds. White fabric for lining 36" wide, 3 yds. White sewing thread. Polyester batting.

DIRECTIONS

Read General Directions for Quilting (see Contents). Quilt is made up of 36 pieced blocks, set with pieced joining strips.

Patterns: See Piecing Diagram, which gives dimensions and shape of each patch piece. Make cardboard patterns for patches. A (3⅜" square), B (half of 5⅛" square), C (2⅜" square), D (half of 2⅜" square), and E (half of 1¹¹⁄₁₆" square).

Patches: For each block, cut one of A, four of B, four of C, and eight of D from print fabric (use one print or combine two or three in a block, as desired); cut 24 of E from white fabric; add ¼" seam allowance all around.

Blocks: Join patches to make block, starting with smaller pieces; see Piecing Diagram. Block will measure 12" square, plus outside seam allowance. Make 35 more blocks.

Assembling: For joining strips, cut 84 pieces 3½" × 12½" from white fabric (measurements include ¼" seam allowance all around). Sew pieced blocks into six horizontal rows of six blocks each, with a white piece between blocks and at beginning and end of each row. Cut cardboard pattern 3" square. Marking pattern on wrong side of fabric and adding ¼" seam allowance all around, cut 49 squares from one print fabric. Sew squares and remaining white pieces into seven horizontal strips, each with seven squares alternating with six white pieces. Assemble quilt top by sewing pieced strips between rows of blocks and at top and bottom of finished piece. Quilt top should measure 93½" square.

Lining: Cut two pieces 31¾" × 93½" and one piece 32¼" × 93½". Sew pieces together on long sides, with widest piece in center and making ½" seams. Press seams open. Lining should measure 93¾" square. Cut batting same size as lining.

Quilting: With ruler and tailor's chalk, mark

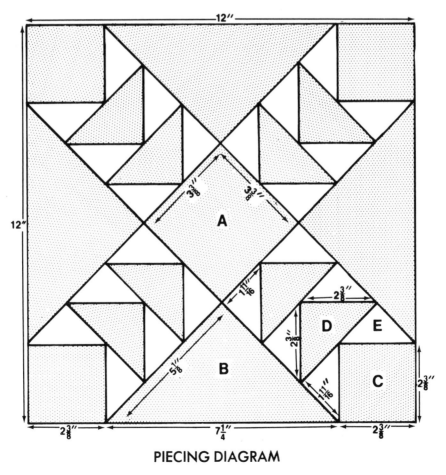

PIECING DIAGRAM

quilting lines ½″ apart over quilt top as follows: On white pieces of joining strips, mark lines diagonally, alternating direction every other strip, both vertically and horizontally; on print squares of joining strips, mark all lines horizontally; on print triangle patches of blocks, mark lines parallel to long side of triangles; on large squares of blocks, mark lines parallel to two opposite sides, alternating direction of lines every other block across horizontal rows of quilt top; on small squares within each block, mark same pattern as large squares, but alternating direction, moving clockwise around block.

Pin and baste lining, batting, and quilt top together, centering layers and following General Directions. Starting in center and working around and outward, quilt on all marked lines; quilt on white triangle patches, ⅛″ in from seams.

Edges: Trim lining and batting to size of quilt top. Cut four 1⅛″-wide strips 94″ long, piecing to get lengths, from same print fabric used for squares in joining strips. Right sides together, sew strips to front of quilt with ¼″ seams. Fold strips to back of quilt, turning in raw edges ¼″, and slip-stitch to lining. Press all edges. ☆

Mariner's Compass Quilt

shown on page 38

SIZE: 78¾″ square.
EQUIPMENT: Light- and dark-colored pencils. Thin, stiff cardboard. Scissors. Ruler. Compass. Tailor's chalk. Tracing paper. Tracing wheel or dry ball-point pen. Dressmaker's tracing (carbon) paper. Sewing and quilting needles. Straight pins. Quilting frame (optional). All-purpose glue.
MATERIALS: Closely woven cotton fabric 36″ wide: dark blue, 5½ yds.; red, 1 yd.; green, 1 yd.; gold, 1 yd.; red and white print, 1⅛ yds.; white, 3 yds. Fabric for lining 44″–45″ wide, 4½ yds. White sewing thread. Polyester batting.

DIRECTIONS

Read General Directions for Quilting (see Contents). Quilt is constructed with nine pieced blocks, set with pieced joining strips and border.

Patterns: Trace the seven actual-size patterns; complete half- and quarter-patterns indicated by dash lines. Patterns for Nos. 2, 3, and 4 are superimposed on No. 1. Glue tracings to cardboard and cut out, for patch patterns. Before cutting patches, check patterns for fit.

Patches: Marking patterns on wrong side of fabric and adding ¼″ seam allowance all around, cut patch pieces as follows: cut 36 of No. 1 from green fabric; 36 of No. 2 from gold; 72 of No. 3 and 9 of No. 5 from red; 144 of No. 4 from red-and-white print; 288 of No. 6 and 36 of No. 7 from white.

Blocks: To piece circle (or "compass") for one block, begin at center and work outward: Sew four No. 7 patches around a No. 5, to form a small circle; sew four No. 1 patches around circle, matching corners to the No. 5 piece; continue with four No. 2 pieces between the No. 1 pieces, eight No. 3 pieces, 16 No. 4 pieces, and 32 No. 6 pieces. Pieced circle should measure 19″ in diameter, plus outside seam allowance.

To complete block, make a cardboard pattern 21″ square. Draw a circle 19″ in diameter in center of square; cut out circle and discard, leaving pattern for "frame." Marking pattern on wrong side of fabric and adding ¼″ seam allowance all around inner and outer edges, cut frame from dark blue fabric. Right sides together, sew pieced circle to frame, for block. Make eight more blocks in same manner. (**Note:** Another method is to appliqué circle to a solid square. However, this is not the way original quilt was made.)

Joining Strips, Border: Cut cardboard pattern 2″ square. Marking pattern on wrong side of fabric and adding ¼″ seam allowance, cut 190 squares from blue fabric. Mark another 2″ square on cardboard, bisect diagonally, and cut on lines for two equal triangle patterns. Cut 380 triangles from white fabric and 12 from blue fabric. Cut a triangle pattern in half to make pattern for small triangle. Cut 24 small triangles from white fabric. Join square and triangle patches into strips as shown in illustration. Make six short strips, each with seven blue squares and 14 white triangles; add one blue triangle at one end and two small white triangles at other end. Make four long strips, each with 24 blue squares, 48 white triangles, one blue triangle, and two small white triangles. Make two longer strips, each with 26 blue squares, 52 white triangles, one blue triangle, and two small white triangles.

Assembling: Join the nine quilt blocks into three horizontal rows of three blocks each, with a short strip between blocks. Join the three rows of blocks with a long strip between rows; add a strip across top and bottom. Join longer strips to remaining sides of piece. Piece should measure 74¼″ square, plus outside seam allowance. Cut four 2½″-wide strips from blue fabric, two 74¾″ long and two 78¾″ long (measurements include seam allowance). Right

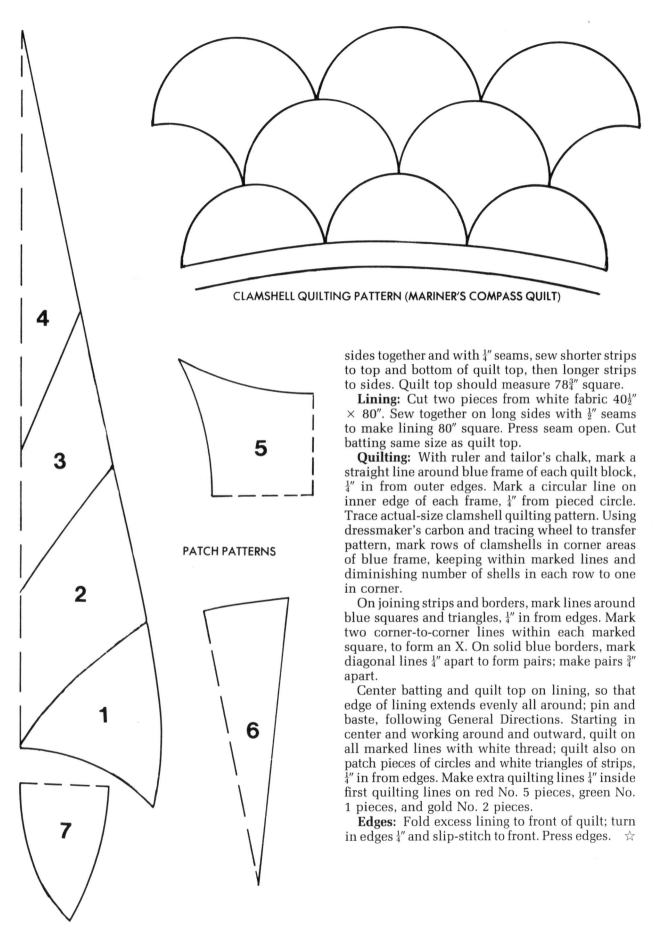

CLAMSHELL QUILTING PATTERN (MARINER'S COMPASS QUILT)

PATCH PATTERNS

sides together and with $\frac{1}{4}''$ seams, sew shorter strips to top and bottom of quilt top, then longer strips to sides. Quilt top should measure $78\frac{3}{4}''$ square.

Lining: Cut two pieces from white fabric $40\frac{1}{2}''$ × 80″. Sew together on long sides with $\frac{1}{2}''$ seams to make lining 80″ square. Press seam open. Cut batting same size as quilt top.

Quilting: With ruler and tailor's chalk, mark a straight line around blue frame of each quilt block, $\frac{1}{4}''$ in from outer edges. Mark a circular line on inner edge of each frame, $\frac{1}{4}''$ from pieced circle. Trace actual-size clamshell quilting pattern. Using dressmaker's carbon and tracing wheel to transfer pattern, mark rows of clamshells in corner areas of blue frame, keeping within marked lines and diminishing number of shells in each row to one in corner.

On joining strips and borders, mark lines around blue squares and triangles, $\frac{1}{4}''$ in from edges. Mark two corner-to-corner lines within each marked square, to form an X. On solid blue borders, mark diagonal lines $\frac{1}{4}''$ apart to form pairs; make pairs $\frac{3}{4}''$ apart.

Center batting and quilt top on lining, so that edge of lining extends evenly all around; pin and baste, following General Directions. Starting in center and working around and outward, quilt on all marked lines with white thread; quilt also on patch pieces of circles and white triangles of strips, $\frac{1}{4}''$ in from edges. Make extra quilting lines $\frac{1}{4}''$ inside first quilting lines on red No. 5 pieces, green No. 1 pieces, and gold No. 2 pieces.

Edges: Fold excess lining to front of quilt; turn in edges $\frac{1}{4}''$ and slip-stitch to front. Press edges. ☆

54

PATTERNS FOR WHIG ROSE QUILT

Whig Rose Quilt

shown on page 39

SIZE: $76\frac{1}{2}''$ square.

EQUIPMENT: Ruler. Scissors. Light- and dark-colored pencils. Thin, stiff cardboard. Tracing paper. All-purpose glue. Dressmaker's tracing (carbon) paper. Tracing wheel or dry ball-point pen. Sewing and quilting needles. Quilting frame (optional).

MATERIALS: Closely woven cotton fabric 36″ wide: green,* $2\frac{3}{4}$ yds.; red, $1\frac{1}{2}$ yds.; yellow, $\frac{1}{8}$ yd.; pink print, $\frac{1}{3}$ yd. White fabric 45″ wide, $4\frac{5}{8}$ yds. (less will be needed if you wish to piece borders). Fabric for lining 40″ wide, $4\frac{1}{4}$ yds. White sewing thread. Polyester batting. *(**Note:** In original quilt, green fabric has a small blue dot.)

DIRECTIONS

Read General Directions for Quilting and How to Appliqué (see Contents). Quilt is made up of nine appliquéd blocks, plus an appliquéd border.

Appliqués: Actual-size pattern for rose appliqué design is on the preceding pages. Trace each numbered part of design, completing quarter-patterns indicated by dash lines. Glue tracings to cardboard and cut out, for appliqué patterns.

Following directions in How to Appliqué, cut and prepare appliqué pieces: From red fabric, cut nine of No. 1, 108 of No. 4, 36 of No. 9, and 36 of No. 11. From green fabric, cut 36 of No. 5, 36 of No. 6, 36 of No. 7 (for No. 6 and No. 7, add only $\frac{1}{8}''$ seam allowance), 144 of No. 8, and 72 of No. 12. From yellow fabric, cut 36 of No. 10. From pink print fabric, cut 36 of No. 2 and 108 of No. 3.

Blocks: Cut nine pieces 22″ square from white fabric, adding $\frac{1}{4}''$ seam allowance all around. On each white square, indicate horizontal and vertical center lines (fold and crease or mark lines with ruler and tailor's chalk). Retrace entire rose appliqué pattern as shown. Using dressmaker's carbon and tracing wheel, transfer main outlines of complete appliqué pattern to each square by matching quarter-pattern lines to marked center lines; the center point of large leaves (No. 5) should fall on marked center lines. Piece large center flowers together, using Nos. 1, 2, 3, and 4. Pin, baste, and slip-stitch pieced center and remaining appliqué pieces in place on the squares, sewing overlapping pieces last.

Assembling: Join the nine finished blocks into three rows of three blocks each, then join rows together for main body of quilt top. Piece should measure $66\frac{1}{2}''$ square, including outside seam allowance.

Borders: Cut four $5\frac{1}{2}''$-wide strips from white fabric, two $66\frac{1}{2}''$ long and two $76\frac{1}{2}''$ long (measurements include $\frac{1}{4}''$ seam allowance). Using same patterns as for main body of quilt top, cut appliqué pieces for border. From green fabric, cut 48 of No. 8 and 24 of No. 12. From red fabric, cut 16 of No. 9 and 12 of No. 11. From yellow fabric, cut 16 of No. 10. To make a pattern for large green pieces of corner motifs, draw around No. 9 pattern on cardboard, then draw another line $\frac{5}{8}''$ away, following contours of first line, to make pattern about $4\frac{1}{4}''$ in diameter. Using this pattern, cut four corner pieces from green fabric. Prepare pieces for appliqué. For vines, cut four $\frac{5}{8}''$-wide bias strips from green fabric, about 80″ long (piece to get this length). For stems, cut 24 bias strips $\frac{5}{8}''$ wide, but varying in length from 2″ to 5″, as desired. Prepare bias strips for appliqué by turning under long edges $\frac{1}{8}''$ to make strips $\frac{3}{8}''$ wide; press carefully without stretching folded edges.

Pin a large green corner piece to each end of the two longer white border strips, $\frac{5}{8}''$ from edges. Lay a long green bias strip between pieces, curving as shown in color illustration; pin in place. In same manner, pin a long bias strip on each of the two shorter white border strips, but with ends of bias strips matching ends of border strips. Pin, baste, and slip-stitch remaining appliqué pieces in place on border strips, following illustration. Then stitch the overlapping vines, stitching along inside curves of vines first, then outside curves.

Sew shorter border pieces to opposite sides of quilt top, then longer border pieces to remaining sides. There will be a small gap in the vine between corner motifs and ends of shorter border strips; fill in with a bias strip. Quilt top should measure $76\frac{1}{2}''$ square.

Lining: Cut two pieces $38\frac{3}{4}'' \times 76\frac{1}{2}''$. Sew together on long sides, with $\frac{1}{2}''$ seams. Press seam open. Cut batting same size as lining and quilt top.

Quilting: Trace large and small quilting patterns; complete quarter-patterns indicated by dash lines. Using dressmaker's carbon and tracing wheel, transfer wreath portion of patterns to white background of quilt top as follows:

Mark large pattern in the four areas where four quilt blocks meet, centering around the corners. Mark half of large quilting pattern (a semicircle) 20 times: mark pattern twice on each edge of main body of quilt top, centering on seam line between blocks; mark pattern midway between all blocks, centering on seam line. Mark quarter-pattern in each of four corners of main body of quilt top. Mark small quilting pattern in remaining large spaces between motifs of appliqués.

With ruler and tailor's chalk, mark triple-line pattern in center of wreaths and over all unmarked areas of white background, making all lines parallel and skipping over appliqués. Extend lines onto white background of border. On appliqués, mark center motifs and large green leaves only with single diagonal lines ¾″ apart; follow same angle as triple lines of white background.

Pin and baste quilt top, batting, and lining together, following General Directions. Starting in center and working around and outward, quilt on all marked lines with white thread. On small leaves, buds, and small flowers, quilt ¼″ in from edge of each appliqué piece. Quilt around main outline of appliqué designs, close to seam.

Edges: Cut four 1⅛″-wide strips 77″ long (piece to get lengths). Right sides together and with ¼″ seams, sew strips to front of quilt. Turn strips to back of quilt, turn in raw edges ¼″, and slip-stitch folded edge to lining.   ☆

Rose of Sharon Quilt

shown on page 40

SIZE: About 84½″ square.

EQUIPMENT: Ruler. Scissors. Thin, stiff cardboard. All-purpose glue. Tailor's chalk. Dressmaker's (carbon) tracing paper. Tracing wheel. Sewing and quilting needles. Straight pins. Pencil. Quilting frame (optional).

MATERIALS: Quilt top: Closely woven cotton fabric 36″ wide: bright pink print, 6½ yds.; yellow print 2 yds.; plain red, ⅔ yd.; plain dark green, 1½ yds. Lining: Cotton fabric 44″–45″ wide, 4⅔ yds. Matching sewing thread. Polyester or cotton batting.

DIRECTIONS

Read General Directions for Quilting and How to Appliqué (see Contents). Quilt is made up of nine appliquéd square blocks, plus wide and narrow borders. Trace appliqué pattern on the following pages, complete quarter-pattern indicated by long dash lines (short dash lines indicate quilting patterns). Make a separate cardboard pattern for each numbered part of appliqué. Following directions in How to Appliqué, cut and prepare appliqué pieces. From yellow print fabric, cut 72 of piece 2 and nine of piece 7; from red fabric, cut 81 of piece 1 and nine of piece 6; from dark green fabric, cut 72 of piece 3, 72 of piece 4, and 36 of piece 5.

For background of blocks, cut nine pieces 21″ square from pink print fabric, adding ¼″ seam allowance all around. On each pink square, indicate

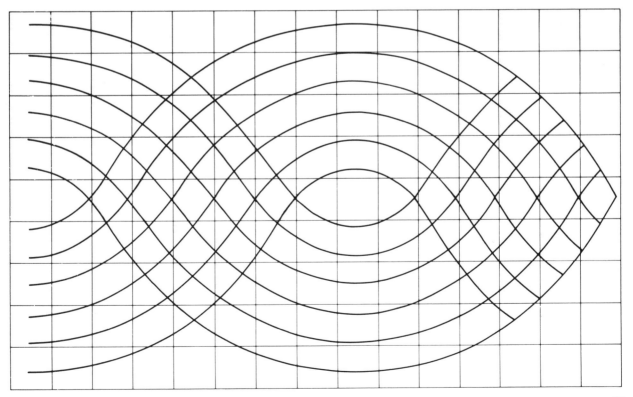

horizontal and vertical center lines (fold and crease or mark lines with ruler and tailor's chalk). Using dressmaker's carbon and tracing wheel, transfer appliqué pattern to each square, centering carefully so there is an equal margin all around; center point of large leaves (piece 5) should fall on the

agonal lines 1″ apart in both directions over pink background of quilt center, skipping over appliqués. Enlarge border quilting pattern on paper ruled in 1″ squares. Using dressmaker's carbon and tracing wheel, transfer pattern to wide pink border,

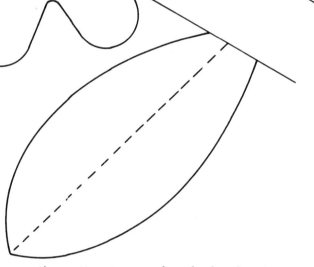

center lines. Pin, baste, and slip-stitch appliqué pieces in place on squares, starting with leaves, then the overlapping stems and flower pieces.

Join the nine finished blocks in three rows of three blocks each, then sew rows together for center of quilt top. Piece should measure 63″ square, plus outside seam allowance.

For narrow borders, cut 12 strips 1¼″ wide: from yellow print fabric, cut two strips 63½″ long, two 65″ long, two 66½″ long, and two 68″ long; from pink print fabric, cut two strips 65″ long and two 66½″ long (measurements include ¼″ seam allowance all around). Sew 63½″ yellow strips to top and bottom of quilt top, right sides together and with ¼″ seams. Sew 65″ yellow strips to sides of quilt top. Sew pink strips on in same manner, then remaining yellow strips. For wide border, cut four strips 9¼″ wide from pink fabric, two 68″ long and two 85½″ long. Sew shorter strips to top and bottom of quilt top and longer strips to sides. Quilt top should measure 85″ square.

For lining, cut two pieces 42¾″ × 84½″. Sew together on long sides with ½″ seams to make piece 84½″ square. Lining will be ½″ smaller all around than quilt top. Cut batting same size as lining.

Quilting: With ruler and tailor's chalk, mark di-

repeating pattern to cover length of each strip; see color illustration.

Pin and baste quilt top, batting, and lining together, following General Directions and centering layers so that quilt top extends ½″ beyond lining and batting all around. Starting in center and working around and outward, quilt on all marked lines; quilt on each appliqué, close to seam line; quilt close to seam lines joining narrow border strips, on both sides of seams.

To bind edges, turn excess fabric of quilt top to back, turning in raw edges ¼″, and slip-stitch to lining. ☆

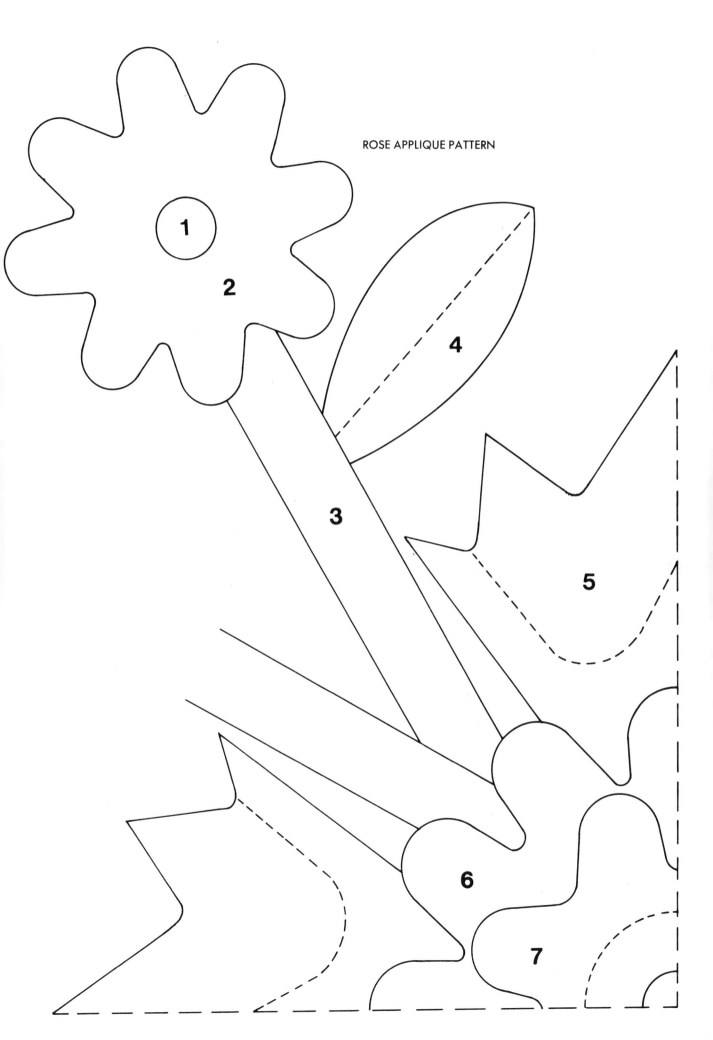

ROSE APPLIQUE PATTERN

Tree Everlasting Quilt

shown on page 68

SIZE: About $80\frac{1}{2}'' \times 85\frac{1}{2}''$.

EQUIPMENT: Thin, stiff cardboard. Ruler. Pencil. Paper for pattern. Scissors. Dressmaker's (carbon) tracing paper. Tracing wheel. Sewing and quilting needles. Straight pins. Quilting frame (optional).

MATERIALS: Closely woven cotton fabric 44"–45" wide: dark blue-green, 2 yds.; red, $1\frac{1}{4}$ yds.; gold, $8\frac{1}{4}$ yds. (including lining). Polyester or cotton batting. Gold sewing thread.

DIRECTIONS

Read General Directions for Quilting (see Contents). Cut nine panels $5\frac{3}{4}'' \times 55\frac{3}{4}''$: five from gold fabric and four from green (measurements include $\frac{1}{4}''$ seam allowance). To make pattern for triangles, cut a piece of cardboard $1\frac{5}{8}''$ square; cut square in half diagonally. Marking pattern on wrong side of fabric and leaving $\frac{1}{4}''$ seam allowance, cut 418 each red and gold triangles. Right sides together, join

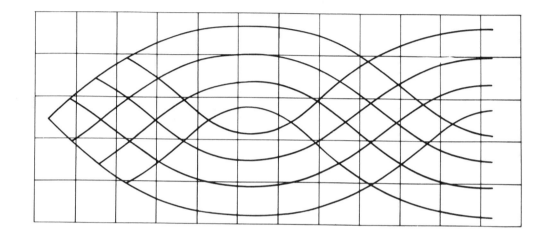

QUILTING
PATTERNS

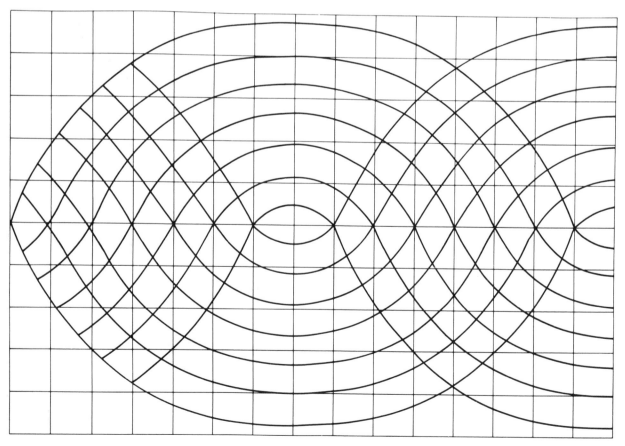

60

red and gold triangles to make 418 squares, matching long sides. Join squares, so that colors alternate, into 10 strips of 34 squares each and two strips of 39 squares each.

Lay the nine gold and green panels out vertically, alternating colors; lay the ten 34-square strips between them and at right and left of outer gold panels; alternate direction of red triangles with every other strip. Right sides together, join strips and panels on $\frac{1}{4}''$ seam lines. Sew 39-square strips across top and bottom. Piece should measure $58\frac{1}{2}''$ × $63\frac{1}{2}''$, plus outside seam allowances.

For border, cut four strips $5\frac{3}{4}''$ wide from green fabric, two 64" long and two $69\frac{1}{2}''$ long (piece where necessary); measurements include $\frac{1}{4}''$ seam allowance. Sew shorter strips to top and bottom, right sides together and making $\frac{1}{4}''$ seams. Sew longer strips to sides. From gold fabric, cut four strips $6\frac{1}{4}''$ wide, two $74\frac{1}{2}''$ long and two $80\frac{1}{2}''$ long (piece where necessary); measurements include $\frac{1}{4}''$ seam allowance. Sew strips to quilt top in same manner as before. Quilt top should measure about $80\frac{1}{2}''$ × $85\frac{1}{2}''$.

For lining, cut two pieces from gold fabric, each $43\frac{1}{4}''$ × $80\frac{1}{2}''$. Join on long edges, right sides together and with $\frac{1}{2}''$ seams. Press seam open. Cut batting same size as lining.

Quilting: Enlarge quilting patterns on paper ruled in 1" squares. Using dressmaker's carbon and tracing wheel, transfer smaller pattern to each green and gold center panel, repeating pattern to cover entire length of panel. Transfer larger pattern to green and gold outer border, $\frac{1}{4}''$ outside of center seam, repeating along entire length of shorter sides and between sides on longer ends.

Pin and baste lining, batting, and quilt top together, following General Directions. Starting at center and working outward, quilt along all marked lines; quilt on each side of seam lines joining triangles, $\frac{1}{8}''$ away; quilt close to seam line on each center panel and around entire pieced center, on green border.

To bind edges, cut four strips $1\frac{1}{2}''$-wide strips from red fabric, two 86" long and two 81" long (piece to get these lengths). Sew strips to quilt top, right sides together and with $\frac{1}{4}''$ seams. Turn strips to back of quilt and slip-stitch to lining, turning in raw edges of strips $\frac{1}{4}''$. Press edges of quilt. ☆

New York Beauty Quilt

shown on page 69

SIZE: 74" × 93".

EQUIPMENT: Scissors. Ruler. Pencil. Thin, stiff cardboard. Tracing paper. All-purpose glue. Compass. Tailor's chalk. Sewing and quilting needles. Quilting frame (optional).

MATERIALS: Closely woven cotton fabric 45" wide: red, $3\frac{1}{2}$ yds.; white, 7 yds.; black-and-white small checked, $3\frac{1}{8}$ yds.; black-and-white striped, 1 yd. (can be 36" wide). Fabric for lining 45" wide, $5\frac{1}{4}$ yds. White sewing thread. Polyester or cotton batting.

DIRECTIONS

Read General Directions for Quilting (see Contents). Quilt is made up of 20 pieced blocks set with pieced joining strips and a plain border.

Patterns: See Piecing Diagram 1 for one block. Draw a 14" square on cardboard. Set compass for $4\frac{1}{4}''$ spread. Place point of compass in one corner of square and draw an arc for pattern B. Set compass for $6\frac{1}{4}''$ and draw an arc in all four corners for pattern A. Trace actual-size patterns of C, D, and E; make several cardboard patterns of each; discard when edges begin to fray.

Patches: Marking patterns on wrong side of fabric and adding $\frac{1}{4}''$ seam allowance all around, cut patch pieces as follows: From red fabric, cut 80 of piece B and 640 of C. From white fabric, cut 20 of A, 560 of D, and 160 of E.

Blocks: Join patch pieces into blocks, following Piecing Diagram 1. To start a block, join eight C pieces, seven D pieces, and two E pieces into a curving strip; join strip to a B piece for corner section. Make three other corner sections in same manner and join the sections to an A piece. Block should measure 14" square, plus outside seam allowance. Make 19 more blocks in same manner.

Joining Strips: To make triangle pattern, draw a rectangle $\frac{7}{8}''$ × $1\frac{7}{8}''$ on cardboard. Mark midpoint on one short side; mark lines from this point to the two opposite corners. Cut out on marked lines for triangle pattern. Marking pattern on wrong side of fabric and adding $\frac{1}{4}''$ seam allowance all around, cut 992 triangles from black-and-white checked fabric and 930 from white fabric. Cut triangle pattern in half and cut 124 small triangles from white fabric. Join 16 checked triangles and 15 white triangles into a strip, sewing triangles together alternately on their long sides; add a small white triangle to each end. Make 61 more triangle strips in same manner.

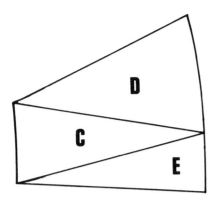

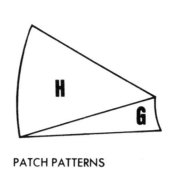

PATCH PATTERNS

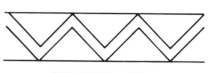

QUILTING DIAGRAM

PIECING DIAGRAM 1

PIECING DIAGRAM 2

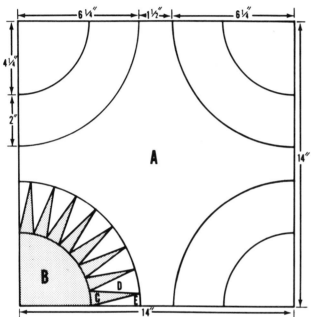

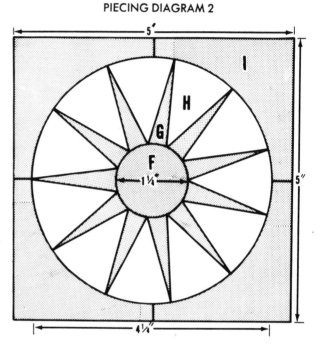

From checked fabric, cut 31 strips $1\frac{1}{4}'' \times 14''$, adding $\frac{1}{4}''$ seam allowance all around. Sew a triangle strip to each long side of checked strip, with base of checked triangles toward center, to make joining strip $5'' \times 14''$, plus outside seam allowance. Make 30 more joining strips in same manner.

Joining Blocks: See Piecing Diagram 2 for one block. For patterns, draw a 5" square on cardboard. Mark horizontal and vertical center lines across square. Set compass for $\frac{5}{8}''$ spread; place point of compass at intersection of center lines and draw around for a circle $1\frac{1}{4}''$ in diameter for pattern F. Set compass for $2\frac{1}{8}''$ and draw another circle in same manner; corner section made is pattern I. Cut on marked lines for patterns F and I. Trace actual-size patterns H and G and make several cardboard patterns of each.

Marking patterns on wrong side of fabric and adding $\frac{1}{4}''$ seam allowance all around, cut patch pieces as follows: From red fabric, cut 48 of piece I, 12 of piece F, and 132 of piece G. From white fabric, cut 132 of piece H.

Following Piecing Diagram 2, assemble 11 G and

11 H pieces into a circle; sew circle to an F piece. Sew four I pieces around circle and to each other, for a joining block 5" square, plus outside seam allowance. Make 11 more joining blocks in same manner.

Assembling: Join large blocks into four vertical rows of five blocks each, with a joining strip between blocks.

Sew remaining joining strips into three vertical rows of five strips each, with a joining block between strips.

Join the four block rows and the three strip rows in alternating fashion for main body of quilt top. Piece should measure $71'' \times 90''$, plus outside seam allowance.

Border: Cut four strips $1\frac{1}{4}''$ wide from black-and-white striped fabric, two $73\frac{1}{2}''$ long and two $92\frac{1}{2}''$ long, adding $\frac{1}{4}''$ seam allowance all around; piece to get lengths. Right sides together, sew shorter strips to top and bottom and longer strips to sides of quilt top; center strips so an equal margin extends at each end. Miter corners; for directions, see Contents. Quilt top should measure $74'' \times 93''$.

Lining: Cut two pieces 37½″ × 93″. Sew together on long sides with ½″ seams; press seam open. Cut batting same size as lining and quilt top.

Quilting: Using ruler and tailor's chalk, mark diagonal lines ⅜″ apart in both directions over white centers (A) of large blocks. Insert tailor's chalk in compass and mark arcs on red corners (B) of large blocks, making arcs ½″, ¼″, ½″, ¼″, etc. apart over entire corner piece.

Mark triangle quilting design on checked strips in center of joining strips, following Quilting Diagram. To make triangle pattern, cut a 1½″ square from cardboard; cut in half diagonally. Place long side of triangle along both long sides of center strips and draw around with tailor's chalk. Mark

same triangle design on border, marking outside triangles along marked seam line.

Following General Directions, pin and baste quilt top, batting, and lining together. Starting in center and working around and outward, quilt on all marked lines and close to seams on all small patch pieces (triangles, circles, and corner [I] pieces of joining blocks). Add extra quilting lines within circles and I pieces, ¼″ apart.

Edges: From red fabric, cut bias strips 1″ wide; sew together for a total of about 335″ for binding. Right sides together and with ¼″ seams, sew binding to front of quilt. Turn binding to back of quilt, turn in edges ¼″, and slip-stitch to lining. Press edges of quilt. ☆

Oak Leaf Quilt

shown on page 70

SIZE: 80″ × 100½″.

EQUIPMENT: Ruler. Scissors. Thin, stiff cardboard. Tracing paper. Dressmaker's tracing (carbon) paper. Tracing wheel or dry ball-point pen. Dark- and light-colored pencils. Sewing and quilting needles. Quilting frame (optional). All-purpose glue.

MATERIALS: Closely woven cotton fabric: blue print 36″ wide, 4½ yds.; white 44″–45″ wide, 5¼ yds. Fabric for lining 44″–45″ wide, 5⅝ yds. White bias binding tape, ¼″ double-folded, 10⅛ yds. White sewing thread. Polyester batting.

DIRECTIONS

Read General Directions for Quilting and How to Appliqué (see Contents). Quilt is constructed with 30 appliquéd blocks, set with appliquéd joining strips.

Appliqués: Actual-size appliqué pattern includes solid lines for appliqués A, B, and C, long dash lines indicating the quarter-block, and short dash lines indicating quilting pattern. Trace solid lines for the three appliqué patterns; complete quarter- and half-patterns for A, B. Glue tracings to cardboard and cut out. Following directions in How to Appliqué, cut and prepare appliqué pieces: From blue fabric, cut 30 of piece A, 120 of B, and 120 of C.

Blocks: For background of blocks, cut 30 pieces 10″ square from white fabric, adding ¼″ seam allowance on each side. On each white square, indicate horizontal and vertical center lines (fold and crease or mark lines with ruler and tailor's

chalk). Retrace appliqué pattern, this time including all lines of complete pattern. Using dressmaker's carbon and tracing wheel, transfer appliqué pattern, matching quarter-block lines to center lines on fabric; do not transfer quilting lines yet. Pin, baste, and slip-stitch appliqué pieces in position on each white square.

Assembling: To frame blocks, cut 120 strips 1½″ wide from blue fabric, 60 10½″ long and 60 12½″ long (measurements include ¼″ seam allowance). Sew shorter strips to opposite sides of each appliqué block, then longer strips to remaining sides. Blocks should measure 12½″ square, including outside seam allowance.

For short joining strips, cut 36 pieces 3¾″ × 12½″ from white fabric (measurements include ¼″ seam allowance). Make six horizontal rows by joining six strips and five blocks in alternate fashion for each row; place blocks so that longer blue framing strips are vertical. For long joining strips, cut seven pieces 4½″ × 80″ from white fabric, piecing to get lengths. Join long strips and horizontal rows, with ¼″ seams, to make piece 80″ × 100½″. To complete quilt top, cut 84 pieces 1½″ × 7½″ from blue fabric. Turn under all edges ¼″ and press. Appliqué pieces to long white joining strips as shown, making an "X" pattern between blocks and on border.

Lining: Cut two pieces from white fabric 40½″ × 100½″. Sew pieces together on long edges with ½″ seams to make lining 80″ × 100½″. Press seam open. Cut batting same size as quilt top and lining.

Quilting: Using dressmaker's carbon and tracing wheel, transfer quilting pattern to appliquéd

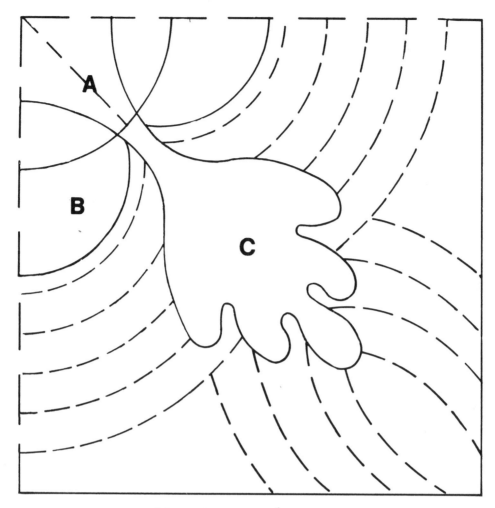

OAK LEAF APPLIQUÉ PATTERN

FLOWER QUILTING PATTERN

blocks. Trace flower quilting pattern; complete half-pattern indicated by dash lines. Transfer flower pattern to each white section surrounding blocks. Following General Directions, pin and baste quilt top, batting, and lining together. Starting at center and working around and outward, quilt on all marked lines and close to all seams, on each side.

Edges: Place edges of quilt between folds of bias binding tape. Slip-stitch edges of binding to front and back. ☆

Lotus Quilt

shown on page 71

SIZE: $87\frac{1}{2}''$ square.

EQUIPMENT: Ruler. Scissors. Dark- and light-colored pencils. Paper for patterns. Tracing paper. Dressmaker's tracing (carbon) paper. Tracing wheel or dry ball-point pen. Sewing and quilting needles. All-purpose glue. Quilting frame (optional).

MATERIALS: Closely woven cotton fabric 44"–45" wide: red, $1\frac{1}{2}$ yds.; light orange, $2\frac{1}{8}$ yds.; green, $2\frac{1}{2}$ yds.; white, $4\frac{1}{2}$ yds. White fabric for lining 45" wide, 5 yds. White sewing thread. Polyester batting.

DIRECTIONS

Read General Directions for Quilting and How to Appliqué (see Contents). Quilt is constructed of 16 appliquéd blocks and a three-color border.

Appliqués: Trace lotus design indicated by solid lines of pattern; complete half-pattern of stem indicated by short dash line. (Dotted lines are quilting pattern and long dash lines outline a quarter-block.) Glue tracing to cardboard and cut on lines, making separate patterns for flower, outer petals (one piece, overlapped by stem), stem, and a leaf. Following directions in How to Appliqué, cut and prepare pieces as follows: Cut 64 flowers from red fabric, 64 petals from orange fabric, 74 leaves and 32 stems from green fabric.

Blocks: Cut 16 pieces 16" square from white fabric, marking squares on wrong side of fabric and adding $\frac{1}{4}''$ seam allowance all around. On each white square, indicate horizontal and vertical center lines (fold and crease or mark with ruler and tailor's chalk). Retrace entire pattern, including dash and dotted lines. Using dressmaker's carbon and tracing wheel, transfer lotus design only to each quarter of white background, matching long dash lines of pattern to center lines of squares and with stem pieces meeting in center of square; leaves will be transferred only twice. Pin, baste, and slip-stitch appliqués in place, overlapping one stem with the other.

Assembling: To frame appliquéd blocks, cut 12 strips $2'' \times 16\frac{1}{2}''$ from green fabric (measurements include $\frac{1}{4}''$ seam allowance). Sew blocks into four horizontal rows of four blocks each, with a green strip between blocks. Cut five strips $2'' \times 69''$ from green fabric. Sew strips between rows of blocks and to top and bottom of piece made. Cut two strips $2'' \times 72''$ from green fabric and sew to sides of piece made. Piece should measure $71\frac{1}{2}''$ square, plus outside seam allowance.

Borders: For first border, cut four strips $3'' \times 77''$ from white fabric (measurements include $\frac{1}{4}''$ seam allowance). Sew strips to quilt top, centering strips on each side so that an equal amount extends at each end. Miter corners; see Contents for directions.

For second border, cut four strips $2'' \times 80''$ from orange fabric. Sew on in same manner as first border, mitering corners.

For third border, cut four strips $3'' \times 85''$ (piecing if necessary) from white fabric and sew on in same manner.

For fourth border, cut four strips $1\frac{3}{4}'' \times 87\frac{1}{2}''$ from green fabric and sew on. Quilt top should measure $87\frac{1}{2}''$ square.

Lining: Cut two pieces $44\frac{3}{4}'' \times 88\frac{1}{2}''$ from white fabric. Sew together on long sides with $\frac{1}{2}''$ seams to make lining $88\frac{1}{2}''$ square; press seam open. Cut batting same size as quilt top.

Quilting: Using dressmaker's carbon and tracing wheel, transfer quilting lines from appliqué pattern to each block. Trace actual-size wave and cable quilting patterns. Transfer wave pattern to each green framing strip and to orange and green border strips, starting in corners where strips meet and repeating waves for length of strips. Transfer cable quilting pattern to each white border strip, starting in corners.

Following General Directions, pin and baste lining, batting, and quilt top together, centering layers so that lining extends $\frac{1}{2}''$ all around beyond batting and quilt top. Starting in center and working around and outward, quilt on all marked lines and around main outlines of appliqué design in each block, close to seams.

Edges: Fold excess lining to front of quilt; turn in raw edge $\frac{1}{4}''$ and slip-stitch folded edge to quilt top. Press edges of quilt. ☆

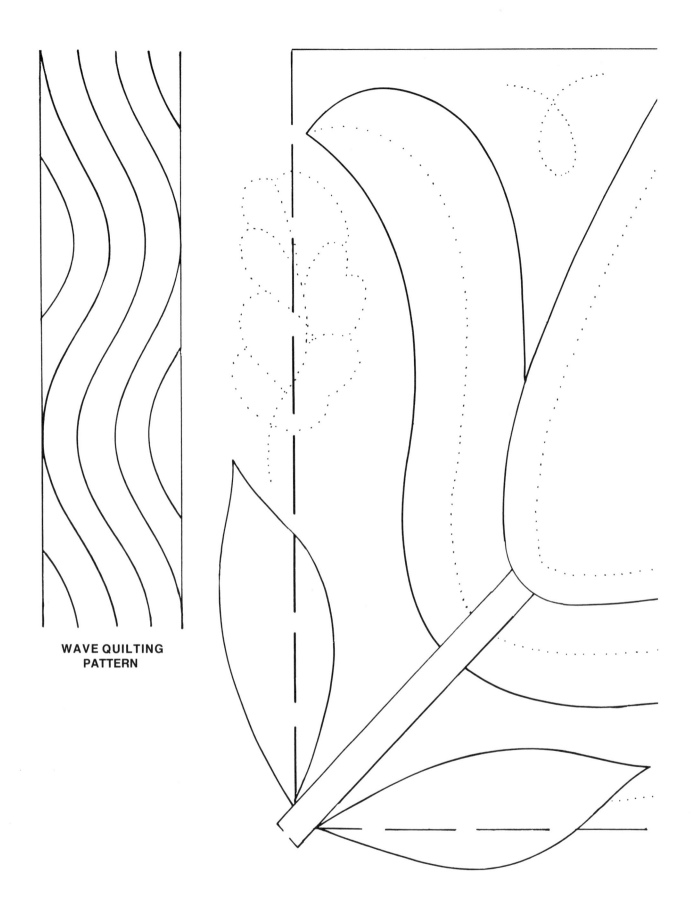

**WAVE QUILTING
PATTERN**

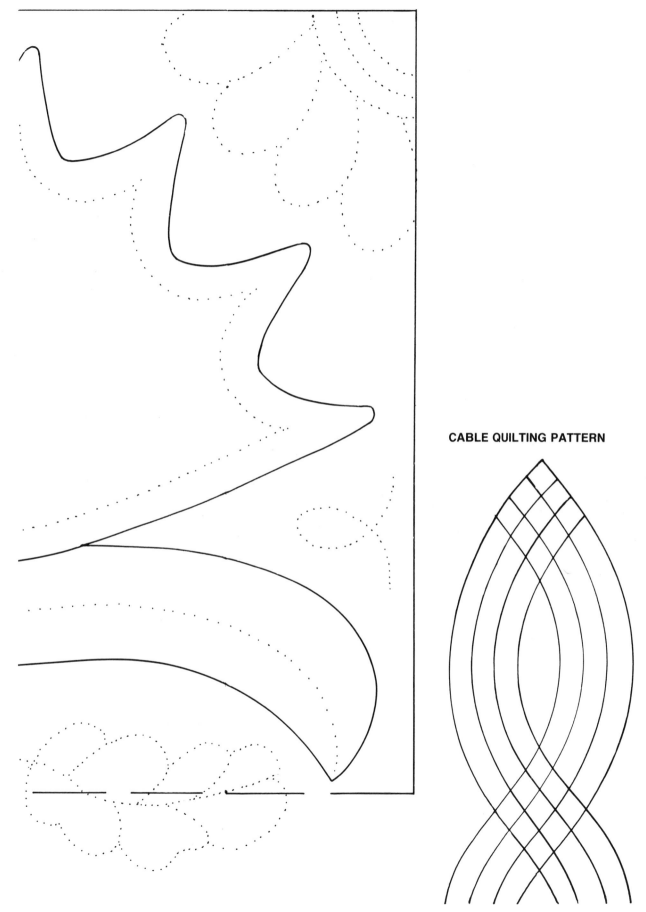

CABLE QUILTING PATTERN

This quilt, made in Pennsylvania ca. 1890, has an affinity with contemporary design. The geometrics are softened by graceful cables, quilted on every panel. This coverlet is unusual because of its border, not typical of the Tree Everlasting Quilt.
For Tree Everlasting Quilt directions, see Contents.

(Quilt courtesy of Tony Ellis and Bill Gallick.)

New York Beauty, despite its name, has an almost Indian flavor. Little triangular segments, needle-sharp, are pieced in arcs to make the spiky wheels. This quilt is for the skilled needleworker only! The interest here is in the piecing; quilting is a simple grid or follows the appliqués. This quilt was made in New York in 1880. For New York Beauty Quilt directions, see Contents. *(Quilt courtesy of Bryce and Donna Hamilton, Tipton, Iowa.)*

Oak leaf motifs in blue are appliquéd to white background blocks, as is the "garden maze" framing. This quilt, unusually large at 80″ × 100″, was made in Vermont, ca. 1860. For Oak Leaf Quilt directions, see Contents.

(Quilt courtesy of Tony Ellis and Bill Gallick.)

The lovely lotus motif, multiplied,
creates a striking overall pattern. Decorative wave
and cable quilting adorns the strips joining
and bordering appliquéd blocks.
This quilt was made in Pennsylvania, ca. 1865.
For Lotus Quilt directions, see Contents.
(Quilt courtesy of America Hurrah Antiques, New York City.)

Sawtooth triangles and stripes are among the oldest of patchwork patterns. Here, plain panels balance the sawtooth panels, all in white and indigo. This quilt was made in New England, ca. 1770–1790. For Sawtooth Stripes Quilt directions, see Contents.

(Quilt courtesy of The Pink House Antiques, New Hope, Pennsylvania.)

This dynamic quilt, made in Missouri ca. 1880, is hung from a high railing to give almost full display to its strong design. Made with a combination of techinques, the quilt's larger blocks are pieced, then framed with fan clusters appliquéd to smaller blocks. For Whig's Defeat Quilt directions, see Contents.

(Quilt courtesy of Bryce and Donna Hamilton, Tipton, Iowa.)

73

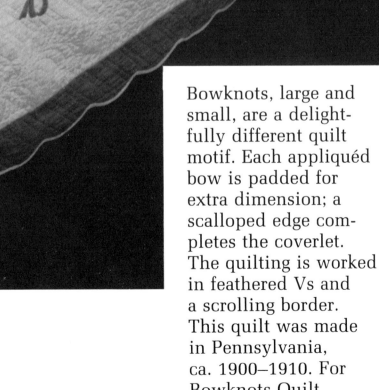

Bowknots, large and small, are a delightfully different quilt motif. Each appliquéd bow is padded for extra dimension; a scalloped edge completes the coverlet. The quilting is worked in feathered Vs and a scrolling border. This quilt was made in Pennsylvania, ca. 1900–1910. For Bowknots Quilt directions, see Contents.

(Quilt courtesy of Pink House Antiques, New Hope, Pennsylvania.)

An imaginative placement of the appliqués
gives this quilt an unusually sensuous
appeal. The background is closely quilted
in a somewhat free-form fashion with leaves
and straight-line patterns. This quilt was
made in Massachusetts, ca. 1840–1850. For
Cockscomb Quilt directions, see Contents.

(Quilt courtesy of George E. Schoellkopf.)

Whig's Defeat Quilt

shown on page 72

SIZE: 83" square.

EQUIPMENT: Pencil. Ruler. Scissors. Thin, stiff cardboard. Paper for patterns. Tracing paper. Dressmaker's tracing (carbon) paper. Tracing wheel or dry ball-point pen. Tailor's chalk. Sewing and quilting needles. Compass. Quilting frame (optional). All-purpose glue.

MATERIALS: Closely woven cotton fabric 44"–45" wide: red, $1\frac{2}{3}$ yds.; dark blue-green, $2\frac{1}{2}$ yds.; white, $5\frac{3}{4}$ yds. Fabric for lining 44"–45" wide, $4\frac{2}{3}$ yds. Polyester batting. White sewing thread.

DIRECTIONS

Read General Directions for Quilting and How to Appliqué (see Contents). Quilt is constructed of nine pieced blocks set with appliquéd blocks and panels.

Pieced Blocks: See Piecing Diagram for one block. To make patterns for patch pieces, draw a $15\frac{1}{2}$" square on cardboard. Set compass for 4" spread; place point of compass in one corner of square drawn and draw an arc for piece B. Set compass for $6\frac{5}{8}$" and draw an arc in all four corners for piece A. Cut along marked lines for patterns. Trace actual-size patterns for pieces C, D, E, and F; glue to cardboard and cut out on marked lines.

Marking patterns on wrong side of fabric and adding $\frac{1}{4}$" seam allowance all around, cut patch pieces as follows: From green fabric, cut 36 B pieces and 252 C pieces. From red fabric, cut 252 E pieces. From white fabric, cut nine A pieces, 216 D pieces, and 72 F pieces.

To make one block, assemble pieces as shown in Piecing Diagram. Join seven C pieces, seven E pieces, six D pieces, and two F pieces into a curving strip, then join strip to a B piece for corner section. Make three more corner sections and join the four to an A piece for a block measuring $15\frac{1}{2}$"

square, plus outside seam allowance. Make eight more blocks in same manner as for first block.

Appliquéd Blocks: Trace actual-size appliqué pattern. Following directions in How to Appliqué, cut and prepare 148 appliqués from red fabric and 104 from green.

For background of blocks, make cardboard pattern 6" × $15\frac{1}{2}$". Marking pattern on wrong side of fabric and adding $\frac{1}{4}$" seam allowance all around, cut 18 blocks from white fabric. On one long side of each block, mark off a center section $2\frac{1}{4}$" wide ($6\frac{5}{8}$" from each end). Place five appliqués in a fan cluster on each block (two green flanking three red), with base of appliqués within marked center section; pin, baste, and slip-stitch in place.

Sew an appliquéd block to two opposite sides of each pieced block, matching appliquéd edge to white edge (piece A) of larger block.

Join the sections made into three rows of three sections each, matching plain edges of appliquéd blocks. Rows should measure 16" × 83", including outside seam allowance.

Appliquéd Panels: For inner panels, cut two pieces from white fabric $12\frac{1}{2}$" × 83" (measurements include $\frac{1}{4}$" seam allowance all around). Appliqué eight fan clusters along edges of each panel in same design as before ($2\frac{1}{4}$" wide at base): Place one fan cluster at each end and three on each long side; to place side clusters, mark points 14" and $41\frac{1}{2}$" from each end. Appliqué two circle clusters to each panel, using four red and four green appliqué pieces for each cluster as shown in illustration and making appliqués slightly more pointed at narrow end where they converge at center of cluster; to place clusters, mark a point $27\frac{3}{4}$" from each end, $6\frac{1}{4}$" from side.

Join the three block rows and the two appliquéd panels together on their long sides, in alternating fashion; side fan clusters of panels should match white edges of square blocks.

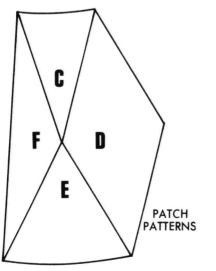

PATCH
PATTERNS

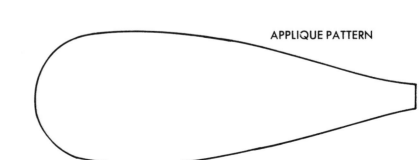

APPLIQUE PATTERN

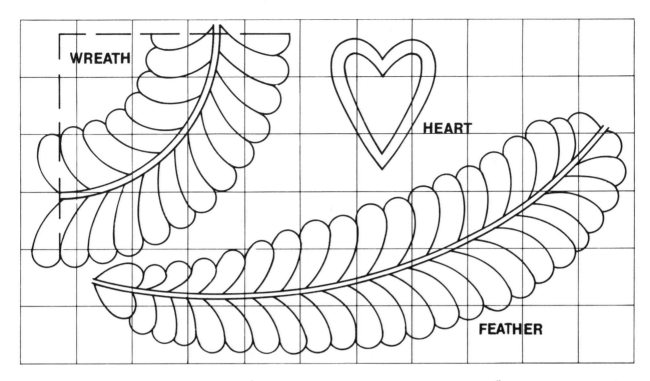

For outer panels, cut two pieces $6\frac{1}{2}'' \times 83''$ from white fabric. Appliqué five fan clusters to each outer panel, placing three on one long edge ($14''$ and $41\frac{1}{2}''$ from each end) and two on the opposite long edge($27\frac{3}{4}''$ from each end).

Join appliquéd panels to both sides of quilt top, matching the three clusters to white edges of square blocks. Quilt top should now measured $83''$ square.

Lining: Cut two pieces $42'' \times 83''$. Sew together on their long sides with $\frac{1}{2}''$ seams; press seam open. Cut batting same size as lining and quilt top.

Quilting: Enlarge wreath, feather, and heart quilting patterns on paper ruled in $1''$ squares; complete quarter-patterns indicated by dash lines. Using dressmaker's carbon and tracing wheel, transfer patterns to quilt top: Place a wreath in center of each white A piece. Place a heart in each side section of A pieces. Place feather four times around each appliquéd circle cluster, making an oval shape. Place feather twice for a half-oval around the eight clusters that edge quilt top. Place a heart inside pointed ends of ovals and half-ovals. Fill in remaining white areas of quilt top with hearts, arranging them in groups of two or four with pointed ends meeting.

Mark concentric circular lines on corner sections of pieced blocks; mark lines $\frac{1}{4}''$ apart in groups of three, making groups $\frac{1}{2}''$ apart.

Following General Directions, pin and baste quilt top, batting, and lining together. Starting in center and working around and outward, quilt on all

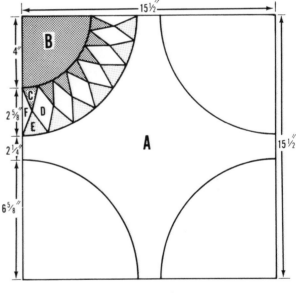

PIECING DIAGRAM

marked lines and around appliqués; within appliqués, quilt two lines $\frac{1}{8}''$ apart.

Edges: Trim corners of quilt slightly for rounded shape. From green fabric, cut bias strips $1''$ wide; sew together for a total of about $9\frac{1}{3}$ yds. for binding. Right sides together and with $\frac{1}{4}''$ seams, sew binding to front of quilt. Turn binding to back of quilt, turn in edges $\frac{1}{4}''$, and slip-stitch to lining. Press edges of quilt. ☆

Sawtooth Stripes Quilt

shown on page 73

SIZE: 83″ × 95″.

EQUIPMENT: Ruler. Scissors. Light- and dark-colored pencils. Thin, stiff cardboard. Tailor's chalk. Sewing and quilting needles. Quilting frame (optional).

MATERIALS: Closely woven cotton fabric: dark blue with small white dot 36″ wide, 4 yds.; white 45″ wide, 4¾ yds. Fabric for lining 45″ wide, 5⅝ yds. White double-fold bias binding tape ¼″ wide, 10 yds. Polyester or cotton batting. White sewing thread.

DIRECTIONS:

Read General Directions for Quilting (see Contents). Quilt is made up of eleven panels of pieced (sawtooth) and plain stripes.

Wide Sawtooth Stripes: Following Piecing Diagram, cut cardboard patterns: Pattern A, half of a 4″ square; Pattern B, half of a 1″ square; Pattern C, half of a 1″ × 1$\frac{1}{16}$″ rectangle.

Marking patterns on wrong side of fabric and adding ¼″ seam allowance all around, cut patch pieces as follows: From blue fabric, cut 45 of A, 495 of B, and 360 of C. From white fabric, cut 495 of B and 360 of C. Following Piecing Diagram, assemble a sawtooth-triangle patch: Make nine 1″ squares by sewing a white B piece and a blue B piece together on their long sides for each square; make eight 1″ × 1$\frac{1}{16}$″ rectangles by sewing a white C piece and a blue C piece together on their long sides for each rectangle. Sew pieced squares and rectangles into strips as shown, adding extra B pieces at ends, then sew strips around an A piece. Finished patch should be a right-angle triangle measuring 7$\frac{7}{16}$″ on each short side. Make 44 more sawtooth-triangle patches in same manner.

For large white triangle patches, make a cardboard pattern by cutting a 7$\frac{7}{16}$″ square in half diagonally. Marking pattern on wrong side of fabric and adding ¼″ seam allowance all around, cut 40 large triangles from white fabric. Cut cardboard pattern in half for medium-size triangle pattern and cut 10 medium-size triangles from white fabric.

Assemble nine sawtooth triangles and eight large white triangles into a strip, fitting pieces together as shown in illustration. At both ends of strip, add a medium-size white triangle. Assemble four more strips in same manner.

Narrow Sawtooth Stripes: To make pattern, mark a rectangle ¾″ × 1⅛″ on cardboard; mark a corner-to-corner diagonal line on rectangle; cut on marked lines for triangle pattern. Marking pattern on wrong side of fabric and adding ¼″ seam allowance all around, cut 420 triangles each from blue and white fabric. Make 420 rectangular patches, sewing a blue triangle and a white together on their long sides for each patch. Join patches into five strips of 84 patches each, with triangles all pointing in the same direction in each strip.

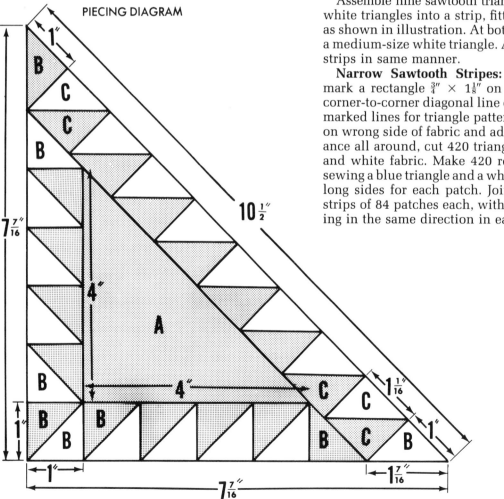

PIECING DIAGRAM

Sawtooth Panels: Join a narrow sawtooth strip to each wide sawtooth strip for five pieced panels; place strips so triangles of both strips are pointing in the same direction. Each panel should measure $6'' \times 94\frac{1}{2}''$, plus outside seam allowance.

Plain Panels: Cut 30 strips $1\frac{3}{4}'' \times 94\frac{1}{2}''$, adding $\frac{1}{4}''$ seam allowance all around: 12 from blue fabric and 18 from white fabric. Join two blue strips and three white strips on their long sides, alternating colors, for a panel $8\frac{3}{4}'' \times 94\frac{1}{2}''$, plus outside seam allowance. Make five more panels in same manner.

Assembling: Join plain panels and sawtooth panels for quilt top, alternating panels and beginning and ending piece with a plain panel. Quilt top should measure $83'' \times 95''$, including outside seam allowance. (*Note:* Outer white stripe has been lost from one side of original quilt, as shown in illustration).

Lining: Cut two pieces $42'' \times 95''$. Sew together on long sides with $\frac{1}{2}''$ seams; press seam open. Cut batting same size as lining and quilt top.

Quilting: With ruler and tailor's chalk, mark quilting lines $\frac{3}{8}''$ apart over quilt; make lines horizontal on sawtooth panels and diagonal (in one direction) on plain panels.

Pin and baste quilt, batting, and lining together, following General Directions. Starting in center and working outward in both directions, quilt on all marked lines.

Edges: Bind edges with white double-fold bias binding tape, slip-stitching to front and then to lining. Press edges. ☆

Bowknots Quilt

shown on page 74

SIZE: $76'' \times 91''$.

EQUIPMENT: Scissors. Ruler. Pencil. Thin, stiff cardboard. Tracing paper. Paper for patterns. Dressmaker's tracing (carbon) paper. Tailor's chalk. Tracing wheel or dry ball-point pen. Sewing and quilting needles. Knitting needle. Quilting frame (optional). All-purpose glue.

MATERIALS: Closely woven cotton fabric 45" wide: $2\frac{3}{4}$ yds. brown; $3\frac{3}{4}$ yds. white. Fabric for lining, 45" wide, $5\frac{1}{8}$ yds. White double-fold bias binding tape, $\frac{1}{4}''$ wide, 10 yds. Polyester batting. Cotton for stuffing appliqués. White sewing thread.

DIRECTIONS

Read General Directions for Quilting and How to Appliqué (see Contents). For white background of quilt top, cut two pieces, $41\frac{1}{2}'' \times 67''$. Sew together on long sides with $\frac{1}{2}''$ seams to make piece $67'' \times 82''$. Press seam open. Turn piece so that seam runs horizontally. Using ruler and tailor's chalk, mark straight lines very lightly on white piece: Mark five vertical lines, the two outer lines $9\frac{1}{2}''$ from sides and the three inner lines 12" apart; mark seven horizontal lines, the two outer lines $9\frac{1}{2}''$ from top and bottom and the five inner lines $10\frac{1}{2}''$ apart.

Appliqués: Trace half-patterns for large and small bows; complete both patterns. Using dressmaker's carbon and tracing wheel (or dry ball-point pen), transfer outline of 18 large bows and 17 small bows to white background where marked lines intersect; alternate large and small bows throughout, both

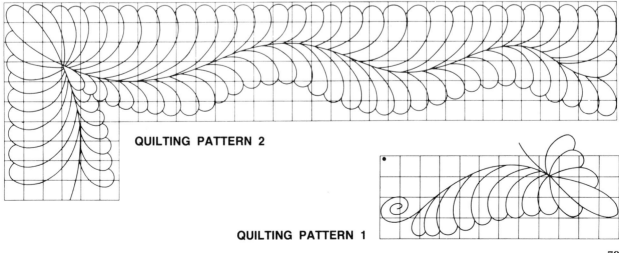

QUILTING PATTERN 2

QUILTING PATTERN 1

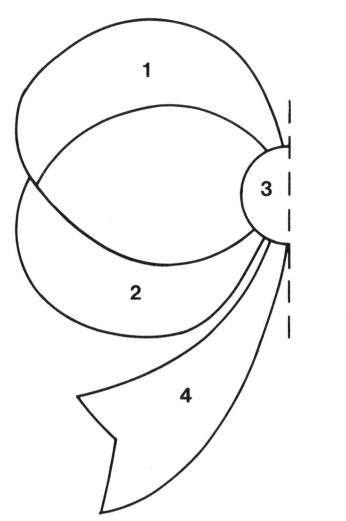

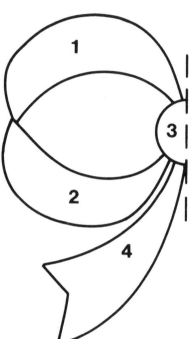

horizontally and vertically, starting in all four corners with a large bow.

Trace patterns again; glue to cardboard. Cut on lines to make a separate pattern for each of the four separate parts of both bows. Following direction in How to Appliqué, cut and prepare appliqué pieces from brown fabric, making 18 large circles, 17 small circles, 36 each of remaining three large pieces, and 34 each of remaining small pieces. Pin, baste, and slip-stitch appliqué pieces in place, centers last; as you baste, stuff in bits of cotton with a knitting needle, so that finished bows are firmly puffed.

Border: Cut four pieces $5\frac{1}{2}''$ wide from brown fabric, two 67" long and two 91" long. Right sides together and making $\frac{1}{2}''$ seams, sew shorter pieces to top and bottom of white center, then longer pieces to sides. Quilt top should measure 76" × 91".

Lining: Cut two pieces $38\frac{1}{2}''$ × 91". Sew together on long sides with $\frac{1}{2}''$ seams to make lining 76" × 91"; press seam open. Cut batting same size as lining and quilt top.

Quilting: Enlarge quilting patterns on paper ruled in 1" squares; complete half-pattern of No. 1 for a curving V-shaped design. Using dressmaker's carbon and tracing wheel (or dry ball-point pen), transfer V-shaped pattern to quilt top 24 times, making six horizontal rows of four patterns each; place each pattern carefully in the open space between four bows so that tops of adjacent V shapes will just touch under a bow.

Place quilting pattern No. 2 all around edge of white background, $\frac{1}{2}''$ from seam; start in corners. At top and bottom of white background, designs should just meet in centers; on sides, add an extra curve to each pattern, so designs will meet.

With ruler and tailor's chalk, mark remainder of quilt top with pairs of diagonal lines in four directions, forming a pattern of concentric diamonds over entire quilt top (skip over appliqués and quilting patterns already marked). Begin by marking an equilateral diamond shape around small bow in center of quilt top, with side points of diamond on center seam; mark another diamond around first one, $\frac{1}{2}''$ outside lines. Mark a second pair of diamonds $1\frac{1}{4}''$ outside first pair. Continue marking concentric diamonds in pairs, working out to brown corners.

Following General Directions, pin and baste quilt

top, batting, and lining together. Starting in center and working around and outward, quilt on all marked lines and around bows.

Edges: To scallop edges, mark 11 points at top and bottom of quilt, placing points 8″ from corners and 6″ from each other. Mark 14 points on each side, 8″ from corners and 5¾″ from each other. Cut curving indentations 1″ deep at points marked. Bind edges of quilt with white bias binding tape, slip-stitching to front and lining ☆

Cockscomb Quilt

shown on page 75

SIZE: About 80″ square.

EQUIPMENT: Scissors. Ruler. Thin, stiff cardboard. Paper for patterns. All-purpose glue. Dressmaker's (carbon) tracing paper. Tailor's chalk. Straight pins. Sewing and quilting needles. Tracing wheel. Quilting frame (optional).

MATERIALS: Closely woven cotton fabric 44″–45″ wide: white, 9 yds. (includes lining); rose, 1 yd.; light green, 2½ yds. Matching sewing thread. Polyester or cotton batting.

DIRECTIONS

Read General Directions for Quilting and How to Appliqué (see Contents). Enlarge appliqué patterns by copying on paper ruled in squares (2″ squares for the flower motif; 1″ squares for border

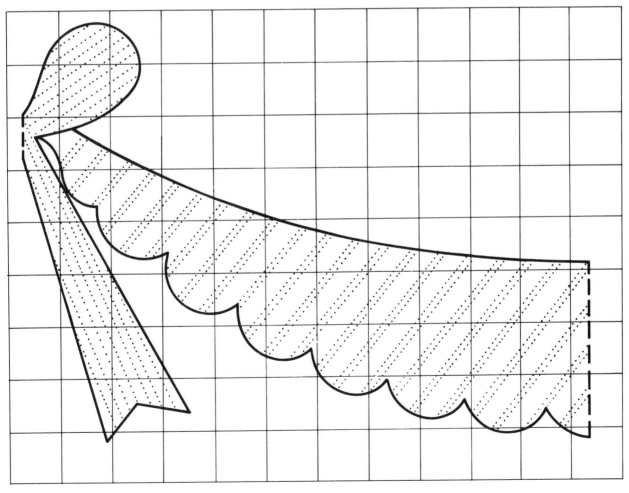

BORDER APPLIQUÉ

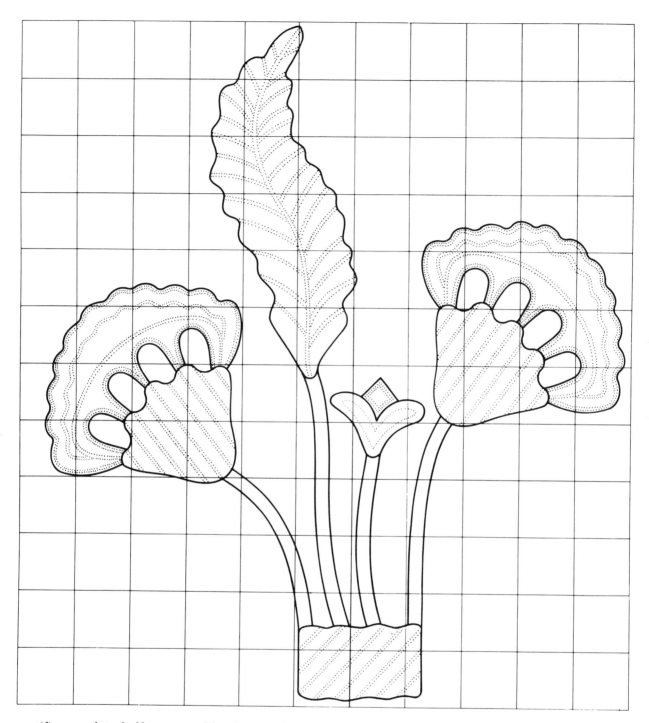

motif); complete half-pattern of border motif indicated by dash lines. Dotted lines indicate quilting patterns. Make a cardboard pattern for each separate part of appliqué motifs. Following directions in How to Appliqué, cut and prepare appliqués as follows: From rose fabric, cut 20 flower tops, 12 buds, and 12 bows; from green fabric, cut 20 flower bases, 12 bud bases, 12 leaves, 9 scalloped rectangles, 12 border swags, 20 flower stems, 12 leaf stems, and 12 bud stems. (*Note:* You may find it easier to substitute straight bias strips for stems cut from pattern. Cut 1"-wide strips on the bias, turn in both long edges $\frac{1}{4}$" to make $\frac{1}{2}$" strips,

and press carefully. Pin in place when appliquéing, curving to fit design.)

For background of quilt top, cut two pieces 41" × 81" from white fabric. Sew together on long edges with $\frac{1}{2}$" seams; press seam open. Pin appliqués in place (do not baste yet) as follows, starting with border: Pin a swag in center of each side, 1" from edge. Pin a swag on each side of center swags, adjusting placement at corners so adjacent swags meet in one continuous curve. Pin on bows where swags meet. Pin a scalloped rectangular piece $\frac{1}{2}$" in from swags on top and bottom and middle swags of sides. Pin flower, leaf, bud, and stem pieces in place along inside edge of each rectangular piece to complete appliqué motifs around sides of quilt top. Pin remaining rectangular piece in center of quilt top; pin remaining appliqué pieces around it (see illustration for placement). At this point, examine overall design carefully and make any adjustments that seem necessary for a pleasing effect; unpin and reposition any part of side and center appliqués as desired. When design is arranged to your satisfaction, baste pieces in place and slip-stitch, starting with stems, then continuing with flower tops and buds and the overlapping green pieces.

For lining, cut two pices 41″ × 81″ from white fabric. Sew together on long sides with $\frac{1}{2}$″ seams. Press seam open. Cut batting same size as lining and quilt top.

Quilting: Using dressmaker's carbon and tracing wheel, transfer dotted-line quilting patterns to each appliqué piece. Using leaf appliqué pattern as a quilting pattern, transfer leaf design to white background where desired. (In original quilt, leaves of varying sizes and shapes were quilted at random over parts of the white background.) Remaining quilting patterns are made with double rows of lines; lines of a double row are $\frac{1}{16}$″ apart, and double rows are $\frac{1}{4}$″ apart. With tailor's chalk, mark two double rows around main outlines of appliqué pieces, including inside curves of swags. Using ruler and tailor's chalk, mark straight double rows over remaining parts of white background; make parallel lines all in one direction or vary as in original quilt (see illustration).

Pin and baste quilt top, batting, and lining together, following General Directions. Trim corners into curves, leaving at least $1\frac{1}{2}$″ between points of corner bows and curves. On quilt top, mark seam allowance all around, $\frac{1}{2}$″ from edge. Starting in center and working around and outward, quilt on all marked lines. Do not quilt beyond seam line marked around edge of quilt.

To finish edges, trim lining and batting to $\frac{1}{2}$″ from edge of quilt top. Turn excess fabric of quilt top to back; turn in raw edge $\frac{1}{4}$″, and slip-stitch to lining. Press edges.   ☆

Sun and Shadow Quilt

shown on page 106

shown on page 106

SIZE: 86″ square.

EQUIPMENT: Light- and dark-colored pencils. Thin, stiff cardboard. Ruler. Scissors. Straight pins. Sewing and quilting needles. Paper for pattern. Tailor's chalk. Dressmaker's tracing (carbon) paper. Tracing wheel or dry ball-point pen. Quilting frame (optional).

MATERIALS: Closely woven cotton, rayon, silk, or crepe fabric, 44″–45″ wide: for patches, $\frac{1}{4}$ yd. each yellow-green, cornflower blue, black; $\frac{3}{8}$ yd. each light green, shocking pink, mauve, blue-green, midnight blue, royal blue (use leftover fabric from border), dark purple, light purple, lavender; $\frac{1}{2}$ yd. each wine, dark green, olive; for border, $4\frac{1}{8}$ yds. royal blue. Fabric for lining 44″–45″ wide, $4\frac{7}{8}$ yds. Black sewing thread. Polyester batting.

DIRECTIONS

Read General Directions for Quilting (see Contents). Quilt is made up of 1089 squares sewn together, plus a plain border. Any combination of colors may be substituted for the ones given in the materials list, as long as the colors progress in the design from light to dark, retaining the shadowed effect.

Patches: Cut cardboard pattern $1\frac{7}{8}$″ square. Cut several patterns and replace as edges begin to fray. Marking pattern on wrong side of fabric and adding $\frac{1}{4}$″ seam allowance all around, cut patches as follows: 85 shocking pink, 88 mauve, 92 wine, 96 dark green, 96 olive, 32 yellow-green, 24 cornflower blue, 84 blue-green, 80 midnight blue, 64 royal blue, 36 black, 84 dark purple, 84 light purple, 84 lavender, 60 light green.

Blocks: Following color illustration, sew patches together in diagonal rows to make a square block, which will be one-quarter of pieced quilt top. Start in a corner with one blue-green patch for first row. Add two royal blue patches for second (diagonal) row, joined to adjacent sides of blue-green patch. Next row is three yellow-green patches, then four olive green patches, etc. Continue sewing on rows of patches, each row one patch longer than previous row, until you reach bottom green row of 17 patches. Continue sewing on rows, following illustration, with each row one patch shorter than previous row, until you reach one shocking pink patch, which is center of quilt. You have now completed slightly more than one-quarter of entire square design.

Mark off a section on color illustration to correspond to block you have sewn, matching rows exactly. Extend your lines on illustration to divide whole square design into four sections; you will note that the three new sections are not identical to the first one marked. Piece three more blocks to correspond to these three sections. Join the four blocks, with single shocking pink patch in center, to make pachwork design about $62\frac{1}{2}''$ square, including outside seam allowance.

Border: Cut four pieces of royal blue fabric, each $12\frac{1}{4}''$ wide: two $62\frac{1}{2}''$ long and two $86''$ long, piecing to get length (measurements include $\frac{1}{4}''$ seam allowance). With right sides facing, sew the two shorter strips to opposite sides of quilt top and the two longer strips to remaining sides, joining ends of shorter strips to sides of longer strips. Quilt top should measure $86''$ square.

Lining: Cut two pieces $43\frac{1}{2}'' \times 86''$. Sew together on long edges with $\frac{1}{2}''$ seams to make lining $86''$ square. Press seam open. Cut batting same size as lining.

Quilting: Using ruler and tailor's chalk, mark diagonal lines in both directions over every patchwork row, going through corners of each patch. For border, enlarge quilting pattern by copying on paper ruled in $2''$ squares. Using dressmaker's carbon and tracing wheel, transfer pattern to each corner of quilt top, $1\frac{1}{4}''$ from edge. Continue design all around border by repeating oval segment of pattern twice more on each side, overlapping flowers at side points of ovals.

Following General Directions, pin and baste quilt top, batting, and lining together. Starting in center and working around and outward, quilt on all marked lines.

Edges: Cut four strips of royal blue fabric, each $2\frac{1}{2}'' \times 86\frac{1}{2}''$. Sew a strip to one side edge of quilt top, with seam $1''$ from edge of quilt and $\frac{1}{4}''$ from edge of strip, right sides together; turn in ends. Fold strip to back of quilt; turn in edge of strip $\frac{1}{4}''$ and slip-stitch to back. Repeat on opposite side of quilt, then on two remaining sides, overlapping ends of strips. ☆

BORDER QUILTING PATTERN

84

Field of Flowers Quilt

shown on page 105

SIZE: About 46″ × 61″.

EQUIPMENT: Pencil. Ruler, Graph paper for patterns. Thin, stiff carboard. All-purpose glue. Compass. Straight pins. Sewing needle. Quilting frame (optional).

MATERIALS: Closely woven cotton fabric 45″ wide: dark red, 1 yd.: rose/blue/off-white print, 1¼ yds. Unbleached muslin 48″ wide, 3 yds. (includes lining). Batting. White sewing and quilting threads.

DIRECTIONS

Read General Directions for Quilting (see Contents). Quilt is made up of 12 pieced blocks; see diagrams for the two block designs.

Patterns: Make three patterns for patch pieces as follows: For pattern A, mark a 3″ square on graph paper; for B, mark a 3″ square, then divide it in half diagonally to make a triangle; for C, mark a rectangle 3″ × 9″. Glue graph paper to cardboard, let dry, then cut on marked lines for patterns, A, B, and C.

Patches: Following General Directions, mark patterns on wrong side of fabric: On white (muslin), mark 42 A, 72B, 12 C. On rose, mark 144 B. On print, mark 42 A, 72 B, 12 C. Cut out patches ¼″ beyond marked lines, for seam allowance.

Blocks: For Block 1, sew together 33 patches, making ¼″ seam and following diagram; first, join rose and white B triangles for B squares, then sew A and B pieces and A and C pieces into rows; join rows for completed block. Make six of Block 1. Make six of Block II, reversing position of white and print pieces as shown. Blocks should measure 15½″ square, including outside seam allowance.

Assembling Quilt Top: Lay out the 12 blocks into four horizontal rows of three blocks each; alternate Blocks I and II throughout. In each row, join adjacent blocks, placing them with right sides facing and making ¼″ seams. Join rows in same manner for quilt top, keeping to alternating pattern. Quilt top should measure 45½″ × 60½″ including outside seam allowance.

Cut lining 45½″ × 60½″ from muslin. Cut batting same size.

Quilting: Quilting pattern for each block is indicated on diagram by dotted lines. For curving lines of pattern, use compass to draw two circles 7¾″ and 8″ in diameter on cardboard; cut out circles for templates. Using tailor's chalk, mark quilting lines very lightly on quilt top: On Block I, mark eight points around perimeter of print section, each 1″ from a corner. Place 8″ template in center of

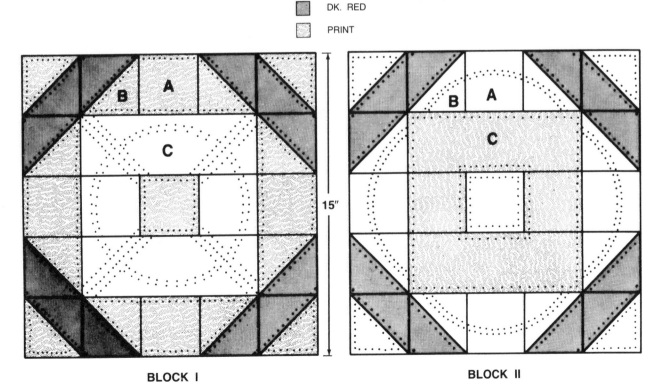

WHITE

DK. RED

PRINT

BLOCK I

BLOCK II

DIAGRAMS FOR QUILT BLOCK DESIGNS

block, then slide it up until sides touch two marked points; mark around upper segment of template for outer curve on upper white section. Mark outer curves on remaining white sections in same manner. Mark inner curves, placing $7\frac{3}{4}''$ template $\frac{1}{8}''$ inside first curves. Using ruler, mark straight lines as shown, $\frac{1}{4}''$ from seams. On Block II, use same templates to mark circles on white section. Mark straight lines as for Block I, but making diagonal lines on white section $\frac{1}{2}''$ apart.

Following General Directions for Quilting, baste lining, batting and quilt top together. Starting in center and working around and outward, quilt on all marked lines.

Finishing: From muslin, cut and piece $1\frac{1}{2}''$-wide strips to equal about 220″. Turn in one long edge of strip $\frac{1}{4}''$ and press in place. On right side of quilt, pin strip around perimeter, right sides of fabrics facing and matching raw edges. Stitch with $\frac{1}{4}''$ seam. Fold strip around edge of quilt to wrong side; slip-stitch pressed edge to lining. ☆

Aunt Sukey's Choice Quilt

shown on page 107

SIZE: 50″ × 73″.

EQUIPMENT: Light- and dark-colored pencils. Ruler. Scissors. Thin, stiff cardboard. Sewing and quilting needles. Quilting frame (optional).

MATERIALS: Closely woven cotton print fabric; small amounts of various patterns of greens, yellows, bright reds, and blues; one dark red pattern, two royal blue patterns, one green-blue pattern, and one turquoise pattern; $\frac{3}{8}$ yd. each of a yellow-on-white and a red-on-white pattern, 36″ wide. White cotton fabric 45″ wide, $1\frac{1}{4}$ yds. Border fabric (see Border directions). Fabric for lining 40″ wide,

$1\frac{1}{2}$ yds. Polyester batting. Yellow double-fold bias binding tape $\frac{1}{4}''$ wide, 7 yds. White, blue, and red sewing threads.

DIRECTIONS

Read General Directions for Quilting (see Contents). Quilt is made up of 12 pieced blocks plus border. All blocks are identical in form (see Piecing Diagram) but are divided by color arrangement into four groups of three blocks each.

Patch Pieces: Make two cardboard patterns for patch pieces as follows: Cut a $2\frac{1}{2}''$ square. Mark

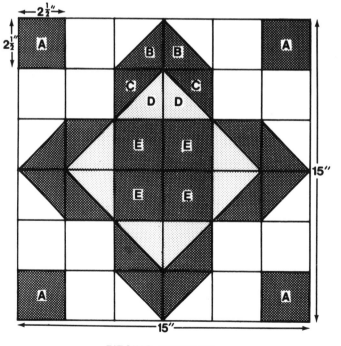

PIECING DIAGRAM

another 2½″ square on cardboard, draw a diagonal line between two opposite corners, and cut on marked lines for triangle pattern.

Marking patterns on wrong side of fabric and adding ¼″ seam allowance all around, cut 144 squares and 96 triangles from white fabric; cut 24 squares each from various green, yellow, bright red, and blue fabrics; cut 24 triangles each from three bright reds, one dark red, two royal blues, one green-blue, and one turquoise fabric; cut 48 triangles each from one yellow-on-white fabric and one red-on-white fabric.

Blocks: Following Piecing Diagram and each color arrangement for Blocks 1, 2, 3, and 4 given in the following paragraph, assemble patch pieces into blocks; join triangle pieces on their long sides to make squares, then join squares for block. Make three blocks in each color group. Block should measure 15″ square, plus outside seam allowance.

Blocks 1: Pieces A, various greens; B, one royal blue; C, second royal blue; D, one yellow-on-white; E, various reds. Remaining pieces are white. Blocks 2: A, various yellows; B, one dark red; C, one bright red; D, one yellow-on-white; E, various blues. Blocks 3: A, various greens; B, one green-blue; C, one turquoise; D, one red-on-white; E, various reds. Blocks 4: A, various yellows; B, one bright red; C, second bright red; D, one red-on-white; E, various blues.

Assembling: Join the 12 blocks into four rows of three blocks each as follows: Row 1: Blocks 1, 2, 1. Row 2: Blocks 4, 3, 4. Row 3: Blocks 3, 4, 3.

Row 4: Blocks 2, 1, 2. Join the four rows in order given for main body of quilt top. Piece should measure 45½″ × 60½″, including outside seam allowance.

Border: For top and bottom borders, cut two pieces 6¾″ × 45½″ from red and blue striped border fabric (measurements include ¼″ seam allowance all around). Fabric used in original quilt is printed with three bands; use similar fabric or piece together three border prints for same effect. Sew strips to top and bottom of quilt top. For sides, cut two pieces 2¾″ × 73″ from red fabric with blue stripe. Sew to sides of quilt top. Piece should measure 50″ × 73″, including outside seam allowance.

Lining: Cut two pieces 37″ × 50″. Sew together on long sides with ½″ seams to make liing 50″ × 73″. Press seam open. Cut batting same size.

Quilting: Following General Directions for Quilting, pin and baste quilt top, batting, and lining together. Starting in center and working around and outward, quilt each block as follows, using either red or blue thread for contrast; quilt around square formed by the four E pieces and around square formed by the D pieces; quilt around entire cross design. Quilt around squares formed by four A pieces and rectangles formed by two outside A pieces of adjacent blocks; quilt around main body of quilt top. Quilt borders at top and bottom between printed bands and side borders along stripe.

Edges: Insert edges of quilt inside fold of yellow bias binding tape; ¼″ wide; slip-stitch folded edges of tape to front and lining of quilt. ☆

Indian Summer Quilt

shown on page 108

SIZE: Approximately 72″ × 90″, to fit twin-size bed. To adjust for larger sizes, lengthen the brown strips that run across the center and correct measurement for brown and off-white fabrics and batting accordingly.

EQUIPMENT: Pencil. Tracing paper. Scissors. Ruler. Thin, stiff cardboard. Dressmaker's tracing (carbon) paper. Tailor's chalk. Sewing and quilting needles. Quilting frame (optional). All-purpose glue. T-square.

MATERIALS: Closely woven cotton fabric, 36″ wide: off-white, 6 yds. for quilt top, 7½ yds. for lining; brown, 2 yds.; ¾ yd. each yellow and orange. Sewing thread: yellow, orange, brown, and off-white or white. Polyester or cotton batting. Brown double-fold bias binding tape ¼″ wide, 9½ yards.

DIRECTIONS

Read General Directions for Quilting and How to Appliqué (see Contents).

Appliqués: Trace actual-size pattern of leaf, omitting stem. Glue tracing to cardboard and cut out for appliqué pattern. Following directions in How to Appliqué, cut out and prepare appliqué pieces for sewing on by hand: From yellow fabric, cut out 29 leaves, then flop pattern and cut 29 more, with leaf tips pointing in the opposite direction. From orange fabric, in same manner, cut out 29 leaves to point left and 29 leaves to point right. From brown fabric, in same manner, cut 28 leaves to point left and 28 leaves to point right.

Cut a stem for each leaf, using same fabrics: On the bias, cut narrow strips ⅞″ wide, then cut stem pieces 1″ in length. Fold under all edges ¼″ except for one short edge, which will be overlapped by leaf.

Panels: Off-white background of quilt top is made up of 22 sections or panels. From off-white fabric, tear off narrow selvages and cut the following: Eight center panels, each 8″ × 32″; a top and bottom panel, each 11½″ × 32″ (to be placed at head and foot of quilt); six side panels, 10″ × 32″; and six outside panels, 11″ × 32″. **Brown strips and borders:** From brown fabric, tear off narrow selvages and cut the following: nine center-panel strips, 2″ × 32″; two border strips, 2⅛″ × 76½″; and two border strips, 2⅛″ × 92½″. Piece strips in the center to obtain the longer lengths. **Assembling center-panels:** With right sides together, pin one brown center-panel strip (2″ × 32″) to one off-white center-panel strip (narrowest of off-white strips) along one long edge. Using off-white thread, machine-stitch them together, ½″ from edge. In same manner, join remaining brown strips and off-white center-panel strips, alternating colors, for striped center piece. Seam top panel (11½″ × 32″) to brown strip at one end of striped piece and bottom panel to brown strip at other end, right sides facing and sewing on long edges.

Stitch three side panels together for each side of center piece: Right sides together, stitch along short sides, making ½″ seam. Press seams flat, then stitch joined side panels to center piece on long edges. Press seams flat, then stitch joined side brown strip. Center and pin a brown leaf, overlapping strip by 1″; point leaf tips away from brown strip toward bottom and outside, at each end. See color illustration for position. Pin a brown stem at top of each leaf, inserting raw end under leaf. Baste stem and leaf in place, curving stem slightly as shown on pattern. **Note:** Half the leaves on quilt point toward bottom left corner of quilt other half point toward bottom right corner, but *all* point toward bottom of quilt, or foot of bed. Hereafter

directions will designate that tips of leaves point either right or left; in all other ways leaves are positioned identically. Include stems in all future references to leaves.

With tiny slip-stitches, appliqué brown leaves at end of each brown strip; stitch around three

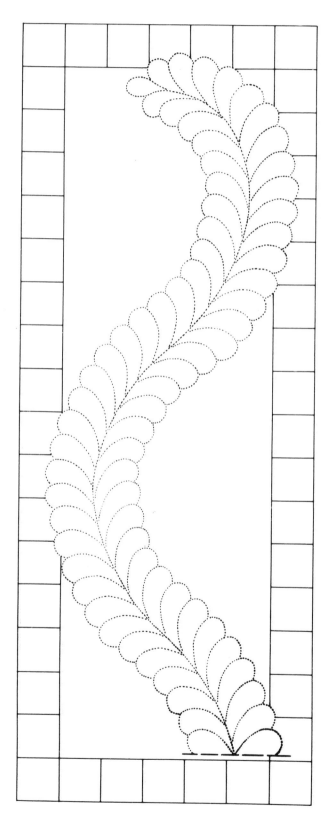

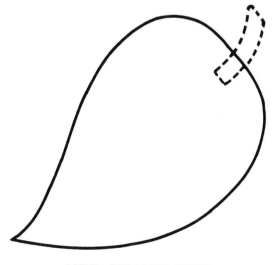

ACTUAL SIZE LEAF PATTERN

visible sides of stem, then all around leaf. Midway between each pair of brown strips and in a vertical line with leaves, appliqué another brown leaf for a total of eight more brown leaves on each side. Appliqué four more leaves, one $1\frac{1}{4}''$ above, one $1\frac{1}{4}''$ below each vertical row of brown leaves. All left-side leaves point left; right-side leaves point right.

Fold top and bottom panels in half widthwise to find the center. Pin one orange leaf $\frac{3}{8}''$ to left of center fold, in a line with brown leaves below bottom brown strip, with tip pointing left. Working toward the left and spacing leaves $\frac{3}{4}''$ apart, all in a straight line parallel to bottom brown strip, appliqué the following: a yellow leaf pointing right, a yellow leaf pointing left, and a brown leaf pointing right. In same manner but in a mirror image, appliqué leaves to the right of center fold on bottom panel: an orange leaf pointing right, a yellow leaf pointing left, a yellow leaf pointing right, and a brown leaf pointing left. (See foot of quilt in color illustration.) Appliqué an identical row on the top panel; remember to have all leaf tips pointing toward foot of bed.

Beside each brown leaf in the vertical row on the left, place a pair of leaves $\frac{3}{4}''$ apart from brown leaf and from each other, left leaf pointing left, right leaf pointing right: Starting at bottom row of leaves, appliqué two orange leaves, then two yellow leaves beside the bottom brown strip. Continue up, alternating orange and yellow leaf pairs and ending with two orange at the top. Repeat on right side of center piece. *Outside panels:* Sew three outside panels together along their short sides, making $\frac{1}{2}''$ seams, for one panel. Make a second outside panel in same manner. Sew outside panels to side panels on long edges. Space a row of leaves evenly along the long raw edge of these sections, parallel to other vertical rows. Along left border, all leaves point left; on the right border, all leaves point right. Starting from the bottom, alternate orange, brown, and yellow leaves in that order; add a yellow leaf at bottom of each row and a brown leaf at top; there will be seven leaves in each of the three sections of assembled outside panels.

Border: Sew brown strips around all four sides of quilt top, making $\frac{1}{2}''$ seams and mitering corners.

Preparing to quilt: *Scrolls:* Enlarge scroll quilting pattern on a 1″ grid and complete half-pattern, indicated by dash lines. Place scroll pattern on quilt top, with dressmaker's carbon paper underneath, to transfer design in each of the following 12 places: centered between brown strips (ends of scrolls should just touch brown leaves); centered on top and bottom center panels; centered on the outside panels between vertical rows of leaves.

Grids: On a piece of paper 10″ square, use a ruler and T-square to mark off lines horizontally and vertically $\frac{1}{2}''$ apart. Lay quilt top out flat. Tie a string from one corner of quilt top diagonally to opposite corner; mark along this line using ruler and tailor's chalk. Place ruled square on quilt top below this line, top and bottom, with dressmaker's carbon paper in between. Transfer grid pattern, on the bias, to quilt top. Lift up paper pattern and replace to left of first grid transfer, matching up lines. Continue all along diagonal, then make a row above the diagonal line. Make a row above and beneath these rows, always matching up lines. Continue in this manner until you have transferred grid design to entire quilt top.

Assembling quilt: Quilt top should measure $72\frac{1}{4}''$ × $90\frac{1}{4}''$. From off-white fabric cut one piece 36″ × $90\frac{1}{4}''$ and two pieces $19\frac{1}{4}''$ × $90\frac{1}{4}''$. With widest piece in the center and right sides facing, sew three pieces together on long edges with $\frac{1}{2}''$ seams to make lining $72\frac{1}{4}''$ × $90\frac{1}{4}''$. Cut batting to same size. Following General Directions for Quilting, pin and baste lining, batting, and quilt top together.

Quilting: Starting in center and working around and outward, quilt as follows: Quilt $\frac{1}{16}''$ outside long edges of brown strips, quilt the scrolls, outline each leaf and stem appliqué, and quilt the diagonal grid lines, skipping over appliqués and scrolls. Use white or off-white thread, except for the brown outside border; quilt this area with brown thread.

Finishing: Enclose edges of quilt within bias tape; slip-stitch folded edges to front and back of quilt. ☆

Butterfly Quilt

shown on page 109

shown on page 109

SIZE: 90″ square.

EQUIPMENT: Ruler. Scissors. Pencil. Thin, stiff cardboard. Paper for patterns. Tracing paper. All-purpose glue. Tailor's chalk (optional). Dressmaker's (carbon) tracing paper. Tracing wheel or dry ball-point pen. Sewing, quilting, and embroidery needles. Quilting frame (optional).

MATERIALS: Scraps of cotton fabrics in prints and

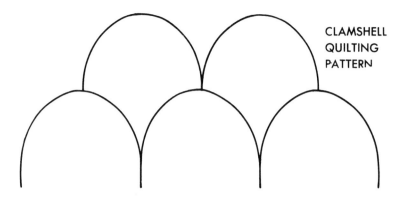

CLAMSHELL QUILTING PATTERN

solids. White cotton fabric 45″ wide, $7\frac{1}{4}$ yds. Green fabric for lining 50″ wide, $5\frac{1}{8}$ yds. Six-strand embroidery floss in black and various colors. White sewing thread. Polyester or cotton batting.

DIRECTIONS

Read General Directions for Quilting and How to Appliqué (see Contents). Quilt is constructed of 30 appliquéd blocks, plus a plain border.

Appliqués: Trace actual-size appliqué pattern (dotted lines are quilting pattern). Make a separate cardboard pattern for each butterfly wing and for body. Following directions in How to Appliqué, cut and prepare 100 bodies from plain scraps and 100 pairs of wings from print scraps, using same fabric for each pair.

Blocks: From white fabric, cut 20 background blocks $16\frac{1}{2}$″ square, adding $\frac{1}{4}$″ seam allowance all around. Indicate horizontal and vertical center lines on each block (fold and crease or mark with ruler and tailor's chalk), dividing block into quarter-sections. Using dressmaker's carbon and tracing wheel (or dry ball-point pen), transfer enlarged butterfly pattern four times to each block, placing pattern in each quarter-section with dash lines on center lines of block.

Following directions in How to Appliqué, pin, baste, and slip-stitch four butterflies to each block, with body overlapping wings.

From white fabric, cut 10 blocks $8\frac{1}{4}$″ × $16\frac{1}{2}$″, adding $\frac{1}{4}$″ seam allowance all around. Indicate crosswise center line and appliqué two butterflies on each block as before; blocks will appear as "half-blocks."

Embroidery: Using three strands of six-strand embroidery floss in needle, embroider blanket-stitch edging (for Stitch Details, see Contents) around butterfly wings and bodies; use black for bodies and a contrasting color for wings.

Assembling: Join square blocks into five vertical rows of four blocks each. Sew a "half-block" to top and bottom of each row, with butterflies positioned in established pattern. Join rows on long sides for main body quilt top. Piece should measure $82\frac{1}{2}$″ square, plus outside seam allowance.

Border: From white fabric, cut four strips 4″ × 90″. Sew a strip to each side of quilt top, centering

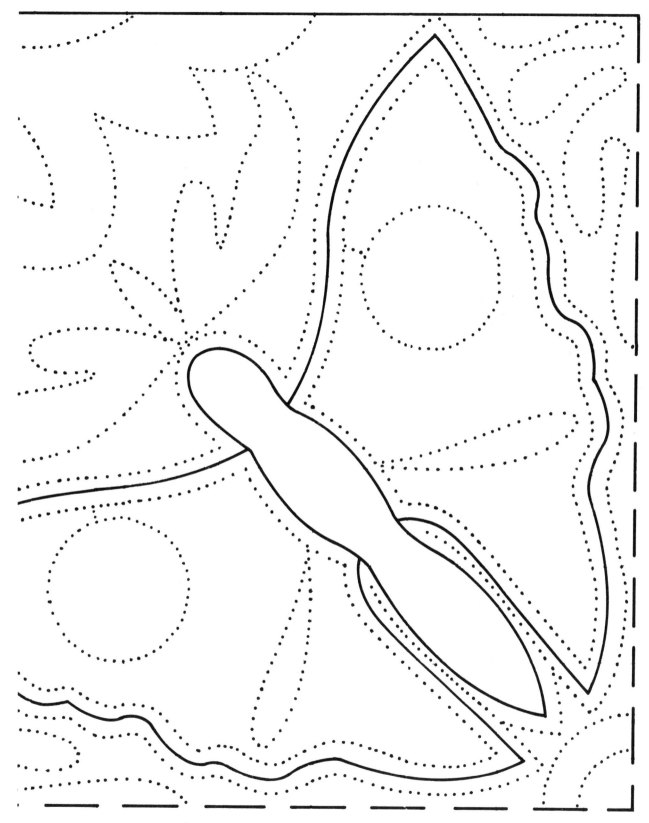

APPLIQUÉ PATTERN

91

so that an equal amount extends at each end. Miter corners (for directions, see Contents). Quilt top should now measure 90″ square.

Lining: From green fabric, cut two pieces $46\frac{1}{4}″$ $\times$ $91\frac{1}{2}″$. Sew together on long sides with $\frac{1}{2}″$ seams for piece $91\frac{1}{2}″$ square; press seam open. Cut batting same size as quilt top.

Quilting: Using dressmaker's carbon and tracing wheel (or dry ball-point pen), transfer dotted-line quilting pattern to each block and "half-block."

Trace actual-size clamshell pattern and transfer to border; start at seam and make four rows of clamshells, curves outward, on each border strip, leaving outer $\frac{1}{2}″$ unmarked

Following General Directions for Quilting, pin and baste quilt top, batting, and lining together, centering so that lining extends $\frac{3}{4}″$ all around from top layers. Quilt on all marked lines, starting in center and working around and outward. (If quilting by machine, use green thread in bobbin).

Edges: Fold excess fabric of lining to front of quilt, turning in raw edges $\frac{1}{4}″$, and slip-stitch (or topstitch) to front. Press all edges of quilt.   ☆

Koala Quilts and Koala Kids

shown on pages 110–111

Beach Koala Quilt

SIZE: $23\frac{1}{2}″ \times 33″$.

EQUIPMENT: Colored pencil. Ruler. Pencil. Paper for pattern. Yardstick. Scissors. Dressmaker's tracing (carbon) paper. Tracing wheel (or dry ball-point pen). Sewing and quilting needles. Large safety pins. Quilting frame (optional). Tailor's chalk.

MATERIALS: Closely woven cotton fabric 36″ wide: pale blue, $\frac{1}{3}$ yd; white-on-lavender small print, $\frac{1}{4}$ yd.; light gold, $\frac{3}{8}$ yd.; tan, $\frac{1}{4}$ yd.; beige with small white dots, $\frac{1}{4}$ yd. Scraps of the following fabrics: white, black, pink, white-on-yellow print, white-on-beige small print, dark gold plaid, pink print, coral print, pale gold-on-maroon small print, maroon-on-pale gold small print, gold-on-white small print, pale gold-on-maroon windowpane check. Fabric for lining: gold with large white dots 45″ wide, $\frac{7}{8}$ yd. Batting. Matching sewing threads. Black six-strand embroidery floss.

DIRECTIONS

Using sharp colored pencil, draw lines across pattern, connecting grid lines. Enlarge pattern by copying on paper ruled in 2″ squares: Heavy lines indicate background and appliqués, light lines indicate embroidery on koala, dotted lines are quilting patterns.

Using dressmaker's carbon and tracing wheel, transfer pattern A to pale blue fabric, B to white-on-lavender print, C to light gold (extending pattern C to top of D); mark on right side of fabric. Cut out each piece on marked lines around outer edges, but $\frac{1}{2}″$ outside marked line of inner edge (horizon between A and B, shoreline between B and C). On B and C, turn under extra $\frac{1}{2}″$ at top of pieces, clipping as necessary, and press. Pin and slip-stitch pieces together, overlapping and matching folded edge of B with marked line on A and folded edge of C with marked line on B; background piece should measure $19\frac{1}{2}″ \times 29″$.

Appliqués: Transfer pattern D to tan fabric and E to white-dotted beige. Cut out each piece on marked lines at side edges, but $\frac{1}{4}″$ outside marked lines of each upper and lower edge. Press under extra $\frac{1}{4}″$ on upper edge of D and both edges of E. Slip-stitch D in place over C, overlapping upper edge of C about $\frac{1}{16}″$; then stitch E in place, matching upper edge of E with marked line on D.

Transfer general outline of remaining appliqué designs to background. Transfer individual appliqué pieces to fabrics, following pattern: F—white-on-yellow print; G—gold plaid; H, I—pink print; J, K, L, M, N—white-on-tan print (face [N] of our bear was cut from reverse side of fabric): O—black; P, Q, R—white; S, T—gold-on-maroon print; U—maroon-on-gold print; V—gold-on-white print; W, X—gold-on-maroon windowpane check; Y—pink; Z—coral print. Referring to How to Appliqué (see Contents) cut out pieces (you need not make cardboard patterns for this quilt). Following directions, prepare appliqué pieces one by one as you pin them in place on background; do not turn under seam allowance where an edge will be overlapped by another piece. When all pieces are pinned in place, baste and slip-stitch pieces.

Replace pattern and transfer embroidery lines to face. Using three strands of black floss in needle, embroider eyes with satin stitch, mouth with outline stitch; see Contents for Stitch Details. Using one strand of black, embroider eyelashes with straight stitches.

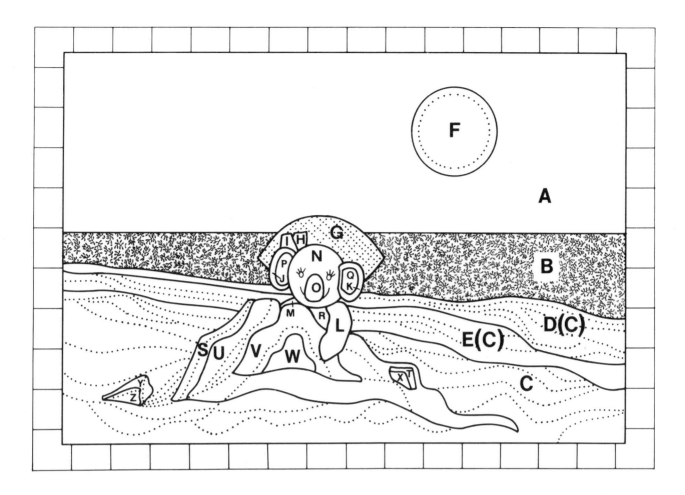

Quilting: Using dressmaker's carbon and tracing wheel, transfer dotted-line quilting pattern; use ruler and tailor's chalk to mark sky pattern, making grid lines $\frac{5}{8}''$ apart.

From dotted gold fabric, cut lining $29\frac{1}{2}'' \times 39''$. Cut batting same size. Lay lining flat, wrong side up; place batting on top. Anchor batting to lining by crossing two long stitches in center. Center appliquéd piece over batting, with 5″ margins all around. Pin and baste in place lengthwise, crosswise, and diagonally in both directions.

Starting in center and working outward in all directions, quilt on marked lines; quilt around each appliqué, close to seams; quilt ocean (B) with gently curving lines about $\frac{1}{2}''$ apart. Use matching threads.

Finishing: Trim away $\frac{1}{2}''$ from batting all around. Turn in edges of lining $\frac{1}{2}''$ all around and press, enclosing edge of batting. Fold lining and batting to front to make padded border $2\frac{1}{2}''$ wide, overlapping top piece $\frac{1}{2}''$. Miter corners (see Contents for directions) trimming away excess batting, and slipstitch border in place along folded edge.

Surfing Koala Quilt

SIZE: 38″ × 58″.
EQUIPMENT: Colored pencil. Ruler. Pencil. Paper for pattern. Yardstick. Scissors. Dressmaker's tracing (carbon) paper. Tracing wheel (or dry ball-point pen). Sewing and quilting needles. Large safety pins. Quilting frame (optional).

MATERIALS: Closely woven cotton fabric 36″ wide: white, $\frac{1}{4}$ yd.; medium blue, $\frac{1}{2}$ yd.; dark blue, $\frac{1}{2}$ yd.; blue-on-white small print, $\frac{1}{2}$ yd.; lavender-on-white small print, $\frac{1}{4}$ yd.; white-on-lavender small print, $1\frac{1}{3}$ yds.; dark red and light blue small print, $\frac{1}{4}$ yd. Scraps of the following fabrics: navy, black, bright yellow, white-on-beige small print, navy-on-beige small print, red-blue plaid, red-navy large print. Red calico for lining 45″ wide, $1\frac{3}{4}$ yards. Six-strand embroidery floss, black and yellow. Matching sewing thread. Batting.

DIRECTIONS

Using sharp colored pencil, draw lines across pattern, connecting grid lines. Enlarge pattern by copying on paper ruled in 2″ squares; heavy lines indicate background and appliqués, light lines embroidery on koala bear; dotted lines are quilting patterns.

Using dressmaker's carbon and tracing wheel, transfer sky pattern to light blue fabric and ocean pattern to white-on-lavender fabric, following dash line; mark on right side of fabric. Cut out each

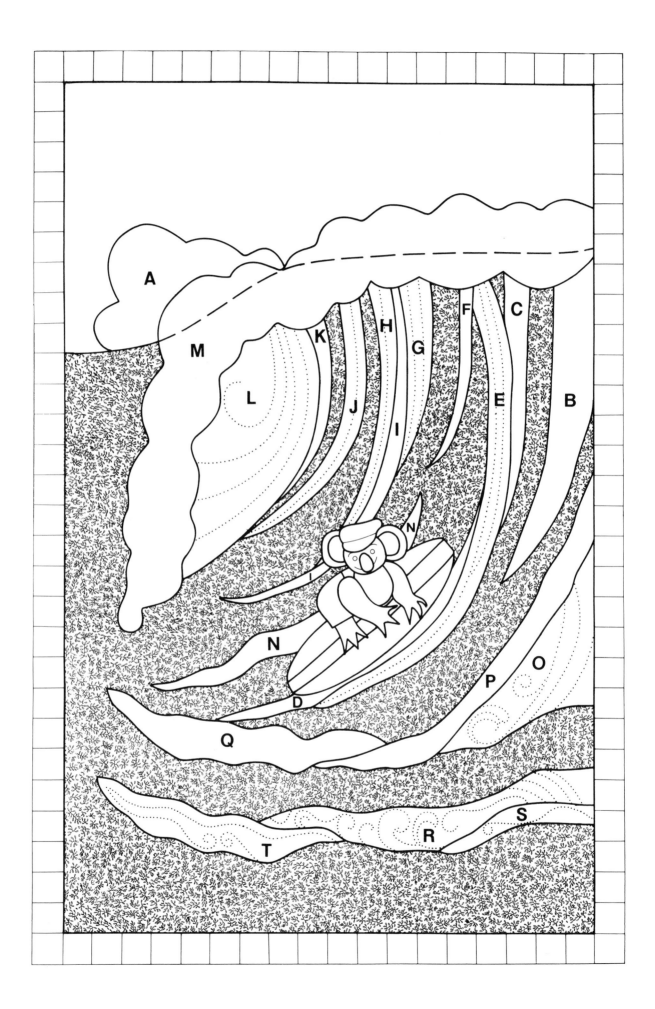

piece on marked lines around outer edges, but $\frac{1}{2}''$ outside marked line of inner edge (horizon). On lavender piece, turn under extra $\frac{1}{2}''$, clipping as necessary, and press. Pin pieces together, overlapping and matching folded edge of ocean with marked horizon of sky; background piece should measure 36″ × 56″.

Appliqués: Using dressmaker's carbon and tracing wheel (or dry ball-point pen), transfer general outline of appliqué design to background. Transfer individual appliqué pieces to fabrics, following pattern: A—white; E, G, N, O, R—medium blue; F, H, L, P, S—dark blue; M, Q—blue-on-white print; B, J, T—lavender-on-white print; C, D, I, K—dark red–light blue print.

Referring to How to Appliqué (see Contents), cut out pieces (you need not make cardboard patterns for this quilt). Following directions, prepare appliqué pieces one by one as you pin them in place on background; do not turn under seam allowance where an edge will be overlapped by another piece. Pin, baste, and slip-stitch pieces in place, starting with A; slip seam allowance along bottom of A under edge of ocean. Slip-stitch sky and ocean together where pinned. Appliqué other pieces in alphabetical order, from B to T.

For koala and surfboard, cut following pieces: foot, arms, back, outer ears, face from white-on-tan print (face of our bear was cut from reverse side of fabric); chest, inner ears from white; bathing trunks from navy-on-tan; nose from black; visor from navy; cap from plaid; surfboard from yellow; stripe from red-navy print. Appliqué pieces in place.

Replace pattern and transfer embroidery lines to face. Using three strands of black floss in needle, embroider eyebrows and mouth with outline stitch, eyes with satin stitch; see Contents for Stitch Details. Using all six strands of yellow, embroider braid on cap with chain stitch.

Quilting: Using dressmaker's carbon and tracing wheel, transfer dotted-line quilting pattern. From red calico, cut lining $42\frac{1}{2}'' \times 62\frac{1}{2}''$. Cut batting same size. Lay lining flat, wrong side up; place batting on top. Anchor batting to lining by crossing two long stitches in center. Center appliquéd piece over batting, with $3\frac{1}{4}''$ margins all around. Pin and baste in place lengthwise, crosswise, and diagonally in both directions.

Starting in center and working outward in all directions, quilt on marked lines; quilt around each appliqué, close to seams; quilt ocean background with gently curving lines about 1″ apart, following contours of appliqués as much as possible. Use matching threads.

Finishing: Trim away $2\frac{1}{4}''$ from batting all around, so batting measures 38″ × 58″. Turn in edges of lining $\frac{1}{2}''$ all around and press. Fold excess lining to front, mitering corners (see Contents for directions) and overlapping top piece $\frac{3}{4}''$; slip-stitch in place along folded edge. ☆

Koala Kids

SIZE: Each Koala: 14″ high.

EQUIPMENT: Sharp colored pencil. Pencil. Ruler. Paper for patterns. Dressmaker's tracing (carbon) paper. Dry ball-point pen. Scissors. Compass. Tape measure. Knitting needle. Small safety pin. Straight pins. Sewing needle. Sewing machine with zigzag attachment. Steam/dry iron.

MATERIALS: *For Each Koala:* Brown plush or short-pile fake fur 60″ wide, $\frac{1}{2}$ yd. Off-white long-pile fake fur, piece 15″ × 9″. Black felt, piece 9″ × 6″. Small amount black six-strand embroidery floss. Heavy-duty sewing thread. Two black round shank-type buttons, $\frac{3}{4}''$ diameter. Polyester fiberfill. All-purpose glue (optional).

For Kirby's Clothes: Red cotton fabric 36″ wide, $\frac{1}{4}$ yd. Plaid cotton flannel, piece 10″ square. Red double-fold bias tape $\frac{1}{4}''$ wide, 1 yd. Flat elastic $\frac{1}{4}''$ wide, piece 15″ long. Red transparent acetate or vinyl, sheet $8\frac{1}{2}'' \times 11''$ (available in most stationery stores). Red sewing thread.

For Katie's Clothes: Yellow calico fabric 36″ wide, $\frac{3}{4}$ yd. Fusible interfacing 18″ wide, $\frac{1}{4}$ yd. Red double-fold bias tape $\frac{1}{4}''$ wide, $\frac{1}{2}$ yd. Red satin ribbon $\frac{3}{8}''$ wide, 1 yd. Flat elastic $\frac{1}{4}''$ wide, piece 14″ long. Two red round shank-type buttons, $\frac{1}{2}''$ diameter. Red and yellow sewing thread.

GENERAL DIRECTIONS

Trace actual-size patterns for koala and clothes, shown on the following pages; complete half-patterns indicated by long dash lines. Use dressmaker's carbon and dry ball-point pen to transfer patterns to wrong side of designated fabrics, placing them $\frac{1}{2}''$ from fabric edges and $\frac{1}{2}''$ apart; reverse all second and fourth pieces. Cut out pieces $\frac{1}{4}''$ beyond marked lines for seam allowance, unless otherwise directed. When cutting additional pieces without patterns, do not add seam allowances. Pin pieces together with right sides facing and raw edges even; stitch on marked lines, making $\frac{1}{4}''$ seams. Clip into seam allowances at curves and across corners; turn to right side and poke out corners with knitting needle. Finish pieces as directed.

KOALAS (for each): Read General Directions. Referring to arrows on patterns for placement on nap, cut the following from brown plush or fake fur: two head fronts, two head backs, four bodies, four ear backs, four arms, and four legs. From off-white fake fur, cut two ear fronts and one tummy. From black felt, cut one nose and four claws, cutting each on marked outline. Mark large dots on wrong side of fur pieces. Mark small dots on wrong side of face, then make tailor's tacks through dots to mark right side. Zigzag raw edges of fur pieces to prevent raveling.

Referring to General Directions, stitch head fronts together at center front between As and Bs. Stitch

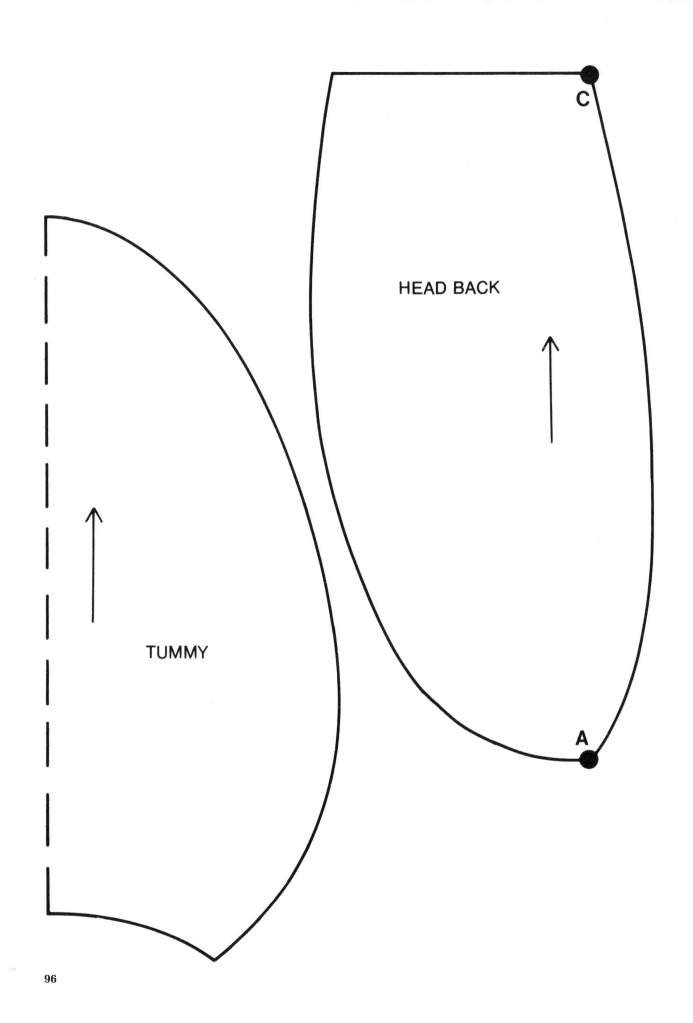

HEAD BACK

C

A

TUMMY

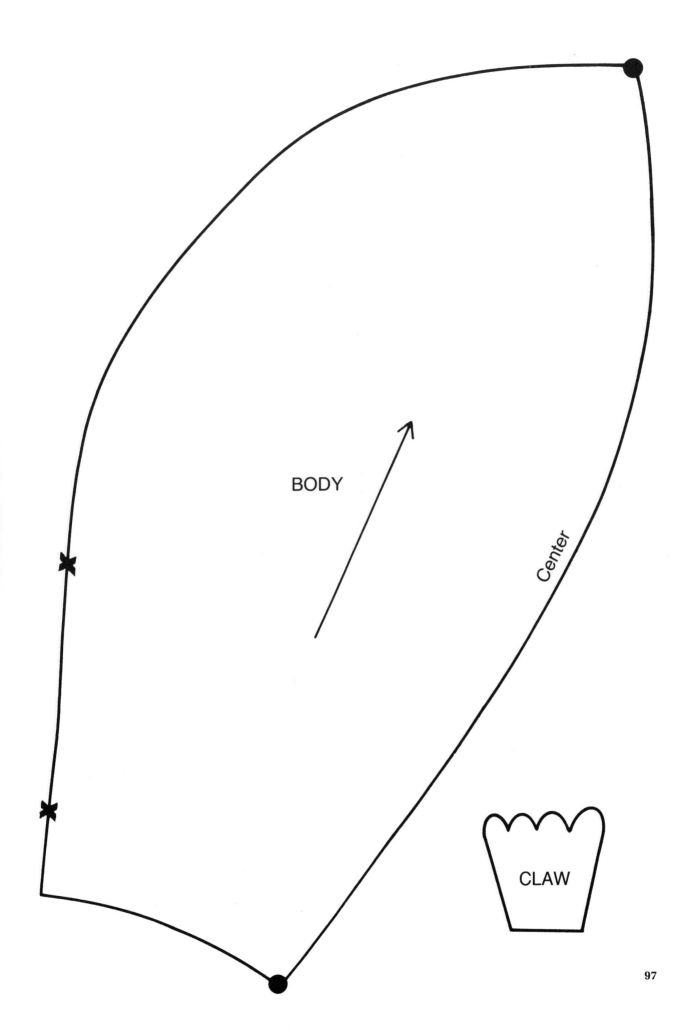

BODY

Center

CLAW

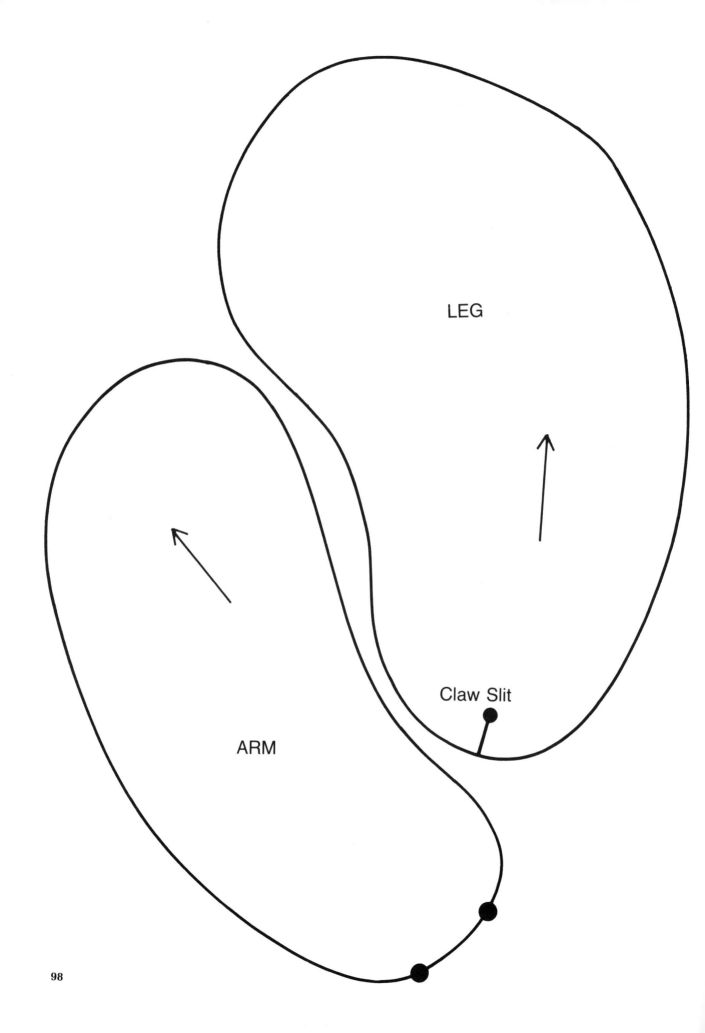

LEG

ARM

Claw Slit

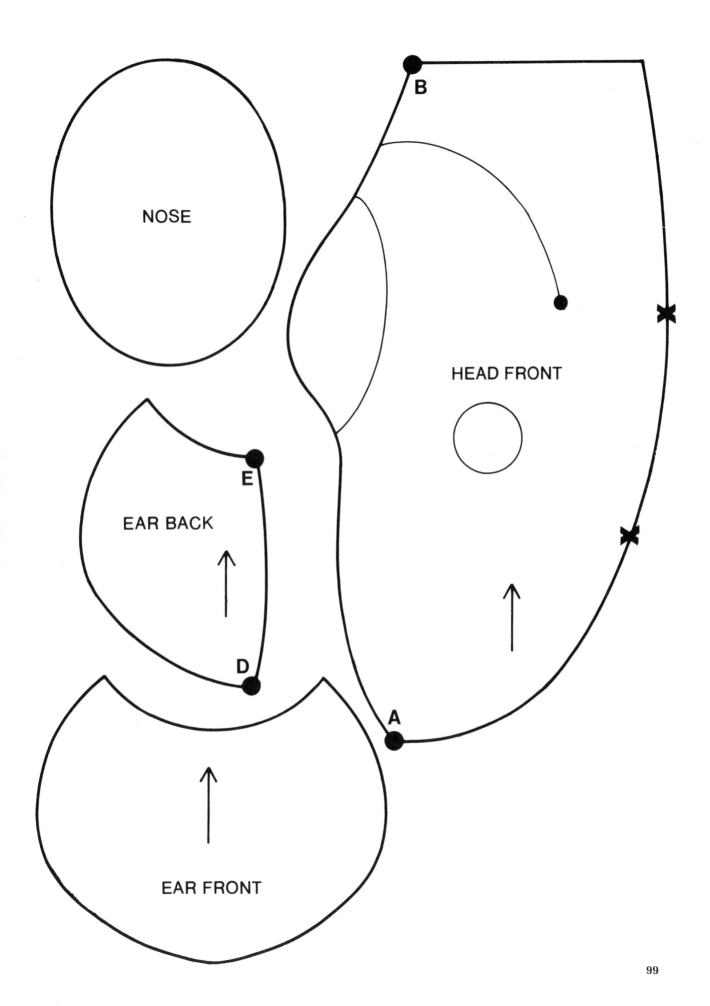

NOSE

HEAD FRONT

B

EAR BACK

E

D

A

EAR FRONT

99

head backs together at center back between As and Cs. Stitch head front and back together, matching As and leaving neck edge open. Machine-baste around neck edge; turn to right side. Stuff head with fiberfill until firm. Pull basting thread gently to gather neck edge. Stitch two pairs of ear backs together at center back between Ds and Es. Stitch each pair of ear fronts and backs together, leaving base open; turn to right side. Turn raw edges $\frac{1}{4}''$ to inside and slip-stitch opening closed. Slip-stitch base of one ear to each side of head between Xs. Baste all around nose. Pull thread gently to gather; stuff lightly. Slip-stitch nose to face where indicated by fine line on pattern. Sew one button "eye" to each side of face where indicated. Double black floss in sewing needle and use all 12 strands to take one or two tiny stitches at one end of mouth (tailor's tack) to secure. Lay floss loosely along face as shown to form mouth. Secure floss at second tack and cut away excess. If desired, secure center of mouth with dot of glue.

Stitch two pairs of bodies together at centers between dots for front and back. Stitch body front to back, matching side seams. Complete body as for head. Using heavy-duty thread, slip-stitch head over neck, matching seams. Turn raw edges of tummy $\frac{1}{4}''$ to inside; baste. Slip-stitch tummy, centered, to body front as shown in color photograph, matching neck edges. Remove basting.

For each arm: Stitch two arms together, with claw in between, matching straight edge of claw with raw edge of arms between dots and pointing "thumb" away from elbow; leave 3" opening in one long side of arm for turning and stuffing. Turn to right side, stuff firmly, and slip-stitch opening closed. Pin one arm against each side of body between Xs with thumbs pointing up; slip-stitch in place.

For each leg: Stitch two legs together, leaving 3" opening in one long side. Cut marked slit for claw through both thicknesses between raw edge and small dot. With wrong side still facing out, fold leg so that seams are centered. Insert claw through 3" opening, bringing straight edge up even with slit; stitch across, $\frac{1}{4}''$ below slit. Complete legs as for arms, reversing position of second claw. Set koala on work surface. Pin one leg against each side, so that seams are at top and bottom, large "toe" is at inside edge, and leg rests on work surface. Repeat for second leg, repositioning legs until koala sits up. Slip-stitch legs in place.

CLOTHES
Read General Directions.

Additional Directions

To Make Waistline Casings: Fold waist edge under $\frac{1}{4}''$; press. Fold under again along short dash line (see patterns); press. Stitch close to both folded edges, leaving 1" opening in bottom edge at one side seam, unless otherwise indicated in individual directions. Use safety pin fastened at one end of elastic to work elastic through casing. Stitch ends to secure, following individual directions; close up casing.

To Bind Edges with Bias Tape: Cut bias tape to size, adding $\frac{1}{2}''$ for overlap. Unfold one long edge of tape; press one short edge under $\frac{1}{4}''$. With right-sides facing and raw edges even, pin tape to garment, beginning at pressed short edge and lapping ends. Stitch along fold; remove pins. Fold tape to wrong side of garment; slip-stitch in place with invisible stitches.

For Kirby: *Shorts:* From red fabric, cut two shorts for front and back, cutting away toned area for each leg opening of front. Stitch front and back together at sides and crotch; press seams open. Turn under leg openings $\frac{1}{8}''$ twice and topstitch. Make waistline casing, following directions above. Thread elastic through casing; overlap ends $\frac{1}{2}''$, and stitch to secure; close casing.

Cap: Cut visor from red acetate or vinyl. Cut 8" length of red bias tape. Enclose curved edge of visor in tape, topstitching $\frac{1}{8}''$ from inner tape edge on narrower side of tape, to catch tape on underside. Use compass to mark 9"-diameter circle on plaid flannel fabric; cut on marked line. Machine-baste around circle $\frac{1}{4}''$ from edges. Pull thread gently to gather; try on koala to fit, then secure threads. Redistribute gathers so that cap is puffed only slightly along a $5\frac{5}{8}''$ section of cap; place visor on outside of cap with straight edge along this section; pin in place. Bind raw edges of cap with bias tape, following directions above and overlapping ends at one corner of visor. Turn visor down.

For Katie: *Sunsuit:* From yellow calico, cut two sunsuits for front and back and two bibs for front and facing. Stitch bib and facing together, leaving bottom edge open; turn to right side; press. With raw edges even, pin and stitch bib to sunsuit front between dots. Stitch front and back together at sides and crotch; press seams open. Turn under leg opening $\frac{1}{8}''$ twice and topstitch. Fold and press waist edges for casing, following directions above; bib will extend beyond waistline after second fold. Stitch casing, leaving 1" opening beyond each side edge of bib. Thread elastic through casing, extending ends $\frac{1}{4}''$ into bib; topstitch open sides of bib to secure. Sew red buttons to upper corners of bib. Cut two 2" × 11" straps from calico.

For each strap: Fold in half lengthwise wrong side out and stitch across one short side and long open side. Trim seam allowance to $\frac{1}{8}''$; turn to right side; press. Machine- or hand-stitch a $\frac{1}{2}''$-long buttonhole perpendicular to and $\frac{3}{8}''$ from finished end of strap. Button straps onto bib. Test-fit sunsuit on Katie, criss-crossing straps at center back and tucking free ends inside waist; pin at waist and at criss-cross point to secure. Remove sunsuit. Machine-stitch straps to waist; tack straps together at center back.

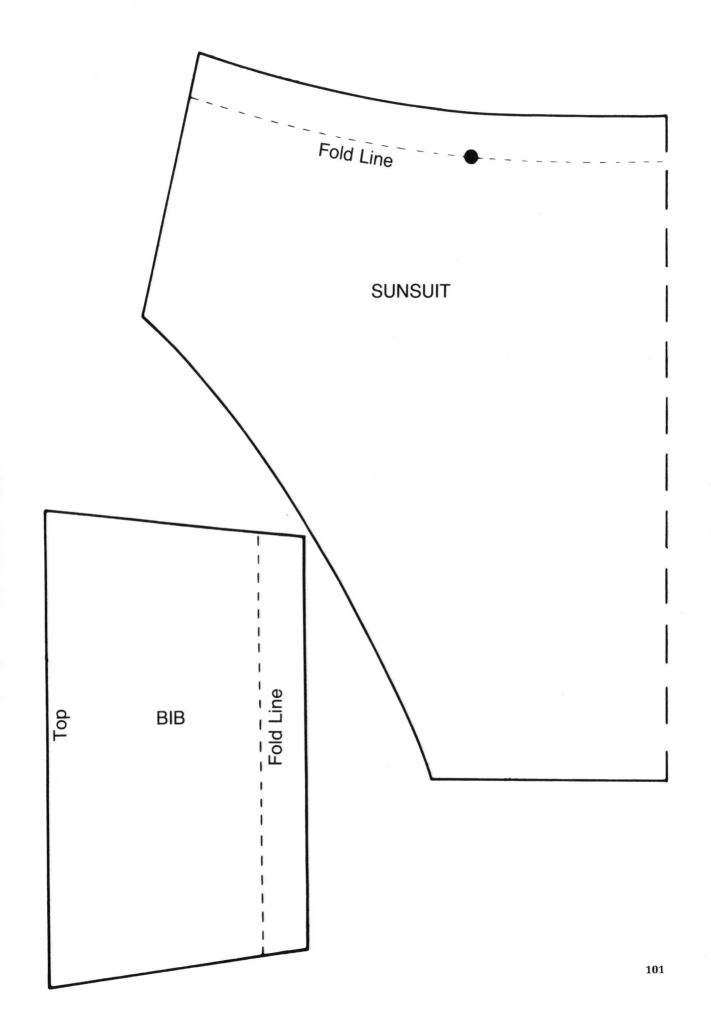

Fold Line

SUNSUIT

Top

BIB

Fold Line

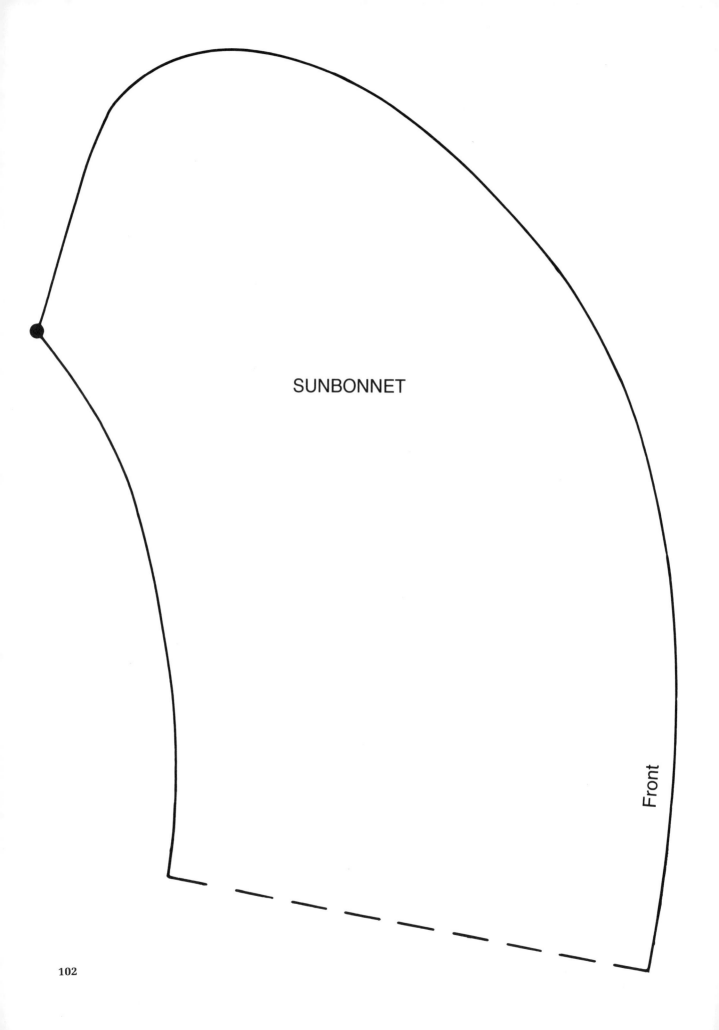

SUNBONNET

Front

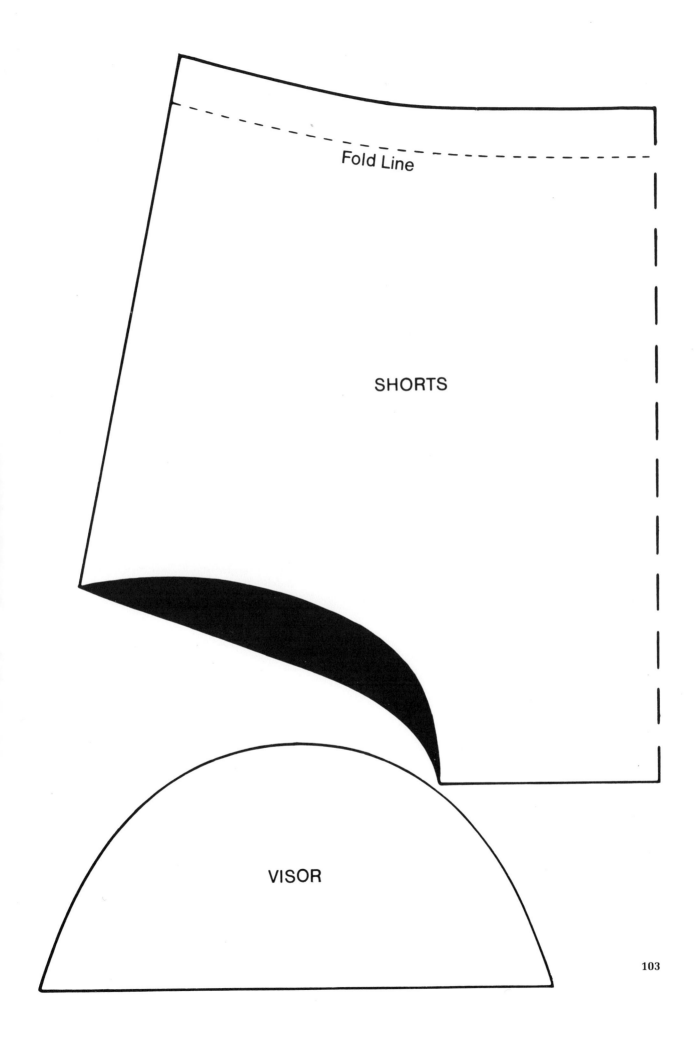

Fold Line

SHORTS

VISOR

Sunbonnet: From yellow calico, cut two sunbonnets for top and lining; also cut one sunbonnet from fusible interfacing, cutting $\frac{1}{8}''$ inside marked outline. Center interfacing on wrong side of lining and follow manufacturer's directions for bonding. Stitch top and lining together all around front between dots; turn to right side; press. Bind raw edges with red bias tape, following directions above and turning under both short edges before stitching. Cut ribbon in half to form two 18″ lengths. Make a decorative bow at one end of each ribbon and tack with matching thread to secure. Stitch one bow to each corner on top of sunbonnet. ☆

Star Quilt

shown on page 112

SIZE: $78\frac{5}{8}'' \times 93\frac{1}{4}''$, plus edging.

EQUIPMENT: Pencil. Ruler. Tracing paper. Paper for patterns (preferably graph paper). Thin, stiff cardboard. All-purpose glue. Scissors. Sewing machine. Quilting needle. Quilting frame (optional).

MATERIALS: Closely woven cotton fabric 44″ wide: black, 4 yds.; red, $2\frac{1}{2}$ yds.; assorted colors (we used about 25), totaling about 5 yds.*; fabric for lining, $5\frac{1}{4}$ yds. Polyester or cotton batting. White and matching sewing threads.

*Includes $1\frac{1}{8}$ yds. for "prairie point" edging.

DIRECTIONS

Read General Directions for Quilting (see Contents). Quilt is made up of 30 pieced star blocks, set with narrow stripping; border is trimmed with "prairie point" edging. Directions given here are for piecing by sewing machine and quilting by hand.

Patterns: Trace actual-size diamond pattern for pieces A, B, and C. For pieces D and E, draw on graph paper a $2\frac{13}{16}''$ square and a 4″ square; on each square, draw a corner-to-corner diagonal line, dividing the square into two triangles. Glue papers to cardboard, let dry, then cut on marked lines for ABC pattern, two D patterns, and two E patterns. When cutting patch pieces, use second D and E patterns after edges of first have begun to fray from repeated use; replace ABC pattern as needed.

Patch Pieces: To cut pieces, place cardboard patterns on wrong side of fabric, with two parallel edges of ABC pattern and right angles of D and E on straight of goods. Draw around pattern with sharp pencil held against it at an outward angle. Mark as many patterns as needed at one time on one color fabric, leaving $\frac{1}{2}''$ between pieces. When

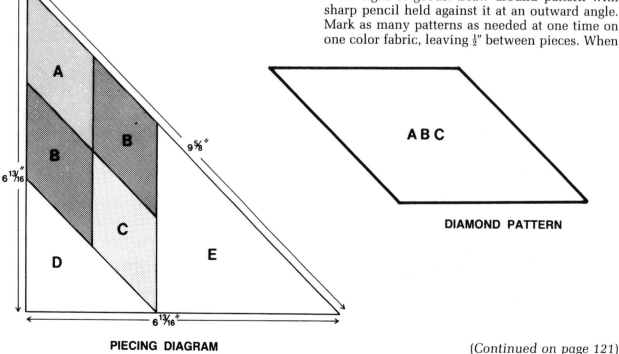

PIECING DIAGRAM

DIAMOND PATTERN

(Continued on page 121)

This dainty quilt (46″ × 61″) looks deceptively intricate, but it's made with only two block patterns! Use chintz floral and solid fabrics. For Field of Flowers Quilt directions, see Contents. *(Quilt designed by Diann Logan.)*

"Sun and Shadow" is a sophisticated display of color and design that
is typically Amish. Construction is simple, consisting merely of
square patches in diagonal rows. Elaborately quilted garlands
decorating the border provide a contrast. (For easier border
quilting, just extend the center quilted grid outward.) This quilt,
from Pennsylvania, was made in the 1930s or early 1940s with modern
dress fabrics. For Sun and Shadow Quilt directions, see Contents.

(Quilt courtesy of George E. Schoellkopf.)

The colorful graphics of a modern-day "Aunt Sukey" depend on a
skillful choice of fabrics. One block is repeated 12 times, with
florals, geometrics, paisleys, and plaids blended in a kaleidoscope
of color. Border stripes appear pieced but are printed in the
fabric. For Aunt Sukey's Choice Quilt directions, see Contents.

(Quilt courtesy of Chardavogne Quilting, Warwick, New York.)

Photographed in the kitchen of Van Cort- landt Manor, our Indian Summer Quilt awaits the coming meal of simple country fare. The appliqué, in fall colors, has a look of rustic simplicity, but the quilting pat- tern is exquisitely detailed. For Indian Summer Quilt direc- tions, see Contents.

Butterflies, four to a block, make a very pretty overall pattern and are a satisfying way to use your most precious scraps of fabric. The butterfly wings, cut from soft and bright prints, are matched with solid-color bodies; blanket stitching gives a finished edge. An intricate quilting design decorates the white background, with clamshell quilting all around to complete the picture. This quilt was made in Illinois in 1960. For Butterfly Quilt directions, see Contents. (*Quilt courtesy of Bryce and Donna Hamilton, Tipton, Iowa.*)

Katie Koala is dressed in a sweet little playsuit and matching sun bonnet. See her playing in the sand in a matching $23\frac{1}{2}'' \times 33''$ coverlet, hand-appliquéd and quilted in sunny cottons.

Kirby Koala, dressed in swim trunks and cap, rides the waves on a yellow surfboard. $38'' \times 58''$ appliquéd quilt is stitched by hand.

For Koala Quilts and Koala Kids directions, see Contents.

(Koala Quilts designed and stitched by Joanne Dzioba Nidositko.)

Piece diamonds into squares—30 squares make a full-sized quilt. So easy! For Star Quilt directions, see Contents.

(Quilt designed by Andrea Shedletsky.)

Even the dreariest days seem
bright in a sunny room. Floral
fabric makes a headboard,
pillow shams, and dust ruffle
radiant! Matching bows blossom
from buttonholes in the pretty
white eyelet cover to add a
dainty touch to the quilt.
For Eyelet & Bows Comforter,
Pillow Shams, Dust Ruffle, and
Covered Headboard directions,
see Contents.

A child's world is butterflies and
birthday cakes, squirrels and seesaws.
Make this quilt your child's very own by
including name and hour of birth on clock,
then, later, an authentic handprint.
Construct in two separate pieces and frame
with bias tape. For Child's World Quilt
directions, see Contents.

(Designed by Maggie-Bet.)

Color wheels spin
a brilliant pattern in
big, bold appliqué.
All wheels have the same colored
spokes in the same order, but each is slightly turned until
all colors come around full circle. Center quilting follows wheel
and spoke motifs; the border is stitched with elegant swags
and darts. For Color Wheels Quilt directions, see Contents.

(Designed by Mary Borkowski.)

114

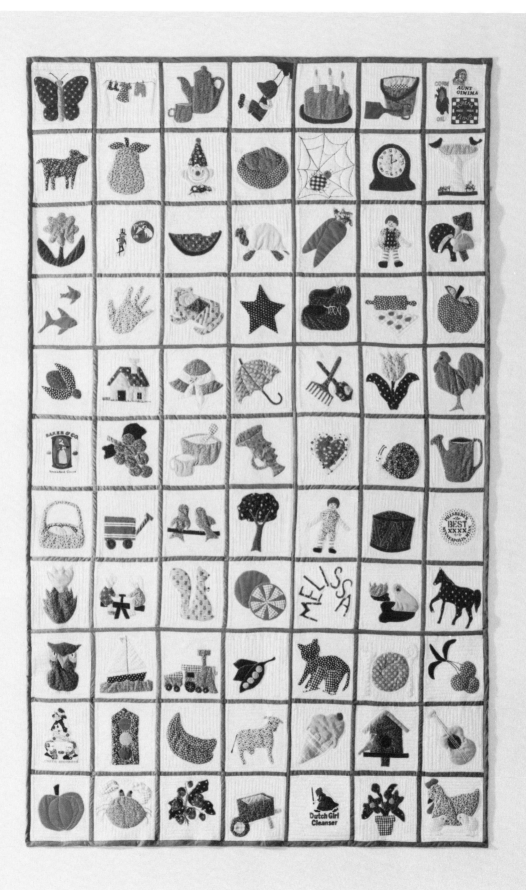

A bright pumpkin is machine-appliquéd
on chintz for a delightful 56″ × 45″
coverlet. For Pumpkin Quilt
directions, see Contents.

Studious youngster, embroidered
in six easy stitches using Persian
yarns, is 18″ × 14″, framed.
For Little Reader directions, see Contents.

(By Doris J. Chaconas.)

Pretty flower portraits—
nine in all—can easily be
your very own! Just paint
them on muslin with textile
paints, add some padding,
and stitch all around to give
them extra dimension. Frame
each with the same soft hue
and combine for a quilt, about
71" square. Select your own
favorites for the pillow
shams. For Painted Quilt and
Pillow Shams directions,
see Contents.

(Designed by Patricia Foxx.)

A perky gingham bunny hops into a child's room on a sunny yellow quilt (45″ × 50″). Bunny and flowers are machine-appliquéd and embroidered on a hand-quilted background, trimmed with gingham petals. Quilt's bunny has a twin—a cuddly toy stitched on a sewing machine. For Bunny Quilt and Toy directions, see Contents.

(Quilt designed by Barbara Clayton.)

Quilt a Christmas pastoral—a wall hanging to warm hearts all year or a Christmas gift to keep the baby you love snug and warm. Either way, this quilt is pure delight in its interpretation of the spirit of Christmas. A variety of calicos and solids is used. All sections are machine-appliquéd. Hand sewing is required only to quilt around the appliqués—good news this busy holiday season! Finished size, 65″ × 48″. For Lion & Lambs Quilt directions, see Contents.

(Quilt designed by Anna J. Monte.)

Three fairy-tale flowers grow giant-sized
on a shining bedspread of polished
cotton. Leaves and flowers are appliquéd
by machine, then embroidered with
two stitches—French knots and couching.
The entire design is quilted by
stitching along the machine appliqué
after the quilt has been assembled.
Overhanging sides are quilted in squares.
The quilt measures 81″ × 125″ and is
trimmed with cording. For Three Flowers
Quilt directions, see Contents.

(Continued from page 104)

all pieces have been marked, cut out each piece $\frac{1}{4}''$ beyond marked line for seam allowance; marked line will be stitching line.

Blocks: Cut 240 each of pieces D and E from black fabric, following directions above. As you construct each block, cut 32 of ABC diamond from three colors as follows: Cut eight of one color for piece A, 16 of a second color for piece B, and eight of a third color for piece C. (*Note:* If you wish to cut some diamonds from red fabric, cut a strip 7″ wide along selvage edge for these pieces, reserving the rest.) Following Piecing Diagram, sew six pieces together for one-eighth of block, placing them with right sides facing and stitching on marked line: Sew A to one B piece and C to other B piece; join the two rows; add black D and E pieces already cut, as shown. Section should measure $6\frac{13}{16}''$ on right-angle edges, plus outside seam allowance. Press seams to one side, under darker color. Make seven more sections in same manner, using same colors for each piece. Sew two sections together along diagonal edges for a quarter-block. Make three more quarter-blocks. Sew quarter-blocks together, aligning A pieces in center, for complete block. The block should measure $14\frac{1}{8}''$ square, including outside seam allowance. Make 29 more blocks in same manner, varying colors of ABC pieces as desired.

Joining Blocks: From red fabric, cut joining strips $1\frac{1}{2}''$ wide, 24 $14\frac{1}{8}''$ long and five $72\frac{5}{8}''$ long; measurements include seam allowance. Lay out the 30 quilt blocks into six horizontal rows of five blocks each; arrange as desired. Place a short red strip between blocks within each row; stitch to adjacent blocks, right sides facing and making $\frac{1}{4}''$ seams. Join rows with long red strips in same manner. Piece should measure $87\frac{1}{4}'' \times 72\frac{5}{8}''$ including outside seam allowance.

Borders: From red fabric, cut border strips $3\frac{3}{4}''$ wide, two $87\frac{1}{4}''$ long and two $72\frac{5}{8}''$ long. From black fabric, cut four pieces $3\frac{3}{4}''$ square. Right sides facing

and making $\frac{1}{4}''$ seams, sew a black square to each end of the long strips. Finish border strips with "prairie points" as follows: Cut about 175 3″ squares from fabric scraps, using the same colors as for stars. Fold each square in half diagonally, right side out, to form a triangle. Fold triangle in half, bringing raw edges together; baste across raw edges; press. To form edging on each border strip, place strip flat with right side up; place points along one side, matching raw edges of points and strip and overlapping points $1\frac{1}{2}''$ (halfway); points will face opposite side of strip. Stitch points in place with $\frac{1}{4}''$ seam. On long strips, continue points out to black corners, then press raw edges to wrong side, so points now extend beyond fabric. Do not press short strips.

Sew short strips to top and bottom of quilt top, then long strips to sides, making $\frac{1}{4}''$ seams. Add two points to each remaining black edge, then press raw edges of short strips to wrong side. Quilt top should measure $78\frac{5}{8}'' \times 93\frac{1}{4}''$, plus edging.

Lining: From lining fabric, cut two pieces $40\frac{5}{16}'' \times 94\frac{1}{4}''$. Sew together on long edges with $\frac{1}{2}''$ seam to make lining $79\frac{5}{8}'' \times 94\frac{1}{4}''$. Press seam to one side. Cut batting same size.

Quilting: Place lining flat, wrong side up; place batting on top. Anchor batting to lining by taking two long stitches in a cross in center. Center quilt top over batting, right side up, and baste generously through all three layers, lengthwise, crosswise, diagonally in both directions, and around perimeter.

Starting in center of quilt and working around and outward, quilt along seams within blocks and around each block; use two strands of white in needle.

Finishing: Trim batting all around to about $\frac{5}{8}''$ from edge of lining. Fold in excess lining $\frac{1}{2}''$, covering edge of batting, and baste in place. Slip-stitch edge of quilt top (under points) to edge of lining. ☆

Eyelet & Bows Set

shown on page 113

Comforter and Pillow Shams

SIZE: Comforter and pillow shams are made for a full/queen bed. For king-size or twin beds and king-size pillows, adjust all measurements.

EQUIPMENT: Scissors. Tape measure. Straight pins. Dressmaker's marking pen. Sewing machine with zigzag stitch or buttonholer.

MATERIALS: *For comforter:* Purchased solid-color full/queen comforter (85″ × 85″). White eyelet fabric, 36″ wide, $4\frac{1}{2}$ yds. White eyelet ruffled trim, $5\frac{1}{2}''$ wide, $6\frac{1}{2}$ yds. Print fabric for 104 bows, 36″ wide, $4\frac{1}{4}$ yds. Thread, white and color to match comforter.

For each pillow sham: Print fabric, piece 36″ × 41″ ($1\frac{1}{8}$ yd.). White eyelet ruffle trim, $5\frac{1}{2}''$ wide, $2\frac{1}{4}$ yds.

DIRECTIONS

Comforter top: Cut eyelet fabric in half cross-wise, then cut one of the halves in half lengthwise. With selvages together and right sides facing, pin smaller rectangles to large rectangle. Machine-stitch, $\frac{1}{4}''$ from selvage edges; press seams open. Piece should measure 71″ × 81″.

To plan for bow placement: If eyelet fabric has a stripe pattern (see illustration), follow these rows for vertical placement of buttonholes. Start 1″ from bottom of first row and mark a dot with dress-maker's marking pen every 10″. Repeat for all odd-numbered rows. On even-numbered rows, stagger the spacing by starting 6″ from the bottom, and thereafter every 10″.

If piece does not have a stripe pattern, fold piece in half lengthwise. One inch from bottom of fold line mark a dot, then another dot ever 10″ along line. Make a parallel fold line 10″ to the right, and mark dots in same intervals. Repeat twice more, then repeat for three rows to left of center fold line. Midway between each row, fold parallel rows; mark a dot 6″ from bottom, then every 10″ until you have seven markings.

At each marking, make a $\frac{3}{4}''$ buttonhole, using buttonholer or zigzag stitch at fine setting (satin stitch).

To make ties for bows, cut out 104 strips, each $2\frac{1}{2}''$ × 20″. On each strip, fold under $\frac{1}{2}''$ on short sides, then fold long edges in to meet at center. Fold in half lengthwise, with raw edges inside; press. Machine-stitch around three open sides, $\frac{1}{8}''$ from edge.

Fold top (short) side of eyelet cover under $\frac{1}{4}''$, then again $\frac{1}{4}''$; stitch top hem. Fold under three remaining sides $\frac{1}{4}''$, then pin each folded edge over bound edge of ruffled trim. Stitch all around. Hem raw ends of ruffled trim.

Place eyelet cover right side up on comforter. Fold ties in half and pin midpoint of each tie to comforter through each buttonhole. Carefully remove eyelet cover and, with a few stitches in color to match comforter, tack each tie in place. Replace eyelet cover, draw ties through buttonholes, and make bows.

Pillow sham: Fold under $\frac{1}{2}''$ on one long side of print fabric, then fold under again 5″ and stitch hem in place. Fold fabric crosswise, right sides together. Stitch along unhemmed and unfolded sides, $\frac{1}{2}''$ from edge. Clip corners, turn, press. To trim: On one side of pillowcase, 5″ from edges, pin bound edge of ruffled trim; slip-stitch in place. Right sides facing, sew ends of trim together.

Dust Ruffle

EQUIPMENT: Tape measure. Scissors. Straight pins. Sewing machine.

MATERIALS: To make dust ruffle for full-size bed: Muslin fabric, 6 yds. Print fabric, 36″ wide, 6 yds. You will need to adjust these measurements for twin, queen, or king-size beds. Twill tape, 40″, plus 40″ if bed has center legs on long sides. Sewing thread to match print fabric.

DIRECTIONS

Measure width and length of box spring. Cut and piece together muslin to make top section of dust ruffle 1″ wider and 1″ longer than these measurements.

Cut muslin for two end sections 1″ longer than width of box spring and 1″ wider than depth of box spring. Cut muslin for two side sections 1″ longer than length of spring and same width as

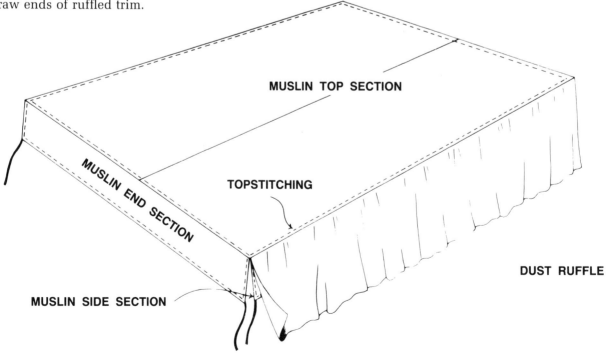

MUSLIN TOP SECTION

TOPSTITCHING

MUSLIN END SECTION

MUSLIN SIDE SECTION

DUST RUFFLE

end sections. Make a $\frac{1}{2}''$ hem along three sides of each piece, leaving one long side unhemmed. Stitch a 10″ strip of twill tape to each finished corner, and a 20″ strip, folded in half, at the center of each side section if the bed has center legs. Place one end section across head of top section, right sides together and raw edges flush, with top section extending $\frac{1}{2}''$ at each side. Stitch together $\frac{1}{2}''$ from raw edges.

To determine depth of ruffle, measure from top of box spring to floor. Cut pieces for ruffle 4″ deeper than this measurement across full width of print fabric. Seam pieces together, matching pattern of fabric until you have one strip $2\frac{1}{2}$ times width of box spring plus 4″ (for end ruffle) and two strips $2\frac{1}{2}$ times length of box spring plus 4″ (for side ruffles). Make a 2″ hem down each short end; turn bottom edge under $\frac{1}{2}''$ and then make a $3\frac{1}{2}''$ hem.

Stitch two rows of machine gathering stitches along top edge of each ruffling strip, placing them $\frac{1}{4}''$ and $\frac{1}{2}''$ in from edge of fabric. Make a mark every 12″ along top edge of muslin end and side sections and every 27″ along top edge of each ruffling strip. Pull up gathering threads of end ruffle until marks match those on muslin end section.

Place right side of muslin end section against wrong side of ruffle, with marks matching and top edges flush; pin together. Place ruffle on top section, right sides together, and stitch $\frac{1}{2}''$ from edge through all three pieces.

Gather side ruffles and attach to top section in same manner, with side ruffles meeting end ruffle at corners. Turn ruffles and muslin end and side sections down and smooth seam allowances to underside of top section. Edge-stitch through top and seam allowances around all four sides.

Place dust ruffle on box spring and tie tapes attached to muslin side and end sections together around legs of bed. Tie tapes around center legs on either side.

Covered Headboard

SIZE: 55″ × 41″, for full-size bed.
EQUIPMENT: Scissors. Tape measure. Pencil. Sewing needle. Saw. Hammer. Thumbtacks. Staple gun. Large-eyed needle. White glue. Optional: Sewing macine with zipper foot attachment.
MATERIALS: Cotton fabric, 36″ wide, 3 yds., or one crosswise half of full-size flat print sheet. Soft cable cord, $\frac{3}{4}''$ diameter, 3 yds. Sewing thread to match. Clear pine 2″ × 2″ in these lengths: one 55″; one 51″; two 39″. Plywood, $\frac{1}{8}''$ thick, 25″ × 55″. Nails, 3″ and 1″ long. Leg glides, two. Tacks. Quilt batting, $24\frac{1}{2}''$ × $54\frac{1}{2}''$, three layers. Cardboard, 2″ wide, one strip 55″, two strips 25″. Optional: Muslin or sheet fabric for back, 27″ × 57″.

DIRECTIONS

Cut wood to sizes given in materials list. Nail one end of each 39″ leg to each end on one side of 55″ length for top. Place 51″ length between legs 16″ from bottom ends; nail in place. Place plywood for headboard front over rectangle formed by tops of legs and cross beams (edges of plywood should be flush with all outer edges of rectangle); nail in place. Hammer glides into bottom of each leg.

From sheet fabric, cut headboard front 28″ × 58″; enough 4″-wide strips to piece a 3-yd. length for headboard edges; two leg pieces each 18″ × 10″; and enough $3\frac{1}{2}''$-wide bias strips to piece a 3-yd. length.

Using pieced bias strips and cable cord, make piping: Lay cable cord along lengthwise center of wrong side of bias strip. Fold strip over cord with raw edges even; stitch along length close to cord, using zipper foot if available.

Sew piping to right side of sheet piece for headboard front as follows: Start at center of one long edge of headboard piece; place piping seamline 1″ from edge of fabric. Having all raw edges facing out and piping facing center of sheet piece, baste piping along half of long side and down the adjacent short side, letting excess piping extend on other half of long side; repeat with other half of piping on other half of sheet piece. At piping ends, cut $\frac{1}{2}''$ off cord ends. Stitch piping in place. Turn casing ends to inside and whipstitch.

Turn all edges of each leg piece under 1″. Baste. Wrap each leg piece tightly around each leg of headboard with lengthwise edges overlapping 1″ on back of legs. Staple along lengthwise edge; remove basting threads.

Place batting layers on plywood front. Place piped sheet front on top with seam allowances lying along headboard sides and piping even with headboard edges at front; smooth and staple seam allowance to sides of headboard. Cut into lower seam allowance to accommodate legs.

To cover sides of headboard, seam 4″ strips together to measure 4 yds., matching patterns if necessary. With wrong side up, place 1″ seam allowance of strip onto front 1″ of headboard sides, along short side, across top side, and down other short side (other 3″ of fabric will fall toward headboard front). Staple strip well to hold it securely. Staple cardboard strips over short sides and top side, with cardboard edges even with edges of headboard sides. Turn sheet strip right side up over cardboard; pull tightly and staple to back of headboard, folding corners to lie smoothly.

To finish back of headboard, fold all edges of fabric under 1″; baste around. Staple onto back; remove basting threads. Install headboard. ☆

123

Color Wheels Quilt

shown on page 114

SIZE: 74″ × 94″.
EQUIPMENT: Paper for pattern. Tracing paper. Pencil. Ruler. Compass. Scissors. Thin, stiff cardboard. Straight pins. Sewing and quilting needles.
MATERIALS: Cotton fabric such as poplin, 44″ wide, 6 yds. white; $\frac{1}{2}$ yd. each of bright blue, purple, dark green, bright yellow, orange, and red; $\frac{1}{4}$ yd. black. Muslin for lining, 44″ wide, $5\frac{1}{2}$ yds. White quilting thread. Sewing thread to match fabric colors. Polyester or cotton batting, 81″ × 96″.

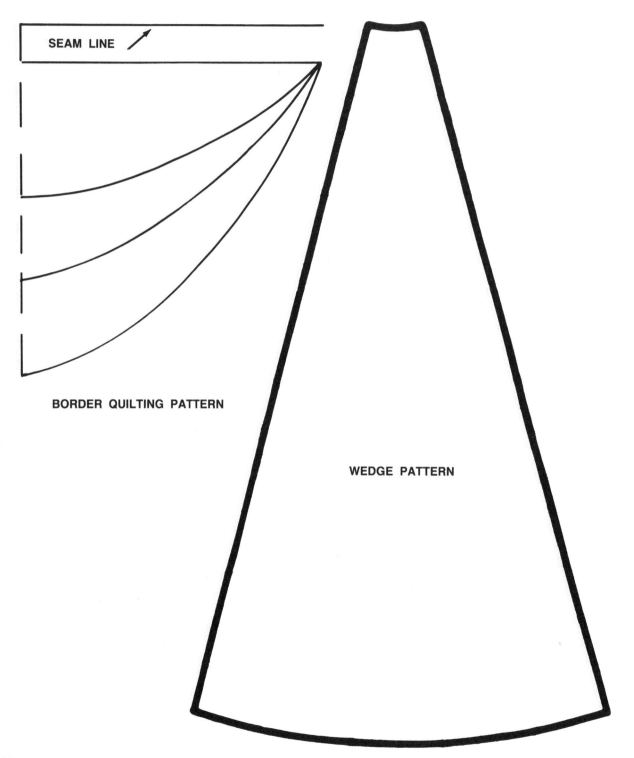

SEAM LINE

BORDER QUILTING PATTERN

WEDGE PATTERN

DIRECTIONS

Read General Directions for Quilting and How To Appliqué (see Contents). Trace actual-size Wedge Pattern. Quilt is made up of 12 18½"-square blocks of white cotton fabric that are appliquéd with colored wedges, then sewn together; next, the border is sewn on and the whole piece is quilted.

To make each block, cut a 19" square of white fabric (this allows for ¼" seams). Trace wedge pattern onto cardboard; cut out. Cut wedges as indicated in General Directions, marking on wrong side of fabric and adding ¼" seam allowance; make sure that the lengthwise center of each piece is placed on the straight of fabric. For each block, cut a wedge of red, orange, yellow, blue, green, and purple. Using compass and light-colored pencil, mark a 2¾"-diameter circle on wrong side of black fabric. Cut out circle, adding ¼" all around. Clip all curves and press ¼" under on all edges.

Lightly mark a 17"-diameter circle on center of white square. Having outer edges flush with marked circle, arrange and pin colored wedges evenly spaced around circle, leaving equal wedge-shaped area of white fabric between each colored wedge (see illustration and quilting pattern). Pin the black circle in center, overlapping ends of wedges and with a small amount of batting under circle to pad lightly. Slip-stitch each piece in place. Make 11 more blocks in same manner, keeping the color sequence the same but moving the colored wedges clockwise into a different position each time.

With right sides facing and making ¼" seams, sew the 12 blocks together in four rows of three across, then sew the rows together to make center of quilt.

For borders, cut four 11"-wide strip of fabric, two 75" long, two 95" long. With right sides facing, sew a long strip to each side of quilt and a short strip to each end, having equal lengths extending at corners. Miter corners (see Contents for directions). Cut off excess fabric to make ½" seam. Round off each corner. Press all seams to one side.

Quilting: Following Center Quilting Diagram, lightly mark quilting lines on quilt top for each color wheel square. Around each 17"-diameter circle, make 17 concentric circles ¼" apart. Outer circles will meet the curved lines from outer circles of adjacent squares (you need not mark if you can work evenly freehand, following circular contour).

For border quilting design, mark a line all around

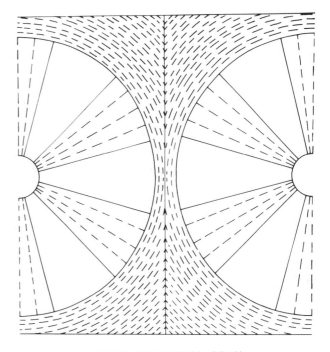

CENTER QUILTING DIAGRAM

border ½" beyond seam line. On each corner, center cardboard wedge pattern, with narrow end at line just marked for quilting; lightly mark around outline of cardboard. Mark another wedge on each side of corner with narrow ends touching (see illustration). Continue marking wedge shapes along border approximately 6½" apart at narrow ends. For swag part of quilted border design, make a cardboard pattern for each curve, completing half-pattern indicated by long dash line. Mark each curve on quilt border between each border wedge.

Cut two pieces of lining fabric, each one-half the width of quilt plus 1" for seam allowances and the length of quilt plus 1" for seam allowances. Making ½" seam, sew the two halves together along long edges. Trim corners of lining edges to match shape of quilt top. Cut batting ½" smaller all around than lining. Pin and baste quilt top, batting, and lining together, and quilt along marked lines and around each 17" wheel as instructed in General Directions for Quilting, quilting the center first. When quilting is completed, turn edges of fabric in ½"; slip-stitch together all around. Remove basting. ☆

Child's World Quilt

shown on page 115

SIZE: 56" × 88".
EQUIPMENT: Scissors. Ruler. Pencil. Thin, stiff cardboard. Paper for patterns. Dressmaker's (carbon) tracing paper. Tracing wheel or dry ball-point

pen. Sewing and embroidery needles. Quilting frame (optional). Straight pins.

MATERIALS: For quilt top, muslin, 36″ wide, 5 yds. For lining, white cotton, 45″ wide 1⅔ yds. Scraps of light and dark closely woven cotton fabrics: a variety of calico, gingham, solids, plaids, and stripes. Blue bias tape: ¼″ wide, prefolded, 31 yds.; ¾″ wide, prefolded, 3 3-yd. packages. White heavy cotton tape, ½″ wide, 2½ yds. Small amounts of embroidery floss in colors desired. Blue and white sewing thread. Cotton or polyester batting.

DIRECTIONS

Read General Directions for Quilting and How to Appliqué (see Contents). Quilt is constructed in two pieces, with machine-appliquéd squares divided by bias tape.

Appliqués: Enlarge all patterns on paper ruled in 1″ squares. Heavy lines indicated appliqué patterns; light lines indicate embroidery; dash lines indicate additional machine-stitching. Make a separate pattern for each appliqué piece. *Note:* Patterns are given for 69 of the 77 motifs. Label appliqués are cut from a printed fabric of choice. To personalize quilt, trace around child's hand, sketch and cut out letters of child's name, and embroider clock hands pointing to hour of child's birth.

Following instructions on How to Appliqué, cut and prepare appliqué pieces using any combination of cotton fabrics.

Quilt Top: Cut muslin for quilt top: one strip 32″ × 88″; one strip 24″ × 88″. Using ruler, mark 8″ intervals across width and along length of first muslin piece. Repeat on second strip.

From ¼″ bias tape, cut and piece six strips 88″ long. Cut and piece ten each 32″ and 24″ long. Press strips open at fold.

Put one 88″-long strip to one side. Center each of the remaining strips over intervals marked across fabric. Do not place a strip at last marking. Pin strips in place along entire length. Using blue thread, machine-stitch bias strips in place, dividing into equal sections. Repeat dividing blue strips across quilt, using corresponding strips with quilt top sections.

Appliqués: Starting with pieces that will be overlapped by others, pin, baste, and slip-stitch appliqués in place on blocks. After slip-stitching, machine-stitch around all pattern pieces close to fabric edge and along dash lines on patterns.

Embroidery: Refer to Stitch Details (see Con-

tents). Using carbon paper, transfer all embroidery lines onto appliquéd squares. To embroider, use two strands of floss for all embroidery, except for facial features and windowpanes; use single strand for these. Work the following stitches in areas indicated.

Chain Stitch: Butterfly antennae, swing rope, dog collar, clock hands, flower mouth, snail antennae, crab legs, strawberry stems. *Outline Stitch:* Clothesline rope, coffee cup rim, clown mouth, clock numbers, turtle eyelid, large fish eye, snail mouth, frog mouth, outline of horse eye, owl eyes, sailboat mast, cat collar and mouth, cherry stems, and banana lines. *Lazy Daisy:* Arrows on clock hands, birdbath flowers and leaves, fish bubbles, watermelon seeds, hat flower, snail eyes, sprinkler holes, Andy's buttons (two each, crisscrossed). *Buttonhole Stitch:* Grass around house. *French Knot:* Spider eye, small fish eye, chick eyes. *Satin Stitch:* House doorknob and all eyes, noses and beaks unless otherwise indicated. *Straight Stitch:* Remainder of embroidery lines on patterns. (*Note:* Guitar strings are long straight stitches anchored with small stitches near opening of guitar).

Lining: Cut two pieces from white cotton, each 44½″ × 56″. Making ½″ seam, stitch together along 44½″ sides. Cut batting pieces same size as each lining piece.

Quilting: Following General Directions for Quilting, pin and baste quilt top, batting, and lining all together. Start in center of quilt and work around and outward. Machine-quilt around each appliqué piece twice: once close to design, and a second line ¼″ away from the first. Quilt ½″ around inside edge of each block.

Referring to illustration, machine-stitch alternate blocks in uneven horizontal and vertical lines approximately ½″ apart. Be sure to consider the alternation of quilting on second quilt top strip before beginning next row of quilting. To finish, stitch along both sides of horizontal and vertical blue strips.

To Join Quilt Top: Align both pieces of quilt top at point where no blue tape divides. Pin and baste remaining blue strip to cover joining. Turn quilt over to wrong side. Pin white ½″-wide tape in place, covering joining. Slip-stitch white tape in place.

Turn quilt to right side and stitch along both sides of blue tape as for other dividers.

Edges: Bind edges of quilt with blue ¾″ binding tape, machine-stitching to front and lining. Press all edges. ☆

Pumpkin Quilt and Little Reader Picture

shown on page 116

Pumpkin Quilt

SIZE: Approximately 56" × 45".

EQUIPMENT: Pencil. Paper for pattern. Dressmaker's tracing (carbon) paper. Ruler. Scissors. Straight pins. Sewing needle. Zigzag sewing machine.

MATERIALS: Chintz fabric, 54" wide: yellow, $3\frac{1}{4}$ yds.; orange and green, $\frac{3}{4}$ yd each. Matching sewing thread. Polyester or cotton batting.

DIRECTIONS

To Prepare Fabric: Enlarge pattern for pumpkin design by copying on paper ruled in 2" squares. Cut pumpkin from orange fabric; cut leaves and stems from green fabric. Cut two quilt pieces from yellow fabric, each 57" × 46" for front and back.

The shorter dash lines on leaves and stems indicate where pieces overlap; the longer dash lines on pumpkin indicate stitching lines. Tape pattern to pumpkin with carbon between. With pencil, go over curved lines to transfer quilting lines to pumpkin fabric.

To Appliqué Quilt Front: Arrange and pin pieces onto right side of one yellow piece. Baste pieces in place all around each piece, close to edges.

To Quilt: Cut two pieces of batting slightly smaller than quilt size. With wrong side of quilt front and back facing, place the batting layers in between. Baste the four layers together, lengthwise, crosswise, and diagonally in both directions, then around all edges. Use zigzag satin stitch on sewing machine and thread to match appliqués. Stitch pumpkin, leaves, and stems to quilt, stitching through all layers along all appliqué edges and on pumpkin along marked lines.

Mark a line $3\frac{1}{2}$" in from quilt edges along each side. Using matching sewing thread, stitch this border line all around with straight sewing machine stitch.

To Finish: Turn front and back edges of quilt under $\frac{1}{4}$"; turn under again $\frac{1}{4}$" to wrong side; press. Topstitch together all around with matching thread.

Little Reader Picture

SIZE: 18" × 14" framed size; $14\frac{1}{2}$" × $10\frac{1}{2}$" design size.

EQUIPMENT: Pencil. Ruler. Paper for pattern. Tracing paper. White dressmaker's tracing (carbon) paper. Dry ball-point pen. White pencil. Masking tape. Embroidery frame or hoop. Embroidery and sewing needles. Embroidery scissors.

For Blocking and Mounting: Brown paper. Soft wooden surface. Thumbtacks. Steam iron. Straight pins. Tack hammer. T-square.

MATERIALS: Dark taupe or brown tightly woven linen-like fabric, 22" × 18". White sewing thread. Three-ply Persian yarn, one 8.8-yd. skein of each color listed in Color Key, except where indicated otherwise in parentheses. Mounting board, $\frac{1}{8}$" thick, 18" × 14". Orange metal strip frame to fit.

DIRECTIONS

With white pencil, lightly mark exact outline of picture area, 18" × 14", in center of fabric, leaving 2" of fabric all around beyond marked outline. (Make a note of actual size of fabric, for blocking.) Take $\frac{1}{4}$" running stitches with sewing needle and white thread over pencil lines, following thread of fabric, to mark guidelines around entire picture.

To Transfer Pattern: Enlarge pattern (on page 130) by copying on paper ruled in 1" squares. Trace entire design. Center tracing on fabric, with dressmaker's carbon paper between. Tape tracing and carbon to fabric to hold in place. Using dry ball-point pen, transfer all design lines to fabric. Remove tracing and carbon. To keep lines clear while embroidering, use sharp white pencil to clarify design lines as needed. Tape edges of fabric to keep them from raveling.

To Embroider: Use two strands of the 3-ply yarn in needle. Place fabric in embroidery hoop. Embroider picture following Stitch Key and Color Key; refer to Contents for Stitch Details. Dash lines in design areas indicate directions of satin stitch and laid stitch. Direction of split stitches follows the contour of area. For a smooth blending of colors in adjacent areas, stitch one color yarn into ends of stitches of the other color yarn. The hay is worked in long straight stitches, using yellow beige, bright gold, and dark gold in a random fashion as illustrated; the hayseed are short straight stitches.

To Block: Tack brown paper to soft wooden surface. Mark the exact size of fabric on paper, being sure corners are square. Stretch fabric right side up over paper; tack, matching marked outlines on fabric and paper. Stretch each side of fabric outline out to marked paper outline and tack a center of each side. Continue stretching sides from center to each corner. Place damp towel over embroidery. With steam iron, lightly steam picture; let dry completely.

To Mount: Smooth fabric over mounting board,

129

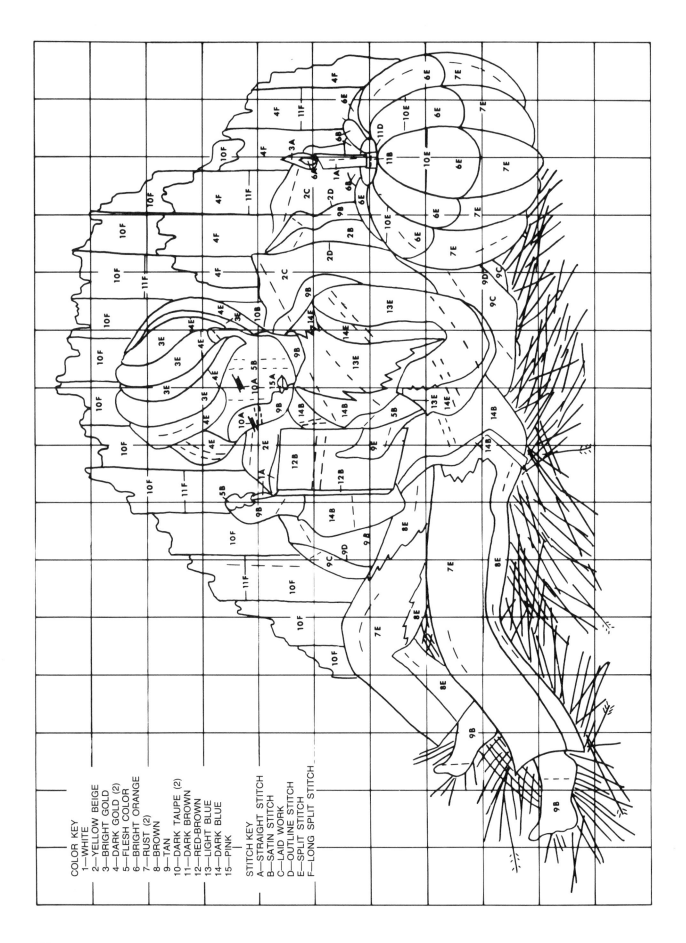

COLOR KEY
1—WHITE
2—YELLOW BEIGE
3—BRIGHT GOLD
4—DARK GOLD (2)
5—FLESH COLOR
6—BRIGHT ORANGE
7—RUST (2)
8—BROWN
9—TAN
10—DARK TAUPE (2)
11—DARK BROWN
12—RED-BROWN
13—LIGHT BLUE
14—DARK BLUE
15—PINK

STITCH KEY
A—STRAIGHT STITCH
B—SATIN STITCH
C—LAID WORK
D—OUTLINE STITCH
E—SPLIT STITCH
F—LONG SPLIT STITCH

130

18" × 14". Starting at corners and center of sides, push straight pins through fabric and into sides of board only part way. Being sure threads of fabric are straight, continue inserting pins about 1" apart all around board. When satisfied that fabric is completely straight, hammer pins in all the way.

To Frame: Assemble metal frame strips together around picture. ☆

Painted Quilt And Pillow Shams

shown on page 117

Painted Quilt

SIZE: 71" square.

EQUIPMENT: Paper for patterns. Ruler. Hard-lead pencil. Dressmaker's tracing (carbon) paper. Thin, stiff cardboard. Flat, stiff paintbrushes in small, medium, and large sizes. Paper plates for mixing paints. Measuring spoons. Straight pins. Sewing machine. Iron.

MATERIALS: For quilt and two pillow shams: Unbleached muslin, 36" wide, 10½ yds. Tightly woven solid-color fabric, 36" wide, 4½ yds. Quilted flannel backing, 36" wide, 4½ yds. Textile paints: brown, yellow, blue, magenta, scarlet, white, green, and extender. Polyester batting, two packages (each sheet 81" × 96".) Sewing thread, black and white.

GENERAL DIRECTIONS

Prewash all fabrics and iron smooth. Enlarge flower patterns by copying on paper ruled in 1" squares. Heavy lines indicate flower outlines; fine lines indicate shading lines. Following directions below, paint and complete all flower panels before assembling quilt and pillows. Using dressmaker's carbon and hard-lead pencil, transfer designs to muslin fabric.

Flower Panels: Cut a 17" square of muslin for each flower panel—nine squares for quilt, one square for each pillow. Lightly mark a 10½" square in center of each for flower area. Transfer a flower design to each square, marking heavy outlines and fine shading lines.

To Paint Flowers: Using paper plates as palettes, dilute paints with a little water to make a consistency that is easy to paint on fabric. Use extender where indicated. Mix paints and apply, following directions for each flower. Use small, medium, or large brush according to size of area being painted. Practice on fabric scrap first and paint from center of area to outline.

Morning Glory: Mix 1 teaspoon blue and 1 teaspoon extender. Paint larger bell portion of flower except star-like centers. Add a little white to blue and paint lower part and arms of star shape. For centers, dilute ¼ teaspoon yellow with water to make pale yellow.

Clematis: Mix 1 teaspoon blue with ¼ teaspoon magenta, a touch of black, and ¼ teaspoon white. Paint all petals completely, but not centers. Use blue paint alone for shading from center outward. Mix ¼ teaspoon each green and yellow to paint centers.

Iris: Mix 1 teaspoon each blue and magenta. Paint all petals, leaving center stripes. Use yellow alone for stripes on petals.

Daffodil: Dilute yellow with a little water for light color to paint entire flower. Use yellow only for lower portion of trumpet and inside area and to shade petals a little.

Poppy: Paint entire poppy yellow. To 1 teaspoon yellow, add a touch of magenta and shade petals. For center, add more magenta to make deep orange color.

Tulips: Dilute yellow with a little water and paint all tulips completely. To the yellow, add a touch of scarlet and water. Shade lower two-thirds of petals with this color. Add a touch of magenta and paint lower end of each tulip.

Day Lilies: Mix 1 teaspoon yellow with ¼ teaspoon scarlet. Paint flowers completely, except center stripes on petals. Use yellow only for stripes.

Crocus: Use yellow alone for one of the flowers, leaving the pistils unpainted. Paint the pistils brown diluted with water. Mix 1 teaspoon each blue and magenta for the other flower; paint the pistils yellow. Dilute brown with a little water to paint one small leaf below each flower.

Nasturtium: Dilute yellow with a little water and paint flowers completely, except center of full flower. Mix a touch of magenta to the yellow for shading at center. Add a bit more magenta and paint lines from center outward. Mix ¼ teaspoon each yellow and green to paint center.

Leaves and Stems: Mix as needed for all leaves and stems, two parts green to one part brown. Di-

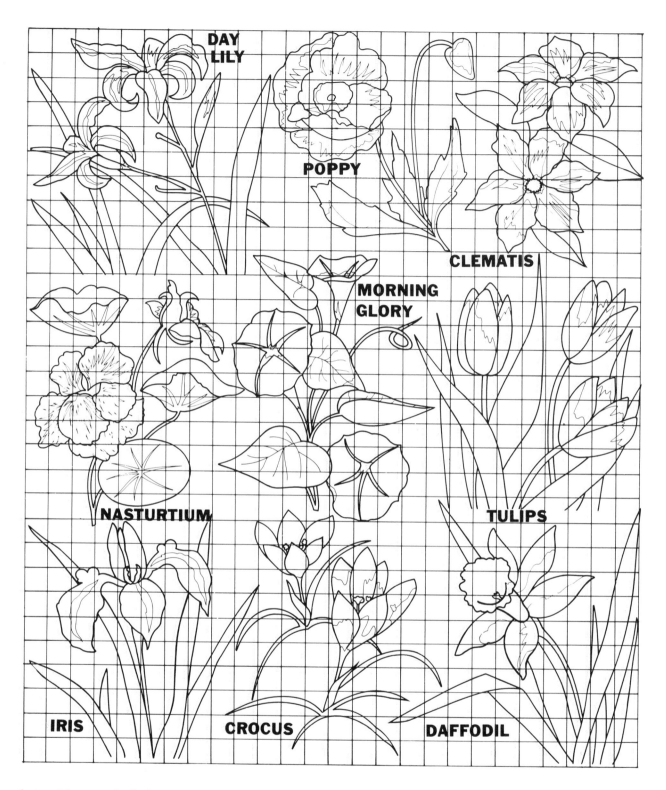

lute with water for lighter areas. Paint some leaves light and some dark; shade others from dark to light.

Let paint dry completely. Set color by ironing on the wrong side for 30 seconds with iron at 350°.

Quilt: To Make Flower Blocks: For each flower panel, cut a 17" square of batting and muslin. Pin painted panel and muslin together with batting between; baste. Release presser foot in sewing ma-

chine for darning, and set stitch length to short. Using black thread, stitch along flower, stem, and leaf outlines (heavy lines on patterns). To begin and end, hold fabric in place and make a few stitches to secure thread.

For border around each flower square, cut four strips of solid-color fabric 3¼" × 14". Turn one long edge of each under ¼" and press. Place the four strips around flower panel right side up, with folded edges overlapping edges of panel and ends of each other (see Fig. 1). Topstitch with white thread through all thicknesses, along folded edges of each strip (dotted lines on Fig. 1). Each panel should measure 16½″ square.

Joining Strips (See Fig. 2): From muslin, cut 12 strips A, 4″ × 17″; cut four strips B, 4″ × 55″; cut four strips C, 9″ × 55″; cut four strips D, 9″ × 63″; cut four pieces E, 9″ square: From batting cut pieces to same measurements in following amounts: six of A; two each of B, C, D, and E. Set aside six of strip A, two each of B, C, D, and square E for lining pieces.

Quilting: Trace actual-size quilting pattern. Trace it a number of times on cardboard as it must be used over and over to repeat pattern along each strip. Discard frayed patterns when necessary. Use dressmaker's carbon and hard-lead pencil with patterns to transfer quilting design to strips.

Fold each of the strips (six of A, two each of B, C, D) in half crosswise and mark center fold. Place pattern with Xs at center mark of strips, leaving equal margin of fabric above and below pattern. Mark pattern on strip. Repeat pattern from center out to end of strip, matching dash lines of pattern for each repeat. For the two 9″ corner squares, mark a 4″ square in center of each. Trace complete motif of quilt pattern twice with lower point of motif placed in the angle of two opposite corners.

Pin each marked strip or square to a matching

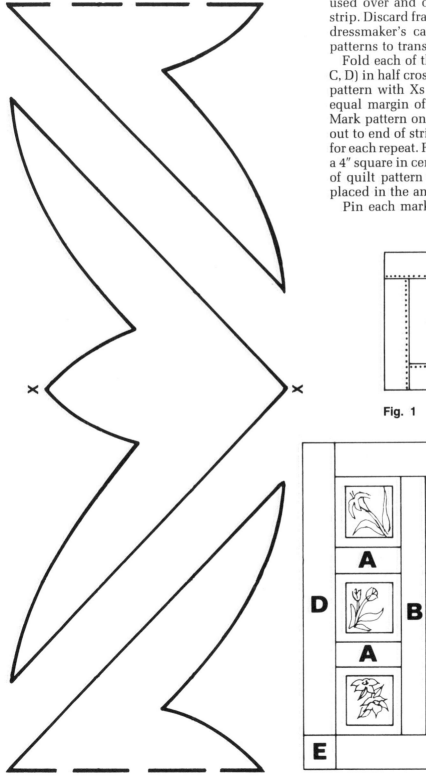

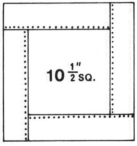

Fig. 1

Fig. 2

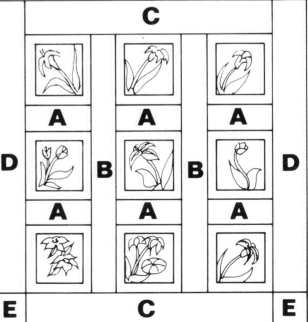

plain muslin strip or square with batting between; baste together. Starting at center, with white thread, topstitch over all traced lines of quilting pattern.

Assembling Quilt: Lay out all parts of quilt following Fig. 2. With right sides facing, stitch pieces together with ½" seams. Start with flower panels and shorter borders. Then stitch joined flower panels to long strips B. Join border C at top and bottom. Then join side borders D. Add corners E last. Trim away batting in each seam.

For back, cut two pieces of quilted flannel 36" × 71". Sew together lengthwise with ½" seams. Pin quilt front to flannel back, wrong sides together. For border edges, cut four strips of solid color fabric; each 72" × 5". Fold long sides under ¼" and fold strips in half lengthwise; press. Encase raw edges of quilt with folded strips; pin. Topstitch along folded edges through all thicknesses along each strip; turn in ends and stitch.

Pillow Sham

SIZE: Fits standard size pillow.

DIRECTIONS

Paint 17" square flower panel for each pillow following General Directions. Cut 27" × 21" rectangles of batting and muslin for backing. Center painted panel on muslin backing, wrong sides facing, with batting between; pin. Stitch over outlines with black thread as for quilt.

For blocks, cut strips from solid color fabric, two 11½" × 5½" and two 21" × 8¾". Prepare as for quilt blocks and stitch shorter strips across top and bottom, longer strips across sides, overlapping ends of shorter strips. For borders, cut muslin strips 4" wide, two 27" long and two 33" long. With right sides facing, sew longer strips along top and bottom with ½" seams and leaving ends equal. Sew shorter strips along sides. Miter corners; see Contents for directions.

For back of pillow sham, cut two pieces of solid color fabric 21" wide, one 24" long and one 15". Hem one 21" edge of each. Overlap hemmed edges with shorter piece on top of longer piece to make a back piece 21" × 27"; stitch together along double top and bottom edges.

Cut quilted flannel strips 4" wide, two 27" long and two 33" long. Stitch strips to solid color back and miter corners as for front. With right sides of front and back facing, stitch together around all sides. Clip corners and turn right side out. ☆

Bunny Quilt and Toy

shown on page 118

SIZE: Quilt, 46" × 50". Toy, 27" tall.

EQUIPMENT: *For Quilt and Toy:* Colored pencil. Pencil. Ruler. Paper for patterns. Tracing paper. Dressmaker's tracing (carbon) paper. Tracing wheel. Dry ball-point pen. Zigzag sewing machine. Iron. Scissors. Small, pointed scissors. Sewing needle. Straight pins.

For Quilt Only: Yardstick. Tailor's chalk. Thin, stiff cardboard. Large safety pins. All-purpose glue. Quilting needle. Quilting frame or hoop (optional).

MATERIALS: *For Quilt:* Finely woven cotton fabrics, such as broadcloth, 45" wide: gold, 2¾ yds.; white, ½ yd.; green, ⅓ yd.; orange, lavender, blue, and hot pink, ¼ yd. each. Coordinating print scrap, 8" × 16". Yellow calico scrap, 3" × 6". Yellow gingham with ¼" checks, 45" wide, 1⅜ yds. Orange double-fold bias seam tape, 13½ yds. Sewing thread: white, orange, royal blue, hot pink, and green. White quilting (strong cotton) thread. Polyester batting and stuffing. *For Toy:* Yellow gingham with ¼" checks, 45" wide, 1 yd. White broadcloth, 45" wide, ½ yd. Scraps of blue and orange cotton fabrics. White, orange, and blue sewing thread. Polyester stuffing.

Quilt

DIRECTIONS

Using sharp colored pencil, draw lines across patterns, connecting grid lines. Enlarge patterns by copying on paper ruled in 1" squares. Cut Border Quilting and Edging Patterns away from Appliqué Pattern and set aside.

Cut two pieces 42¾" × 46¾" from gold fabric for quilt top and lining. Center Appliqué Pattern on wrong side of quilt top and transfer all solid lines, using dressmaker's carbon and tracing wheel; use dry ball-point pen to transfer small areas. Hand-baste a general outline around bunny to mark position on right side. Turn quilt top to right side. Cut an 18" × 31" piece from both white fabric and yellow gingham; press pieces. With right sides facing up and matching edges, place white piece first, then gingham piece on right side of quilt top to cover basting outline. Pin or baste layers in place.

To Appliqué Bunny: Step One: Thread sewing machine with white thread and set for small straight

petal

leaf

EDGING

BORDER QUILTING

APPLIQUÉ PATTERN

stitches. Working on wrong side of quilt top, stitch over all marked lines, except tail, inner eyes, and nose. Turn quilt top to right side and, using sharp pointed scissors, cut away excess of both fabrics from bunny outline (except tail), close to stitching ($\frac{1}{8}''$ or less). Carefully cut away gingham only from tail, inner ears, chest, tummy, and eyes, exposing white fabric. Cut two $2\frac{1}{2}''$ squares from blue; press. On right side, pin blue squares over eyes. On wrong side, stitch around tail and pupils, including com-

mon lines of rump and eye outlines already stitched. Turn to right side and cut away excess fabric as before. Using a 3″ square of orange fabric, appliqué nose in the same manner. **Step Two:** Trace bunny face and body from enlarged pattern, including dash lines. Placing pattern right side down, transfer dash lines only to gingham bunny on right side. Thread machine with hot pink thread and set for close, wide zigzag (satin) stitch. Working on right side of quilt top and starting at base of straight ear

135

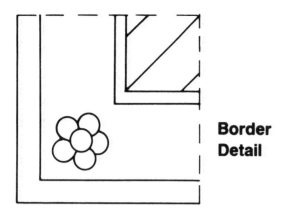

**Border
Detail**

on outside, stitch around straight ear, covering fabric edge and straight stitching; stitch across top of head and around bent ear, continuing stitching over dash line and across top of inner ear. Stitch around rest of inner ear and around second inner ear. Stitch completely around face, including dash line. Stitch bunny body in same manner, working over dash lines to make a continuous outline where desirable. Stitch around nose. Change to blue thread and stitch eye outlines; stitch eyebrows and mouth over dash lines.

To Appliqué Flowers: On wrong side of quilt top, baste a circle around each flower about ½" beyond outline. Cut two 8" squares each from white, orange, and print fabric, for flowers; cut two 5" squares each from lavender, blue, and hot pink and two 3" squares each from hot pink, yellow calico, and blue, for large and small flower centers. Following illustration for placement, pin one flower, one large center and one small center on right side of fabric over each basted circle. Reset sewing machine for short straight stitches and switch to white thread. On wrong side of quilt top, stitch small flower centers, then trim excess on right side; stitch large centers, then trim; stitch flowers, then trim; remove basting. Baste around leaves and stems on wrong side. Cut a 6" square for each leaf and a 2"-wide strip for each stem segment from green fabric. Pin leaf pieces in place and stitch outline, including common outline of flower already stitched; trim excess fabric on right side. Pin strips in place and appliqué stem segments in same manner. Reset machine for zigzag stitching. Working on right side of quilt top and using hot pink thread, stitch around both centers of each print flower, print flower outlines, both centers of each white flower and orange flower outlines; stitch around both centers of each orange flower with blue; stitch around white flower outlines with white; stitch leaf and stem outlines with green.

Quilting Pattern: Lay quilt top right side up on work surface. Following Border Detail and using yardstick and tailor's chalk, draw first border line 1" in from fabric edges; draw second line 3¼" in from first, and third ½" in from second. Draw a

diagonal line from lower left corner of inside border to upper right corner, skipping over appliqués. Continue to draw diagonal lines over background, 1½" apart and parallel to first.

Transfer border quilting motifs to wide border area, centering them between first and second border lines as follows: One flower in each corner (see detail); one flower in center of each side and top and bottom; on sides only, one flower midway between center and each corner flower; on top and bottom, one flower 10½" in from each corner flower. Also on top and bottom, transfer one triple scroll to each side of center flower; reversing scroll for second side of each flower. Transfer two double scrolls between all other flowers around edge.

Quilting: Lay quilt lining on flat surface, wrong side up. Cut two layers of batting same size, and lay on top, smoothing out any bumps or wrinkles. Place quilt top on batting, right side up. Pin all layers together to hold temporarily, using large safety pins. Baste generously through all thicknesses, lengthwise, crosswise, diagonally, and around perimeter, remove pins. If desired, attach to quilt frame or hoop, or quilt in your lap, working over a small area at a time.

Using quilting thread and taking small running stitches, quilt close to outside of all zigzag stitching, working around bunny, flowers, and leaves. Stitch diagonal lines, working from center of quilt out. Stitch border lines and border motifs.

Edging: Trace petal and leaf patterns. Glue tracings to cardboard; let dry and cut out. Use as templates to mark 136 petals on yellow gingham and 24 leaves on green fabric. (If templates become bent or frayed, make new ones.) Cut out petals and leaves on marked lines. Reset sewing machine for small straight stitches. Pin two petal pieces together, wrong sides facing and edges even. Cut a 7" length of seam tape; leaving top straight edges free, sandwich curved edges of petal between folded edges of tape; topstitch with orange thread. Lightly stuff petal with fiberfill and "pleat" top edge between dots; tack pleat in place. Make 67 more petals in same manner. Pin two leaf pieces together, right sides facing. Leaving top straight edges open, stitch, making ¼" seam; turn to right side. Lightly stuff and pleat as for petal. Make 11 more leaves.

Following sequence given here, place petals and leaves on right side of quilt top, so that all raw edges are even and petals and leaves point inward quilt center. Overlap pieces slightly to fit. For top and bottom edges, place 3 petals, 1 leaf, 5 petals, 1 leaf, 5 petals, 1 leaf, 3 petals. Adjust pieces so that center leaf is lined up with center border flower and each leaf overlaps a petal on each side. Pin pieces in place to quilt top only and stitch ⅜" in from raw edges, being careful not to catch batting or lining in stitches. Place and stitch side edge pieces in same manner, adding one more petal to each end. Press all raw edges to wrong side of quilt top, so that petals and leaves point outward. Trim batting and fold raw edges of quilt back $\frac{3}{8}''$ to wrong side. Pin in place and topstitch through all thicknesses $\frac{1}{8}''$ in from folded edge.

Toy

DIRECTIONS

Cut an 18″ × 31″ piece from both white and gingham fabric. Following Quilt Directions, enlarge bunny pattern only and transfer to wrong side of white fabric (bunny backing). Baste gingham, right side up, to right side of white fabric, edges even. Appliqué bunny as for quilt: For Step One, include tail in first stitching. Do not cut excess fabric from bunny outline. Carefully cut away gingham from inner areas as directed, including tail (to expose white fabric). Add blue eyes and orange nose. Work Step Two as for quilt. Trim excess fabric $\frac{3}{8}''$ beyond bunny outline; use as pattern to cut back from gingham. Pin back to front, right sides facing and edges even. Reset sewing machine for straight stitching and sew pieces together, stitching close to zigzag outline; leave a 3″ opening at inside edge of each ear and at bunny bottom. Clip into seam allowance to ease curves and turn to right side. Stuff ears first, then slip-stitch ear openings closed. Stuff head and body; slip-stitch bottom opening closed. ☆

Lion & Lambs Quilt

shown on page 119

EQUIPMENT: Paper and lightweight cardboard for patterns. Ruler. Pencil. Scissors. Tracing paper. Tailor's chalk. Dressmaker's tracing (carbon) paper. Dry ball-point pen. Straight pins. Sewing needle. Zigzag sewing machine.

MATERIALS: Calico print cotton or blend fabrics: large scraps for lion, lambs, leaves, bird, moon, stars, of various colors as shown or as desired. (In quilt shown, the largest amount of one calico needed is $\frac{1}{2}$ yd. of 45″ wide fabric for 59 leaves.) Solid, closely woven cotton or blend fabric, 45″ wide, in colors shown or as desired in the following amounts: $\frac{5}{8}$ yd. for tree; 1 yd. for foreground hill; $\frac{7}{8}$ yd. for background hill; $5\frac{1}{2}$ yds. for sky, borders, and backing. Thin muslin 45″ wide, $1\frac{3}{4}$ yds. Matching or contrasting thread. Batting.

DIRECTIONS

Enlarge pattern by copying on paper ruled in 2″ squares. Heavier pattern lines are cutting lines; finer lines within pieces indicate machine stitching.

Trace each part of quilt separately.

Two basic lamb patterns are given (each facing different direction), two basic leaf patterns, one star pattern; cut several of each of the patterns from cardboard; discard frayed patterns as necessary. Using patterns, cut tree trunk; cut two hills out of appropriate fabric, adding $\frac{1}{2}''$ to side and bottom edges.

Press all fabrics smooth. Cut sky, adding $7\frac{1}{2}''$ to top edge for complete sky and $\frac{1}{2}''$ along each side and bottom. Trace outline of each appliqué piece to appropriate fabric, marking on right side with tailor's chalk or pencil. Transfer fine lines of stitching with carbon and dry ball-point pen. Cut 59 leaves using the two basic patterns; during cutting, the sizes can be varied slightly. Cut nine sheep facing left and seven facing right. Cut five stars and one moon.

Cut piece of muslin 59″ × 43″. Pin all pieces of design to muslin as illustrated. Baste securely in place. Using close zigzag, satin stitch all around pieces and on inner lines of appliqués using matching or contrasting thread.

Cut two border strips 59″ × 7″ and two 55″ × 7″. Pin and sew longer borders to sides of quilt front, right sides facing, making $\frac{1}{2}''$ seam. Pin and sew remaining borders to shorter ends of quilt. Cut piece of batting 65″ × 49″. Lay quilt top out flat and smooth, right sides down; center and pin batting to wrong side.

For backing, cut two pieces of fabric 44″ × $30\frac{1}{2}''$. Stitch together on 44″ edges, right sides facing and making $\frac{1}{2}''$ seam. Pin back to quilt, centered on top of batting; stitch together all around close to edge of back.

Fold borders to back leaving 3″ wide border on front, 3″ wide border on back; turn in raw edges $\frac{1}{2}''$; slip-stitch border in place on back.

Using thread to match fabric and short running stitches, quilt by hand around all appliqué pieces close to machine stitching; quilt all sides just inside border. ☆

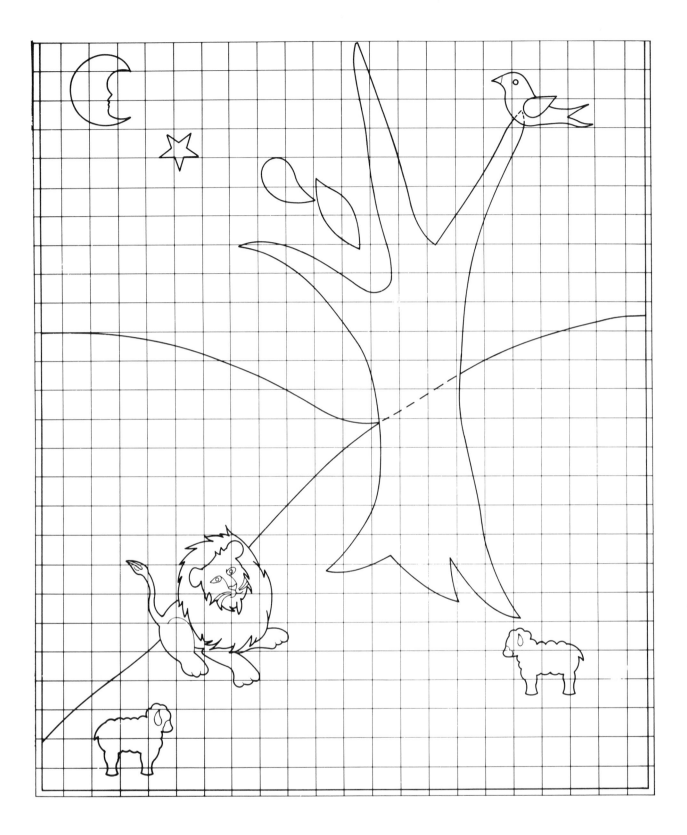

138

Three Flowers Quilt

shown on page 120

SIZE: 81″ × 125″.

EQUIPMENT: Paper for patterns. Pencil. Ruler. Scissors. Tape measure. Straight pins. Sewing machine with zigzag attachment. Thin, stiff card-board. Tailor's chalk. Dressmaker's carbon paper. Large-eyed embroidery needle.

MATERIALS: Polished cotton 44″ wide: White, 14 yds.; dark yellow-green, 3¼ yds.; medium yellow-

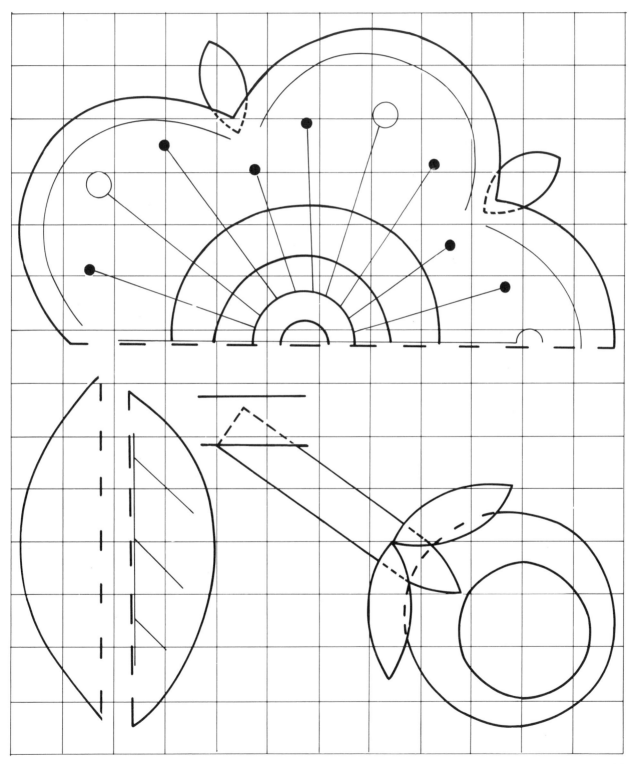

green, $\frac{1}{2}$ yd.; peach, $\frac{3}{4}$ yd.; dark pink $\frac{1}{4}$ yd. Sewing thread to match and white. Six-strand embroidery floss: 4 strands each of green and purple. Quilt batting, queen size. Cable cord $\frac{1}{4}''$ thick, 10 yds.

DIRECTIONS

Read General Directions for Quilting and How to Appliqué (see Contents). Enlarge appliqué patterns by copying on paper ruled in 1″ squares; complete half-patterns indicated by long dash lines. Make a separate cardboard pattern for each part of flower and bud designs and leaves. Cut and prepare appliqué pieces as directed.

From dark yellow-green fabric, cut three strips 1″ wide, 100″ long for stems; cut 15 bud stems with pointed ends; cut 15 tiny leaves around large flowers; cut 15 pairs of leaves below buds; cut 27 large plain leaves. From medium yellow-green fabric, cut 27 large leaves with veins. From peach fabric, cut three large flowers (outer line); cut 15 buds (outer line). From pink fabric, cut three large flower centers; cut 15 bud centers. From remaining dark yellow-green fabric, cut bias strips $1\frac{1}{2}''$ wide, with diagonal ends. Join strips to make 10-yd. piece for cording.

For quilt top, cut two pieces of white fabric 44″ wide and 125″ long. Seam together along long edges with $\frac{1}{2}''$ seam allowance. Press seam open. Repeat for lining. Spread quilt top on a large surface. Measure in 21″ on each long side of quilt top and make a line of basting from top to bottom end as a guide for design area. Measure 18″ in from top end and baste a line across fabric for top guideline. Following diagram and illustration, place stems and all pieces on quilt top with large flowers touching top guideline and leaves touching side lines. Space buds, bud stems, and leaves evenly. Pin all pieces in place. Appliquéing is done on machine, using fairly wide zigzag stitch set at satin stitch setting. Appliqué pieces to quilt in three stages, since some pieces overlap others. Baste only those pieces being appliquéd in each step. leaving rest pinned in place. First do buds, then bud stems and all leaves, including tiny leaves around large flowers and bud leaves; then do large flowers, buds, and centers for both. Use matching thread and work carefully over edge of each piece to ensure even coverage and smoothly curving lines. Roll quilt up from both ends while working, leaving only small area flattened on machine. To avoid turning whole quilt around, sew on pieces in two motions where possible. Pull thread ends through to back and tie. Finish all appliquéing before doing embroidery.

With dressmaker's carbon, mark radiating lines and circles on large flowers. Using purple floss, embroider all lines in couching (see Contents for Stitch Details). Use four pieces of the full six strands for laid lines and couch with six strands. Couch circles at end of radiating lines, starting at center and working around in rounds to outside. Make dots in French knots using six strands doubled.

Mark vein lines on medium yellow-green leaves and couch with green floss in same manner as for flowers. When embroidery is finished, press fabric and lining pieces.

Quilting: Pin and baste quilt top, batting and lining together, following General Directions for Quilting. For machine stitching, push a table up against machine to rest quilt on so it will not drag against the needle. With matching thread, topstitch around each appliquéd piece just inside satin stitching. Work slowly and carefully to avoid puckering.

Round off bottom corners of quilt, using a quarter of a 2½″ circle of cardboard. The side overhangs are quilted in squares with white thread. To prepare for quilting, with tailor's chalk, mark vertical and horizontal lines across fabric 3″ apart, with first line just outside leaves. Topstitch along each line to within ½″ of outside edge (for hem allowance).

To finish edges, trim away ½″ of batting and lining all around. Turn in ¼″ on top edges; turn over to back and topstitch hem all around.

Using zipper foot, make cording with the green bias strip over the cable cord. Trim the edges of cording and sew by hand around sides and bottom fo quilt along hemline, with seam of cording hidden underneath the cording. ☆

Window Wall Hanging

shown on page 145

SIZE: 73″ × 44″.

EQUIPMENT: Pencil. Colored pencil. Scissors. Yardstick. Paper for pattern. Tracing paper. Dressmaker's tracing (carbon) paper. Dry ball-point pen. Straight pins. Large safety pins. Sewing needle. Zigzag sewing machine. Quilting foot (optional). Iron.

MATERIALS: White cotton/polyester fabric 45″ wide, 4⅛ yds. Bleached muslin 45″ wide, 2⅛ yds. Cotton fabric 36″ wide: flower print ¾ yd.; light blue, ⅔ yd.; small-scale green print, ½ yd.; pink and brown, ¼ yd. each; scrap of black. Polyester or cotton batting. Matching sewing threads, plus deep pink and blue.

DIRECTIONS

Using sharp colored pencil, draw lines across pattern, connecting grid lines. Enlarge pattern on paper ruled in 4″ squares; dotted lines indicate overlapped pieces; fine lines indicate quilting design. Make a separate pattern for each part of design, including fine lines for quilting.

Using dressmaker's carbon and dry ball-point pen, transfer outline of sky pattern to right side of light blue fabric and outline of ground pattern to right side of flower-print fabric; use outer lines of window frame for the straight edges. Cut out pieces, cutting on marked lines for straight edges and ½″ beyond marked lines for curving edges. On flowered ground piece, fold under extra ½″ and press. Place folded edge along marked line on blue sky piece; pin and baste. Zigzag-stitch pieces together, sewing close to folded edge. Piece should be about 31″ × 43½″.

Transfer leaf design to ground-sky piece for placement. Using patterns, cut out leaves from green print and zigzag-stitch in place; see How to Appliqué (refer to Contents) for method.

From muslin, cut four strips 2½″ × 43½″ (cut all muslin strips on lengthwise grain of fabric). Fold long edges in ⅝″ to form 1¼″-wide pieces. Press. Place two strips along sides of ground-sky piece, matching outer edges and with smooth side out; pin. Baste along outer edges of strip; straight-stitch along inner edges, ⅛″ from fold. Position remaining strips vertically so piece is divided into three equal parts; stitch along both long edges of each strip.

From muslin, cut five strips 2½″ × 31″. Fold and press as before. Using patterns and referring to color illustration, mark notches and pointed ends where needed. Cut away excess fabric ¼″ beyond marked lines; turn the ¼″ to wrong side; press. Sew the five strips horizontally across ground-sky piece in same manner as before, dividing into four equal sections and positioning notches over intersected strips; fold in inner corners of top and bottom strips for a mitered effect.

Cut two black birds and appliqué to upper left windowpane, in same manner as for leaves.

Transfer portion of figure between dash lines (from bottom of window to shoulder) to appliqué window piece. Cut out figure, ¼″ from marked line. Turn ¼″ to wrong side; press; baste.

From white cotton/polyester, cut background 44″ × 73″. Position window as indicated on pattern; pin and baste. Straight-stitch around outer edges of window, continuing stitching around cut-out figure. (If necessary, trim edges of ground-sky under window frame).

Cut two hair pieces from brown fabric and two sashes and two bows from pink, marking patterns on wrong side of fabric and adding $\frac{1}{4}''$ seam allowance all around. For each appliqué, place the two pieces with right sides facing and stitch around on marked seam line, leaving an opening for turning. Turn right side out; turn in seam allowance of opening; press piece flat.

Transfer head outline to window and position hair appliqué. Straight-stitch all around, close to edge. Appliqué bow and sash in same manner.

Transfer fine-line quilting design to hanging.

Assembling: Cut cotton/polyester lining and one layer of batting, both the same size as hanging. Place lining down flat, wrong side up. Place batting on top and secure to lining with two long stitches in a cross. Place hanging over batting, right side up. Pin all layers together temporarily with large safety pins. Baste generously through all thicknesses, using a sturdy thread and a large needle. Baste first on the lengthwise and crosswise grain of fabric, then diagonally across in two directions and around all sides.

Quilting: Adjust sewing machine so that pressure is slightly heavier than for medium-weight fabric. Work with the bobbin thread a little loose.

Set stitch length to 12-to-inch for fine areas (hair), 8-to-inch for long straight lines (wall). Although a quilting foot is not essential, it may be useful for making curved lines. Start in center of hanging and work outward in circular fashion as much as possible, to prevent fabric from bunching in any one area. When quilting parallel lines, alternate direction of stitching.

With deep pink thread in needle, quilt lines in bow. With white thread, quilt hair lines, then around hair and sash; quilt lines of shoulders and outer arms, around windowpanes, birds, and leaves, ground-sky line, then around window frame; quilt remaining lines of dress, starting with inner arm. With blue, quilt wall lines. With black, quilt baseboard and floor.

Edges: From muslin, cut four strips 4″ wide, two 73″ long and two 44½″ long. On each strip, fold long edges under $\frac{1}{4}''$ and press. Pin a 73″ strip to each long edge on lining side, with a folded edge of strip $1\frac{3}{4}''$ from edge of hanging. Stitch $\frac{1}{4}''$ from folded edge. Turn strip to right side of hanging and pin. Stitch $\frac{1}{8}''$ from folded edge. Repeat with 44½″ strips on top and bottom edges of hanging, turning in extra $\frac{1}{4}''$ at each end of strips. ☆

Quilted Primitives

shown on pages 146–147

EQUIPMENT: Paper for patterns. Tracing paper. Pencil. Ruler. Dressmaker's tracing (carbon) paper. Scissors. Tailor's chalk. Hard-lead pencil. Straight pins. Sewing and embroidery needles. *For Mat:* X-acto knife; metal edge.

MATERIALS: Unbleached muslin 36″ wide, 1 yd. for each. Polyester or cotton batting (see individual directions). Pieces of cotton print fabrics for backgrounds (amounts given in individual directions). Large and small pieces of print and plain fabrics as illustrated or as desired that are suitable for the appliqués. Six-strand embroidery floss (colors given in individual directions). Sewing thread to match fabrics. Print fabric for each mat, 36″ wide, $\frac{5}{8}$ yd. Mounting cardboard and mat board (same size as matted size, given in mat directions). Rubber cement. Double- and single-faced masking tape.

GENERAL DIRECTIONS

First read How to Appliqué (see Contents). Instead of slip-stitching appliqués, sew pieces together and in place with tiny running stitches $\frac{1}{4}''$ apart, using double strand of matching sewing thread. When working embroidery, refer to Embroidery Stitch Details (see Contents).

To Make Patterns: Enlarge complete patterns (on pages 144 and 153) by copying on paper ruled in 1″ squares. The heavier lines on pattern indicate pieces to be cut out and appliquéd. The dash lines indicate pieces that are to be tucked (see directions for Farm Scene). The finer lines indicate what is to be embroidered. Trace pattern for each appliqué piece.

To Make Background: Cut the background fabrics as indicated in individual directions. Cut batting and muslin for backing the same size: $11\frac{1}{2}'' \times 17\frac{1}{2}''$ for Hearth, $13\frac{1}{2}'' \times 18''$ for Farm. Place the muslin on back of batting; place background fabrics on top of batting, overlapping the lower piece of background on upper piece $\frac{1}{2}''$. Turn top edge of lower fabric under $\frac{1}{4}''$ and, with running stitch and double strand of thread, sew together through all layers where they overlap.

Quilt background with double strand of matching sewing thread and tiny running stitches. Use a random pattern for quilting or select a pattern appropriate to the design (note that stitching pattern on sky in farm scene suggests cloud formations).

To Make Appliqués: Place separate patterns on the particular fabric for a specific part of the scene with carbon between; transfer the outline with hard lead pencil to the fabric. Cut the individual pieces out of fabric, adding $\frac{1}{4}''$ all around each piece. Fold under $\frac{1}{4}''$ along each edge of each piece; press, then appliqué each piece in place on background with tiny running stitches spaced $\frac{1}{4}''$ apart, using double strand of matching sewing thread. Embroider parts as indicated in individual directions.

To Embroider: Embroidery is done in satin stitch with all six strands of floss in needle unless otherwise indicated. Embroider through top background layer of fabric only; do not work through all layers.

To Make Border: Cut four strips of print fabric each 3″ wide: two the width of design plus 2″ and two the length of design plus 2″. Fold each strip in half lengthwise and turn in $\frac{1}{4}''$ on each long edge; press. Insert $\frac{1}{4}''$ along each side of picture between turned-in edges of border strips. With two strands of sewing thread and tiny running stitches, sew border strips to each side $\frac{1}{16}''$ in from fold. Repeat with remaining two strips at top and bottom of picture.

To Make Mat: Cut opening in center of mat board using X-acto knife and straight edge: 15″ × 19½″ for Farm, 13″ × 19″ for Hearth. Spread rubber cement over one surface of mat and cover with fabric; pull excess fabric over outer edge to other side and cement in back to secure. Clip into center of fabric and cut out 1½″ away from inner edges of mat. Clip into corners to mat; fold fabric over to back and cement. Tape finished fabric scene to center of mounting cardboard. Place double-faced masking tape around edge of mounting cardboard; place mat over picture and cardboard and press to secure. Frame as desired.

Farm Scene

MATTED SIZE: $19\frac{1}{2}'' \times 23\frac{1}{2}''$

Using separate patterns, cut fabric background pieces for sky and ground, adding $\frac{1}{4}''$ to top, side, and bottom edges. Assemble following General Directions.

Cut out all individual pieces for appliqués as indicated on pattern. Cut cow and lady out of muslin; cut skirt of fabric and appliqué to muslin lady.

(Continued on page 153)

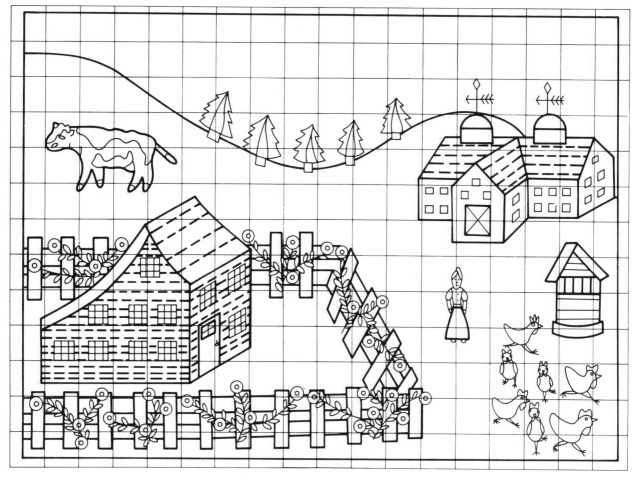

Every picture tells a story, and this beautiful wall hanging
seems to whisper a young girl's most romantic dreams. Capture the
gentleness of such moments with soft colors and delicately printed
cotton fabrics. For a personal touch, match hair color of a
special child to make the hanging hers. Window Wall Hanging,
73" × 44", uses machine appliqué and quilting. For
Window Wall Hanging directions, see Contents.

(Designed by Laurie Swim.)

145

Two charming scenes—a fanciful
farm and an old-fashioned hearth—
are captured in an enchantingly
primitive style. The print and
polka dot backgrounds are quilted;
delightful details are appliquéd
with running stitches, or floss-
embroidered—or both! Mat size of
hearth is $23'' \times 17\frac{1}{2}''$; farm is
$19\frac{1}{2}'' \times 23\frac{1}{2}''$. For Quilted Primitives
directions, see Contents.

(Designed by Susan Hesse.)

Children's drawings are too delightful to be left on plain old paper! Have children draw directly on fabric for adaptation to wall hangings, pillows, or even clothes—or trace a favorite drawing yourself. For more fun, children can draw themselves—a super gift for Grandma! Picture and wall hanging are painted with ballpoint paint tubes, then machine-quilted and bordered in a pretty print. Plump pillow has pop-up figures and calico backing. For Children's Art directions, see Contents.

(*Designs from Muriel Hassan.*)

Felt doll,
the artist herself,
sticks to wall hanging
with Velcro. Child
is wearing an
original design,
easily painted on a
cotton T-shirt.

(Designs from Muriel Hassan.)

"Still Life" patchwork begins with square patches in traditional fashion—but the way they're put together and the final result are far from usual. Do piecing and quilting in sections, working from a chart. Stuff the bowl and fruit sections of the "painting" if this king-sized quilt is to be used as a wall hanging. For "Still Life" Patchwork directions, see Contents.

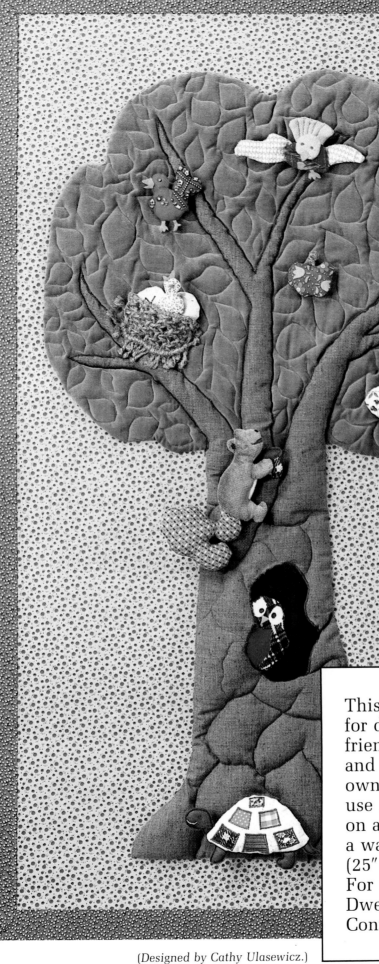

This quilted tree is home for delightful little friends that can be removed and rearranged at the owner's whim. Any way you use it—as a "pack-up" toy, on a bed, or mounted on a wall—the Tree Quilt (25″ × 42″) is irresistible! For Quilted Tree and Tree Dwellers directions, see Contents.

(Designed by Cathy Ulasewicz.)

Crisp white sails billow against a blue sky on a fire screen that can be displayed on a stand or on the wall. Sails and ship are separate pieces hand-appliquéd over padding. Detailing is satin stitch and quilting. For Schooner Screen directions, see Contents.

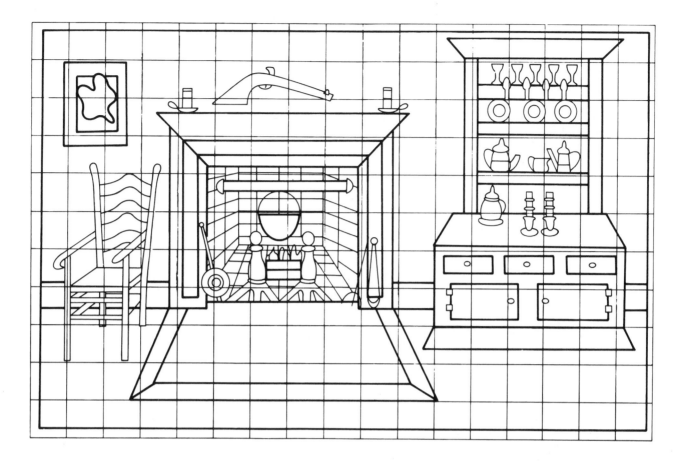

(Continued from page 144)
Sew to background. Cut horizontal strips of fence; sew these down first, then cut and sew vertical strips on top.

For farmhouse and barn roofs, use pieces of muslin twice the height of appliqué patterns; do the same with printed fabric for farmhouse roof; do not cut shape out of fabric yet. Make ¼″ horizontal tucks across pieces to resemble clapboards (see color illustration). Cut the separate pieces, adding ¼″ so that tucks will be angled correctly for perspective when lines meet. Sew the two house pieces together; sew roof to house. Sew barn pieces together; sew roof to barn. Then sew each structure in place on background. Assemble parts of the well and sew to background.

Embroider the trees, working satin stitch in opposite directions on each side of center to suggest branches. Embroider the spots, hooves, and features of cow in satin stitch. The flowers are all satin stitch; do the centers in pink first, then do the petals. Embroider stems and leaves in straight stitches. Work chickens in satin stitch; do the legs and feet in outline stitch. Fill in the windows and doors of barn in white satin stitch. Work weather vanes in straight stitches, with satin stitch top.

Make the lines in windows and on doors of both structures in outline stitch. Fill in the lady's hair and blouse in satin stitch over muslin.

Hearth Scene

MATTED SIZE: 17½″ × 23″

Cut and join the wall and floor as for Farm Scene background. Cut a strip of muslin the width of scene for molding; sew in place. On floor fabric, use ruler and tailor's chalk to mark diagonal quilting lines ½″ apart (to imitate floor boards). Appliqué hearth to floor and add muslin border. Quilt background (including hearth) following General Directions. Cut the pieces for cupboard and sew them all together as appliqués before sewing complete cupboard to background.

Assemble and sew the individual parts of fireplace together before appliquéing to background: first cut out piece for interior, then add muslin frame. Embroider all the lines on interior of fireplace, the fireplace tools, and the pot handle in outline stitch. Use satin stitch for the remaining details. ☆

Children's Art

shown on pages 148–149

EQUIPMENT: Pencil. Ruler. Scissors. Pins. Zigzag sewing machine. Embroidery and sewing needles. Tracing paper. Iron. Cardboard.

MATERIALS: *For Small Hanging:* White satin, cotton print, and white cotton fabrics 45″ wide, $\frac{1}{2}$ yd. of each. Batting piece 12″ × $18\frac{1}{2}$″. White lace edging $\frac{5}{8}$″ wide, $1\frac{1}{2}$ yds. Felt scraps for hangers. Small amount of white embroidery floss, $1\frac{1}{4}$″-diameter wooden dowel, 2′ long. *For Large Hanging:* White satin, cotton print, and white cotton fabrics 45″ wide, $\frac{2}{3}$ yd. of each. Batting, piece $18\frac{1}{2}$″ × $42\frac{1}{2}$″. Scraps of felt and embroidery floss to match cotton-print fabric. *For Doll:* Felt scraps in colors to match figure in small hanging (see Small Hanging directions). Matching embroidery floss. Polyester fiberfill. Velcro, two pieces each, 1″ square. Toothpick. *For Pillow:* White satin fabric 45″ wide, $\frac{1}{2}$ yd. Two coordinating calico cotton prints 45″ wide, one $\frac{5}{8}$ yd., one $\frac{1}{8}$ yd. Scraps of brightly colored cotton fabric, felt, and yarn. Jumbo rickrack to match calico, $\frac{3}{4}$ yd. Polyester fiberfill. 1″-diameter wooden dowel, 4′ long. *For T-Shirt:* Washable, 100% cotton t-shirt. *For All:* Sewing thread to match fabrics. All-purpose glue. Tubes of ball-point paint suitable for fabric, in various colors.

Note: Sewing directions are given for drawings shown. Adjust measurements for the drawings you are using.

DIRECTIONS

For Small Hanging ($13\frac{1}{2}$″ × 21″): Cut 11″ × $18\frac{1}{2}$″ pieces from satin and from white cotton fabrics. With pencil, mark off a 10″ × $17\frac{1}{2}$″ design area in center of right (shiny) side of satin. Have child draw a picture (which should include a doll figure or any shape that can be made into a toy) or copy one already drawn with ball-point paint tubes; let dry. Place white backing cotton under satin picture with batting between; pin. Using white or contrasting thread, machine-stitch around large shapes in picture, sewing through all thicknesses; make stitched outline general rather than detailed.

Cut cotton print into four strips; two 4″ × $21\frac{1}{2}$″, two 4″ × 11″. Fold both long edges of each strip under $\frac{1}{4}$″; press. Fold strips in half lengthwise, wrong side inward; press. Pin, then baste one short strip to one short side of quilted picture, with $\frac{1}{2}$″ of picture between edges of strip. Repeat with remaining short strip on other short side of picture, then with long strips on long sides of picture, centering picture between top and bottom; be sure to encase raw edges of short strips. Turn in extending raw edges of long strips; slip-stitch closed. Slip-stitch top and bottom of "frame" to sides, on front and back. Cut a 56″ length of lace edging. Place along cotton print "frame," $\frac{1}{8}$″ from inner edges; overlap where ends meet. Topstitch along inner edge of lace, through all thicknesses.

Make four hanging loops, cutting the following three pieces from a different color felt for each loop: 7″ × 1″; $7\frac{1}{2}$″ × $\frac{3}{8}$″; heart shape (see pattern). Center narrow felt strip on wide strip, allowing $\frac{1}{2}$″ of narrow strip to extend at one end (front); glue. Glue heart centered on front end; see color illustration. Fold completed strip crosswise. Pin loops to long top edge of hanging, spacing them evenly and with "frame" between felt and hearts facing front; glue to both sides of frame. With six strands of floss in needle and stitching through all thicknesses, embroider five lazy daisy stitches (see Contents for Stitch Details) in center of heart, forming a daisy. Insert dowel through loops to hang picture.

For Large Hanging ($21\frac{1}{2}$″ × $45\frac{1}{2}$″): Make as for small hanging with the following changes: Cut $18\frac{1}{2}$″ × $42\frac{1}{2}$″ pieces from satin and white cotton fabrics. Mark $17\frac{1}{2}$″ × $41\frac{1}{2}$″ design area. Do not paint doll shape (doll will be made separately of felt); mark doll outline with pencil and quilt on line. Cut cotton print fabric into the following strips: two $4\frac{1}{2}$″ × 46″; two $4\frac{1}{2}$″ × 22″. Omit lace edging.

For each hanging loop, cut a $2\frac{1}{2}$″ × 5″ strip from cotton print. Fold strip in half lengthwise, right side inward; stitch $\frac{1}{4}$″ from long raw edges. Turn to right side; press, with seam centered along one side. Make seven loops. Pin loops along top edge of hanging, spaced evenly apart and enclosing 1″ of frame. Zigzag-stitch along each bottom raw edge, through all thicknesses. Using pattern, cut seven daisies from felt. Pin one to bottom of each loop, covering stitching (see color illustration). Using six strands of floss in needle, secure each daisy with one large cross-stitch in center, stitching through all thicknesses. Insert dowel through loops to hang picture.

For Doll: Trace quilted outline of doll on large hanging, then trace the following parts, making a separate pattern for each: face, complete head (with hair), dress, arms, hands, legs, feet. Add $\frac{1}{4}$″ to neck of dress and to both ends of arms and legs. Pin patterns to felt, using colors in small hanging. Cut one face. Cut two of everything else. Put identical felt hands together; with machine set for a close zigzag, stitch along outside edge, leaving an opening at wrist; stuff and set aside. Repeat with other hand. Make both arms the same way, leaving one short end open for stuffing; use pencil to stuff, if necessary. Insert one end of each arm $\frac{1}{4}$″ inside a wrist opening; zigzag-stitch closed. For feet, slit center of top piece of each pair enough to accommodate leg end. Stitch feet and legs together as for hands and arms; stuff; zigzag-stitch closed. Insert one end of each leg into a foot slit; hand-stitch

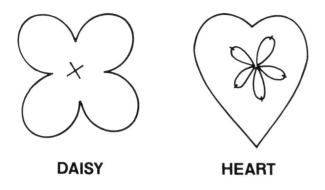

DAISY   **HEART**

closed. Place two dress pieces together; insert leg and arm ends ¼″ in between dress pieces and pin; see color illustration. Zigzag-stitch along edges of dress, being sure to catch leg and arm ends; leave neck open for stuffing. Stuff dress and set aside. Embroider features on face in desired stitches using six strands of floss in needle and with illustration as guide. Zigzag-stitch embroidered face to one head piece (approximately from ear to ear). Zigzag-stitch head front to head back, just along edges of hair; leave bottom open. Stuff head, using a pencil if necessary to push stuffing into hair ends. Insert dress ¼″ into head-neck opening; pin. Zigzag-stitch opening closed, being sure to catch in dress.

For stick in hand, wrap toothpick with embroidery floss; leave ½″ uncovered. Cut two small diamond shapes (about 1″) from felt. Glue diamonds together, with uncovered end of toothpick inserted in one end. Stitch toothpick onto doll's hand. Hand-stitch 1″ Velcro square to back of doll's head; stitch the other Velcro piece to corresponding place on doll outline of hanging.

For Pillow (16″ square): From white satin, cut a 14″ square. With pencil, mark off a 13″-square design area on right (shiny) side of satin. As for wall hangings, have child draw or copy a drawing within design area with ball-point tube paints; let dry. Trace outline of figures in drawing; pin tracings to remaining satin. Cut out satin figures, adding ¼″ all around for seam allowance. Pin satin figures to back of satin picture, each directly behind its "twin." Topstitch each in place, ¼″ from edges and leaving an opening for stuffing; stuff and stitch closed. To frame satin picture, make four strips, each 2″ × 13½″. Cut two from smaller amount of calico; make other two a patchwork of same calico and other cotton scraps (see color illustration). Cut two 13½″ pieces of jumbo rickrack; topstitch to center of calico strips. Cut four 2″ squares from felt scraps. With right sides facing and raw edges flush, pin a square to each short end of calico strips; stitch ¼″ from ends, being sure to catch rickrack. With right sides facing and raw edges flush, pin patchwork strips to opposite ends of satin picture; stitch ¼″ from raw edges. Repeat with calico/felt strips and other edges of picture. Set machine for close zigzag (satin) stitch, and stitch over all seams. Attach yarn trim with embroidery floss to center of patchwork strips if desired (see illustration).

Cut a 16½″ square from larger yardage of calico. With right sides facing and raw edges flush, pin to pillow front; stitch all sides ¼″ from raw edges, leaving an opening for turning and stuffing. Turn to right side; stuff. Slip-stitch closed.

For T-Shirt: Insert cardboard into shirt to make smooth painting surface and to prevent bleeding onto back of shirt. Have child use ball-point paint tubes to paint design; let dry. ☆

Schooner Screen

shown on page 150

SIZE: 23″ × 20″ unframed.

EQUIPMENT: Paper for pattern. Tracing paper. Hard- and soft-lead pencils. Ruler. Scissors. All-purpose glue. White dressmaker's tracing (carbon) paper. Tracing wheel. Sewing and embroidery needles. Straight pins. Staple gun. Iron.

MATERIALS: Closely woven polished cotton fabric, 36″ wide: light tan 1 yd.; medium light blue ½ yd.; royal blue ⅛ yd.; small pieces of red, orange, dark tan, and ecru. Sewing thread to match all fabrics. Six-strand embroidery floss, one skein each of dark brown, medium brown, dark tan, ecru, yellow-gold, red, light blue, royal blue, and black.

Piece of batting 23″ × 20″, plus scraps. Wooden canvas stretcher 23″ × 20″. Staples.

DIRECTIONS

Design is made up of appliqué, embroidery, and quilting. Read How to Appliqué (by Hand) and refer to Embroidery Stitch Details (for both, see Contents). Use sewing thread to match fabric when appliquéing or sewing pieces together.

To Make Patterns: Enlarge patterns by copying on paper ruled in 1″ squares. On ship pattern, heavy solid lines indicate pieces to be appliquéd; fine lines indicate lines and areas to be embroidered;

Inside the banner: *Don't Give Up the Ship*

dash lines indicate lines to be quilted. Trace each separate part of boat design, omitting quilting and embroidery lines; complete pieces where they overlap. Glue tracings to cardboard and cut out for appliqué patterns.

To Prepare Background: Cut light blue fabric for sky 16″ × 16¼″; cut royal blue fabric for sea 3½″ × 16¼″. With right sides facing, sew together along 16¼″ edges, making ¼″ seam. With dressmaker's carbon and tracing wheel or dry ball-point pen, trans-

fer main outline of appliqués to background piece, omitting quilting and embroidery lines.

To Appliqué: Following directions in How to Appliqué, cut and prepare appliqué pieces for red banner and oval rear of ship, orange pennant, light tan sails, ecru ship hull (upper portion), dark tan ship hull (lower portion). Pin, baste, and slip-stitch pieces into position; place small amounts of batting under sails, pennant, and banner.

To Embroider: Retrace appliqué patterns and

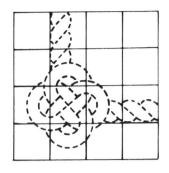

include quilting and embroidery lines. Transfer these lines to appliqués. Work satin stitch all around edges of red oval with four strands of yellow-gold floss. Do the same along the two cross lines. Fill small square windows on oval and letters on banner in satin stitch with four strands of light blue floss. With one strand of light blue floss, make small running stitches on banner. With four strands of red floss, work vertical satin stitch along top and bottom edges of ecru ship hull. With four strands of black floss, make all cannons in vertical satin stitch; with four strands of royal blue floss, make the rectangular cannon openings in horizontal satin stitch. With one strand of dark tan floss, make running stitches along curved lines on each sail. Do not embroider the straight diagonal lines across sails or sky; these are quilting lines.

Embroider masts in horizontal or vertical satin stitch with four strands of dark brown floss.

To Make Border: Cut light tan fabric 27″ × 24″. Transfer outer line of ship pattern to center of tan fabric for rectangular outline with rounded corners. Mark a second line $\frac{1}{4}$″ inside first line. Cut out center of tan fabric on inner line. Turn $\frac{1}{4}$″ center margin to wrong side of fabric, slashing at curves for a smooth fit. Press. Pin and baste tan border piece over appliquéd ship piece. Slip-stitch all around inner edge.

To Quilt: With dressmaker's carbon and tracing wheel (or dry ball-point pen), transfer rope-knot motif to each corner of border $\frac{1}{2}$″ away from seam line. Continue rope design between knot motifs to complete border. Transfer quilting lines to background: waves, clouds, and ropes.

Cut batting and lining 23″ × 20″. Pin and baste ship piece, batting, and lining together, vertically, horizontally, diagonally in two directions, and around perimeter. Quilt through all thicknesses by hand with short running stitches, using two strands of floss in needle. Use ecru floss for waves and clouds; use medium brown for rope lines across sails and sky; use dark tan floss for rope border.

To Mount: Assemble canvas stretchers to 23″ × 20″ rectangle. Place design over stretcher; pull fabric tautly and evenly to back and staple. Trim away excess fabric. Frame as fire screen or as desired. ☆

Quilted Tree and Tree Dwellers

shown on page 151

Quilted Tree

SIZE: 25″ × 42″ unmounted.

EQUIPMENT: Paper for pattern. Pencil. Ruler. Scissors. Tracing paper. Dressmaker's tracing (carbon) paper in light color. Tracing wheel or hard-lead pencil. Pins. Zigzag sewing machine.

MATERIALS: Green velveteen, piece 24″ × 28″. Brown homespun or similar coarse fabric 45″ wide, $\frac{3}{4}$ yd. Scrap of dark brown burlap, 10″ square. Unbleached muslin for lining 45″ wide, $\frac{3}{4}$ yd. Cotton or polyester batting. Green and brown sewing thread.

DIRECTIONS

Enlarge complete tree pattern by copying on paper ruled in 2″ squares. Fine lines indicate lines to be quilted by machine. Dash line at tree trunk top indicates end of foliage area (which is to be cut of green velveteen). Dash line at trunk hole

indicates pattern for pocket lining. Trace complete pattern with quilting lines. Cut entire tree out of unbleached muslin for lining.

With dressmaker's carbon and tracing wheel or hard-lead pencil, transfer tree foliage pattern onto green velveteen and trace trunk and branches on brown homespun, including all lines to be quilted. When cutting out fabric, add $\frac{1}{2}$″ seam allowance only around outside edges of foliage and trunk, but not around tree branches. Cut out the foliage and trunk pieces from fabric, then cut out hole in trunk indicated by shading. For pocket, cut a piece of burlap to fit across tree under trunk hole opening; pin in place behind trunk hole.

To Quilt Tree: Cut a piece of batting the size and shape of muslin lining; cut a second layer just for tree trunk. Place muslin lining on working surface and cover with batting. Place green foliage and trunk on top of batting, right side up. Under "pocket" of trunk hole, add a piece of batting and

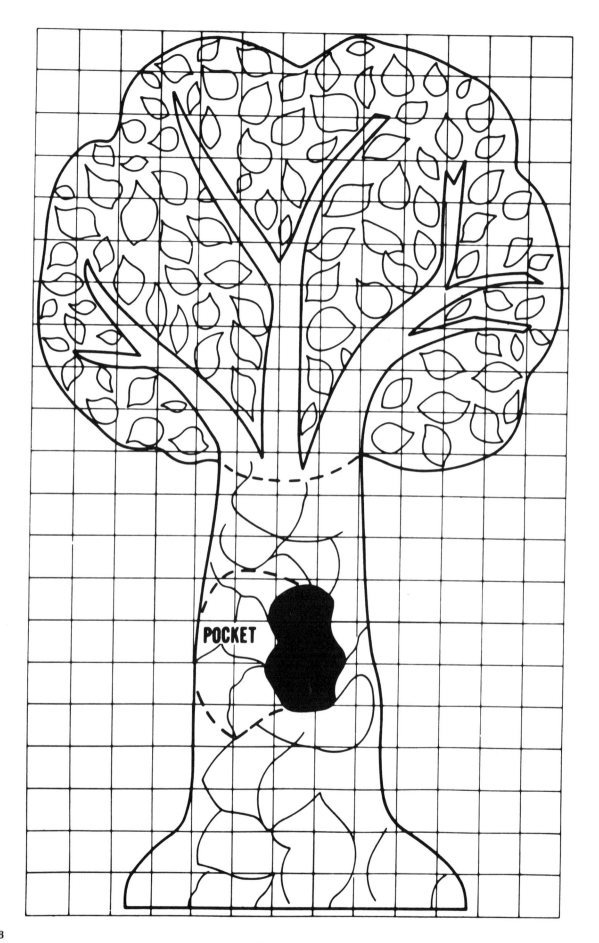

POCKET

a scrap of brown homespun for lining. Baste layers of pocket together. Using matching thread, quilt along lines of pocket area only by machine. Stitch along left edge of hole with close zigzag satin stitch. Add extra batting under tree branches. Smooth out wrinkles. Pin and carefully baste layers of tree together. Turn $\frac{1}{2}''$ seam allowance to back along edges and slip-stitch on back of lining.

Starting from center and working outward, machine-quilt leaf motifs on tree foliage with matching thread. In trunk area, skip pocket of trunk hole, but quilt remainder of tree trunk with matching thread. Do not cross a line of stitching, and do not backtrack. To secure ends of quilting stitches, bring thread ends to back of work (lining side) and knot with bobbin thread ends close to fabric; trim thread ends. Using matching thread and close zigzag stitch, satin-stitch around tree branches and around remaining edges of trunk hole, keeping pocket flap free from trunk on left side. Stitch brown burlap through all thicknesses inside pocket to secure in place.

Tree Dwellers

EQUIPMENT: Paper for patterns. Pencil. Ruler. Tracing paper. Scissors. Straight pins. Sewing and embroidery needles. Zigzag sewing machine.

MATERIALS: Scraps of printed and solid-color fabrics in a variety of colors and textures as shown or as desired; scraps of felt; rope scraps (for worm in bird's mouth and apple stems); scrap of fake fur (for squirrel's tummy); rope macrame or natural burlap (for nest). Polyester fiberfill batting for stuffing. Small amounts of six-strand embroidery floss in various colors. Small Velcro patches for attaching creatures to tree.

GENERAL DIRECTIONS

Enlarge patterns by copying on paper ruled in 1" squares. Make a separate pattern for each part of each item; dash lines indicate where pieces are overlapped.

For main parts of each item, pin pattern on doubled fabric; cut out, adding $\frac{1}{4}''$ all around for seam allowance. Cut other outlined parts of each from contrasting or different textured fabric. Stitch these pieces to the main part with zigzag satin stitch. Pieces of felt need no seam allowance and may be stitched close to edge, leaving an opening for stuffing. For pieces made of woven and knit fabrics, place right sides together and stitch front and back together with $\frac{1}{4}''$ seam, leaving a small opening for turning and stuffing. Trim excess fabric; clip into seam allowance at curves. Turn to right side; stuff with fiberfill. Turn edges of opening in and slip-stitch closed. Slip-stitch pieces of Velcro onto backs; slip-stitch pieces of Velcro onto tree to hold items in place. Cut and sew small pieces of Velcro to attach acorn to squirrel paw.

Refer to Stitch Details (see Contents) for embroidery.

Birds: Use prints, woven or knit fabrics. Construct body, wings, and tail separately, then slip-stitch pieces together as illustrated; make separate head for larger bird. Cut feet and beaks of gold-color felt; enclose feet in seam when stitching; whipstitch beaks in place. When completed, embroider eyes with French knots. For worm, use 2" piece of rope and attach with a few stitches under beak of larger bird.

Chick, Eggs, and Nest: Use prints, woven or knit fabrics. Use a piece of rope macrame or burlap for nest; sew to branch. "Crack" in egg is close zigzag stitch. Embroider chick eye with French knot. Whip felt beak in place.

Owl: Use corduroy and felt. Zigzag-stitch all parts in place before stitching main body sections together. Enclose felt feet in seam when stitching.

Apples: Use corduroy for one, print for other. Secure patch on apple with close zigzag stitch. For stems, use rope $1\frac{1}{4}''$ long and enclose in seam when stitching.

Butterfly: Use print fabric. Top wings are cut in one piece; bottom wings in two pieces. When sections are completed, slip-stitch together at center. Slip-stitch wool or rope to center for body, head, and antennae.

Squirrel: Use knit and corduroy fabrics. Complete body and tail separately, then slip-stitch together. Embroider features on face with satin stitch. Slip-stitch fur tummy in place.

Turtle: Use woven fabrics and felt. Zigzag-stitch around shell patches before sewing body sections together. Make separate felt head, legs, and tail (cutting two pieces for each). Make eye with French knot and mouth with outline stitch before sewing head sections together. Stitch felt pieces together; stuff. Enclose in seam when stitching body sections together.

Tree Mounting

SIZE: 30" × 50".

EQUIPMENT: Ruler. Pencil. Scissors. X-acto knife. Staple gun. Straight pins. Sewing needle. Staples.

MATERIALS: Wooden canvas stretchers, two each in the following sizes: 30" and 50". Thin, stiff cardboard. Calico fabric in two different prints and two contrasting colors, 36" wide: $1\frac{1}{2}$ yds. for background and $1\frac{1}{2}$ yds. for border. Masking tape. Nylon transparent thread.

DIRECTIONS

Assemble wooden stretchers. Center background fabric over stretchers; smooth over sides and staple to back, beginning at centers and working to corners; pull fabric tautly as you staple; miter corners.

Cut four calico border strips, two each with the

NEST

following dimensions: 4″ × 54″ and 4″ × 36″. With X-acto knife, cut four cardboard strips, two each with the following dimensions: ½″ × 47″ and ½″ × 27″; piece cardboard strips by taping together to form desired length. Place shorter calico border strips face down along top and bottom stretchers with fabric edge ½″ over inside stretcher edge. Place shorter cardboard strips on calico fabric borders, even with stretchers, covering the ½″ fabric edge; staple cardboard and fabric strips in place. Bring fabric over cardboard stripping and to back of stretchers, pulling tautly; staple onto stretcher backs.

Repeat with longer strips of fabric border and cardboard, mitering fabric at corners (see Contents for How to Miter Corners).

Center completed tree onto background fabric.

Pin in place. With nylon thread, hand-sew tree in place: take small, close stitches so that tree is securely attached. ☆

"Still Life" Patchwork

shown on page 150

SIZE: 106″ × 127½″.

EQUIPMENT: Ruler. Scissors. Thin, stiff cardboard. Dark- and light-colored pencils. Sewing needles. Sewing machine. Clear nail polish.

MATERIALS: Paper for patterns. Closely woven, printed cotton or cotton-blend fabrics, 36″ wide, in the following colors and amounts: light blue, A on piecing diagram, 1½ yds.; dark blue, B, ⅝ yd.; green and blue-green, C, 4¼ yds. ¼ yd. each of the following: Yellow-green, D; bronze-green, E; gold, G; red-brown, J; purple, K; lavender, L; magenta, M. ½ yd. each of yellow, F; orange, H; peach and pink, N. Red, I, ⅓ yd.; black and white, O, 1⅞ yds.; beige and tan, Q, 1⅝ yds. 45″-wide fabrics in solid colors: black, P, ⅛ yd.; white, ½ yd.; navy, 2 yds.; medium blue for lining, 9 yds.; fabric for inner lining, about 7 yds. Navy sewing thread. Polyester or cotton batting.

DIRECTIONS

Bowl of fruit design is pieced entirely of square patches; corners are appliquéd. Each square on piecing diagram represents one square patch of design. To make patterns for patches, cut several 1¾″ squares from cardboard; coat edges with clear nail polish to keep them from fraying. Mark squares on wrong sides of fabrics and add ¼″ seam allowance all around each one. Cut square patches as follows: 457 patches of light blue, A; 142 of dark blue;, B; 837 green and blue-green, C; 46 yellow-green, D; 59 bronze-green, E; 120 yellow, F; 49 gold, G; 127 orange, H; 149 red, I; 34 red-brown, J; 43 purple, K; 28 lavender, L; 26 magenta, M; 99 peach and pink, N; 480 black and white, O; 23 black, P (or cut one strip 23 squares long); 401 beige and tan, Q.

Quilt is pieced and quilted in sections, starting in the center and working outward. Sections are indicated by heavy outlines on piecing diagram. Begin with bunch of grapes, left of center. Following piecing diagram, stitch I, J, K, L, and M patches together into rows, then stitch rows together to form a section. Cut batting and inner lining same size as pieced-together grape section. Turn under

outside seam allowance of pieced section and press to wrong side. Center lining and batting on pieced section; pin and baste all three layers together. Set sewing machine for wide, close zigzag stitch. Machine-stitch over seams dividing color areas, indicated on diagram by light lines; use navy thread. Trim lining to match folded edge of pieced section; trim batting ⅛″ smaller than pieced section all around. Make pieced sections H, N, I, and E and join; do not turn under outside seam allowances. Cut batting and inner lining ⅛″ larger than these and all other sections; center, pin, and baste all three layers together. Quilt seams indicated by heavy lines in the piecing diagram, in same manner as for grape section. To join the two completed sections, place edge of grape section on second section, overlapping edge of second section ¼″; baste together. Zigzag-stitch the pieces together, then remove basting thread. Make and join D and N sections at left of grapes and quilt on seam dividing sections. Join to left side of grapes; when joining sections, always overlap edges as before. Make and join O and P sections to make bowl, but do not quilt on seam joining O and P. Join bowl section to completed fruit section. Make and join sun, right-hand window, bananas, apple stem, and leaf sections; quilt on heavy dividing lines. Join completed corner section to I, E, and O sections of fruit and bowl. Make and join remaining sections in the following order: wall section C at right to sections B and O; table section Q to O, P, and C; small wall section C at left to section D, O, and Q; left hand window section to D and C; upper wall section C to window and fruit sections. Trim edges of lining and batting to match outside seam allowance of quilt.

Inner border: Cut four strips of white fabric, each 2¼″ wide; cut two 88″ long and two 112½″ long; measurements include ¼″ seam allowances all around. Using straight stitch and with right sides together, sew 88″ strips to sides of quilt, ¼″ from raw edges, then sew longer strips to top and bottom of quilt. For second border, cut four strips from navy fabric, each 8¼″ wide: cut two 91½″ long

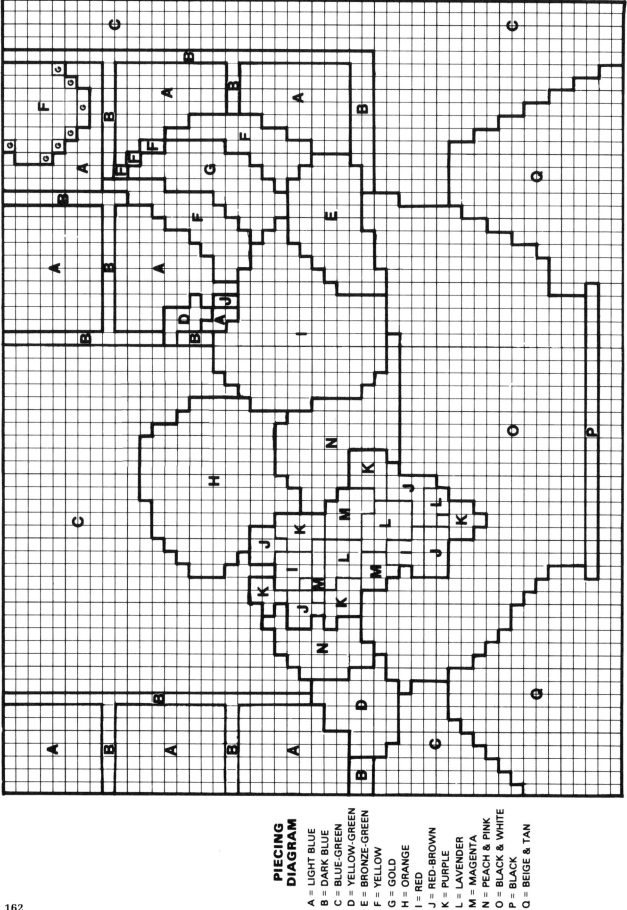

PIECING DIAGRAM

A = LIGHT BLUE
B = DARK BLUE
C = BLUE-GREEN
D = YELLOW-GREEN
E = BRONZE-GREEN
F = YELLOW
G = GOLD
H = ORANGE
I = RED
J = RED-BROWN
K = PURPLE
L = LAVENDER
M = MAGENTA
N = PEACH & PINK
O = BLACK & WHITE
P = BLACK
Q = BEIGE & TAN

and two $112\frac{1}{2}''$. Cut four pieces $8\frac{1}{4}''$ square for corners. To make appliqués, enlarge fruit patterns on paper ruled in 1″ squares. Make a cardboard pattern for each separate part of each design. Mark patterns on wrong side of fabric and add $\frac{1}{4}''$ seam allowances all around each piece; cut appliqués out. Pin and baste each one in place on corner square and straight-stitch around marked outline. Trim excess fabric to $\frac{1}{8}''$. Using close zigzag stitch, stitch around each appliqué, covering straight stitching and $\frac{1}{8}''$ margin. Join a square to each end of the two longer navy strips by stitching $\frac{1}{4}''$ from raw edges. Stitch the 88″-long navy strips to sides of quilt, then longer strips to top and bottom, using straight stitch for all seams. Quilt should measure $106\frac{1}{2}'' \times 127\frac{1}{2}''$, plus outside seam allowance. Turn $\frac{1}{4}''$ seam allowance to wrong side and baste.

If completed design will be used for a wall hanging, fruit and bowl sections of design may be given extra dimension with padding. (If it will be used as a bed covering, the padding is best omitted.) To do so, turn work wrong side up. Slit inner lining only in center of each fruit and bowl section. Stuff with extra batting, then slip-stitch slits closed.

Lining: Cut two pieces $107'' \times 43\frac{1}{2}''$ and one piece $107'' \times 43''$ from medium blue fabric. With raw edges flush, stitch the two $43\frac{1}{2}''$-wide pieces to the 43″-wide piece on long sides $\frac{1}{2}''$ from raw edges. Lining is $107'' \times 128''$; turn $\frac{1}{4}''$ seam allowance to wrong side of lining and baste. Cut batting 106″ $\times$ 127″. Place pieced quilt wrong side up; center batting on top of pieced quilt; center lining on top of batting, enclosing edges of batting between the two layers. Folded edges of pieced quilt and lining should be flush. Pin and baste all three layers together. Use zigzag stitch to quilt along inner and outer seam lines of white border, around corner squares, and $\frac{1}{4}''$ in from folded edges of quilt. If using completed design as a wall hanging, do not stitch $\frac{1}{4}''$ from folded top edge; this will be slip-stitched closed after loops for hanging are inserted.

Loops: Cut seven $5\frac{1}{2}'' \times 7''$ pieces from blue lining fabric. With right sides facing, fold each strip in half lengthwise. Stitch $\frac{1}{4}''$ from long raw edges of each strip; turn strips to right side and press. Stitch along both long edges of each strip $\frac{1}{8}''$ from edges. Fold strips in half crosswise and stitch $\frac{1}{4}''$ from raw edges. Raw edges of strips are inserted $\frac{1}{2}''$ between front of quilt and lining and stitched to lining. Pin one strip to lining $\frac{1}{4}''$ in from each side edge; space five remaining strips evenly between them. Baste strips to lining; zigzag-stitch in place. Slip-stitch front of quilt to lining at top edge, enclosing raw edges of strips. ☆

Balloon Wall Hanging

shown on page 182

SIZE: 26″ × 20″.

EQUIPMENT: Paper for patterns. Ruler. Dressmaker's tracing (carbon) paper. Pencil. Scissors. Straight pins. Sewing, large-eyed embroidery, and tapestry needles. Sewing machine with zigzag attachment. Iron. Drill with $\frac{1}{2}''$ bit. Paintbrush.

MATERIALS: *For dolls:* Calico print fabric scraps 10″ × 15″ for each. Scraps of white cotton fabric. Six-strand embroidery floss: one skein or less of black, pink, red, and green. Crewel yarn: yellow and brown for hair. *For hanging:* Light blue cotton fabric, $26\frac{1}{2}'' \times 20\frac{1}{2}''$; medium blue, $26\frac{1}{2}'' \times 20\frac{1}{2}''$; olive-green, 21″ square; apple green, 22″ × 21″; red, two pieces 8″ × $10\frac{1}{2}''$; scrap of red calico, 11″ × 6″; scraps of light brown, blue and white. Fusible webbing. Dowel $\frac{1}{2}''$ in diameter, 22″ long. Two wood balls $1\frac{1}{2}''$ diameter. Red enamel paint. One spool of gold-color pearl cotton size 3. Stiff cardboard 25″ × $19\frac{1}{2}''$. All-purpose glue. *For both:* Layer of batting. Sewing thread to match fabrics.

GENERAL DIRECTIONS

Enlarge patterns on paper ruled in 1″ squares; complete all half-patterns indicated by long dash lines. Heavy solid lines indicate cutting lines; fine lines indicate stitching and draped pearl cotton. Short dash lines indicate where pieces are overlapped. With the exception of balloon trim and clouds, add $\frac{1}{4}''$ to all pattern pieces for seam allowance. Make separate pattern for each piece.

Dolls

For each doll, cut two sacques, two arms, two head-body pieces from calico print and two faces from white fabric. Cut two large dolls and one small one. With right sides facing, fold each arm in half along half-pattern line; sew edges together, leaving top end of arm open. Clip into seam allowance at curve; turn to right side and stuff. With embroidery floss, wrap arm $\frac{3}{4}''$ from end to form

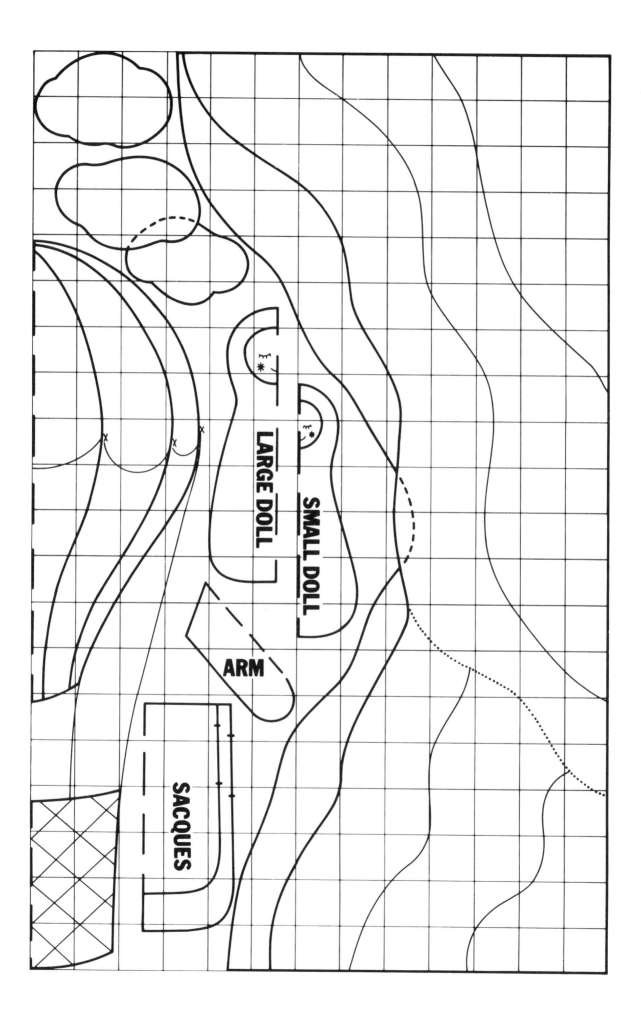

LARGE DOLL

SMALL DOLL

ARM

SACQUES

hand; knot floss. Place two sacques together with right sides facing; place arms inside between crosslines with hands pointing inward; pin. Stitch edges together with $\frac{1}{4}''$ seam; leave top edge open. Clip corners and turn right side out. Make $\frac{1}{8}''$ hem at top edge, then fold top in $\frac{7}{8}''$. To make casing, machine-stitch all around top $\frac{1}{4}''$ from fold and then $\frac{3}{16}''$ below stitching. Cut 12" piece of red or green six-strand floss. With tapestry needle, insert floss into casing from center of one side; go through casing and bring floss out close to starting point. Knot ends.

Sew head-body pieces together with $\frac{1}{4}''$ seam, right sides facing and leaving $1\frac{1}{2}''$ on bottom open. Clip curves; turn right side out. Stuff and slip-stitch opening closed. With three strands of floss in needle, embroider one face piece: make eyes in outline stitch with black floss (plus three or four straight stitches for lashes), mouth in outline stitch with red floss, and cheeks in star stitch with pink floss (see Contents for Stitch Details). With right sides facing, stitch faces together, leaving opening at top for turning. Clip curves; turn right side out. Press and slip-stitch closed. Slip-stitch face in place. For one large doll's hair, make turkey work loops along forehead line with two strands of yellow crewel yarn. Clip loops and trim. For another large doll's hair, make double French knots along top of face with two strands of brown crewel yarn. For the small doll's hair, cut 30 $3\frac{1}{2}''$ strands of yellow crewel yarn. Tack center of strands to center top of head and at sides of head; tie full six strands of red floss around yarn hair at sides. Insert doll in sacque, pull floss to gather, and tie into bow.

Wall Hanging

Drill a $\frac{1}{2}''$ hole $\frac{3}{4}''$ deep in each of the wooden balls. Paint balls and dowel with red enamel paint.

While paint is drying, cut two red balloons, two red calico balloon trims, and two light brown baskets from fabric. Cut fusible web same size as balloon trims. Place trims on right side of fabric balloon with fusible web between. Following package instructions, fuse trim to balloon. With small white zigzag (satin) stitch, stitch around balloon trim. Cut two layers of batting same size as balloon. Pin batting to wrong side of appliquéd balloon; pin balloons together, right sides facing. Stitch all around with $\frac{1}{4}''$ seams, leaving a 5" opening along side. Clip curves; turn right side out and press. Using illustration as a guide, pin balloon to blue fabric, tilted to right of center and with bottom of balloon 14" from bottom of fabric. Topstitch bal-

loon in place with red thread, turning opening raw edges under.

For basket, pin and stitch basket pieces together, right sides facing and leaving an opening for turning along side. Clip corners; turn. Press and slip-stitch opening closed. Using ruler and pencil, mark inner basket lines on one side of basket. Wind pearl cotton on bobbin and thread top of machine with matching sewing thread. Stitch along inner basket lines, leaving 1" of pearl cotton and sewing thread at the beginning and end of each line. Do not backtrack. Fold pearl cotton ends to thread side and tack down. On the back of blue fabric, draw two straight lines from the bottom of the balloon to the basket area (see pattern). With bobbin wound with pearl cotton and top with sewing thread, stitch along pencil lines. Pin pearl-cotton side of basket face up on blue cotton, leaving enough space so doll fits snugly in basket. With gold-color sewing thread in machine, sew basket to fabric with wide zigzag stitches, couching a strand of pearl cotton 27" long from side of balloon to and around basket to other side of balloon. String 15" pearl cotton evenly and loosely across middle of balloon; tack at balloon stripes at Xs.

To make tassel, cut eight 3" strands of pearl cotton. Fold in half; with matching sewing thread tie strands together $\frac{1}{4}''$ from fold. Knot and trim ends even. Tack to balloon on either side.

Cut three clouds, two from medium blue and one from white cotton fabric. Cut fusible web the same size. Position clouds on light blue background; apply hot iron. With matching thread, make small zigzag (satin) stitches around each cloud.

Cut two foreground hills from olive green, two background hills from apple green, and two layers of batting for each. Using carbon, transfer quilting lines to right side of one of each. Pin matching batting to wrong side of one olive green hill. Pin olive green hills together, right sides facing; stitch all the way around, leaving one side open. Turn right side out and slip-stitch opening closed. Stitch along all fine lines. Repeat for apple green hills. Pin hills together (apple green in the back); then pin to light blue fabric. Stitch along dotted line through all thicknesses. Pin medium blue fabric to light blue, right sides facing. Stitch all around with $\frac{1}{4}''$ seams, leaving top and $1\frac{1}{4}''$ down on either side unsewn. Turn right side out; press; insert cardboard. Stitch across opening $1\frac{1}{4}''$ from top. Pin back to front at top turning in raw edges $\frac{1}{4}''$; top-stitch together along edge.

Slide dowel in opening. Glue dowel ends and insert into wood balls. Insert dolls into pockets. ☆

Quilted Sun and Moon Pictures and Pillows

shown on pages 183–184

SIZES: Pillows, 17½″ diameter. Pictures 27″ square.

EQUIPMENT: Colored pencil. Pencil. Scissors. Paper for patterns. String. Ruler. Straight pins. Sewing needle. Sewing machine (with cording or zipper foot for pillows). *For Pictures:* Mat knife. Heavy objects for weighting.

MATERIALS: Unbleached muslin 36″ wide; 1 yd. for each pillow; 2½ yds. for each picture. Off-white sewing thread, several spools. Batting. ***For Each Pillow:*** Cotton cording ¼″ diameter, 1½ yds. ***For Each Picture:*** Two pieces of heavy cardboard, each 27″ square. All-purpose glue. Masking tape. Frame to fit (27″ rabbet).

GENERAL DIRECTIONS

Patterns: With pencil, draw lines across patterns, connecting the grid lines. Enlarge patterns by copying on paper ruled in 1″ squares. Complete half-patterns for sun rays indicated by long dash lines. Large dot on each moon pattern indicates center of completed design.

Quilting: For each design, refer to individual directions to mark shape on muslin in size specified for top piece of pillow or picture; cut out. Also find and mark center of each top with a pin. To draw a circle, use string, pencil, and pin as follows for a compass: Tie one end of string to a pencil. Cut string so that its length equals radius of required circle (8½″ radius for pillows and 10¾″ radius for pictures). Pin free end of string to center of fabric and swing pencil around to mark circle.

Tape pattern to a flat surface and center muslin top piece over pattern (for moon designs, mark center point of muslin circle and match to center dot of pattern); tape to secure. With pencil, lightly mark pattern lines (which will be visible through fabric) on muslin; use ruler to mark all ray lines, continuing lines of moon designs out to edge of circle.

For each muslin top piece, cut an additional piece of muslin and two pieces of batting, all the same size as top. Place the muslin pieces together, with marked side of top facing up and the two layers of batting between. Smooth out layers and pin together temporarily. Baste through all thicknesses, first on lengthwise and crosswise grains, then diagonally in two directions.

For quilting, use straight machine stitch: Set machine at 10 stitches per inch for long straight ray lines, 8 stitches per inch for large curved lines (including outer marked circle), and 12 stitches per inch for smaller feature lines. Stitch along all lines, always working from the center out. When all the stitching is complete, remove basting stitches.

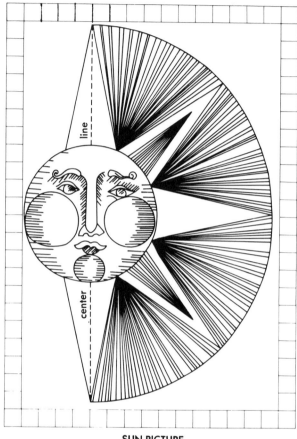

SUN PICTURE

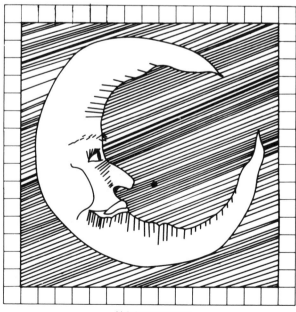

MOON PICTURE

166

Finish pillows and pictures, following individual directions.

Pillows

For each pillow top, mark a 17"-diameter circle on muslin; cut out, adding ½" seam allowance all around. Mark pattern in circle, cut remaining pieces, and quilt; see General Directions. For pillow back, cut another piece of muslin the same size as top.

For welting, cut 1½"-wide bias strips from remaining muslin. Join strips at short ends with ⅛" seams to make one strip long enough to fit circumference of pillow with ½" overlap. Lay cotton cord on wrong side of muslin strip, centering lengthwise. Fold strip over cord and stitch along length close to cord, using cording or zipper foot attachment.

With raw edges facing out, baste welting to right side of quilted pillow top, keeping seam along marked circle and easing along curve as necessary. Overlap ends ½"; trim excess. To fit ends together, cut off one end of cord ½" inside muslin casing; turn in casing ¼". Insert other end of casing and slip-stitch both ends together.

Place pillow top and back together with right sides facing and welting enclosed; stitch together with ½" seam, leaving an opening large enough for stuffing. Clip curves and turn to right side; stuff fully with batting and slip-stitch opening closed.

Pictures

For each picture, cut muslin 30" square for top piece; mark 21½"-diameter circle in center. Mark pattern in circle, cut remaining pieces, and quilt; see General Directions. To mount, center 27" square of cardboard on wrong side of quilted picture; fold excess muslin onto cardboard, pulling all sides taut; tape, making certain that picture remains centered.

For padded mat, cut another 30" square from muslin and two 27" squares of batting; glue batting pieces together. In center of remaining 27" square of cardboard, draw a 21"-diameter circle. Cut away circle with mat knife. Cut away batting at opening, leaving 1" for overhang all around. Clip into overhang and wrap to back of mat; tape batting to cardboard.

Center padded mat, battting side down, on wrong side of muslin square; wrap excess muslin to back of mat and tape in place. Cut out muslin in opening, leaving 1" for overhang. Clip and tape muslin overhang in place. Center and glue padded mat over mounted design; weight until dry. Frame as desired. ☆

MOON PILLOW

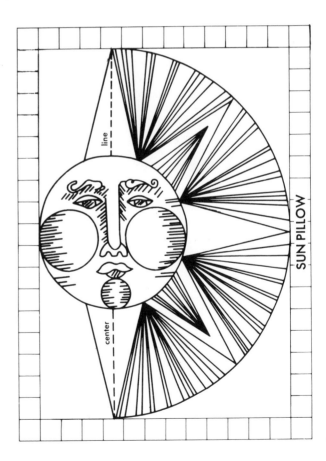

SUN PILLOW

Bicentennial Patchwork

shown on page 187

EQUIPMENT: Pencil. Thin cardboard. Ruler. Tape measure. Scissors. Light-colored pencil. Sewing machine. Sewing needle. Straight pins.

MATERIALS: For patchwork: Red, white, and blue cotton or cotton-blend fabrics (all should be the same weight), 45″ wide; see individual directions for amounts. (*Note:* Yardage is based on piecing of backings and edgings and careful cutting of the patches.) Matching sewing threads. Any additional materials listed under individual directions.

GENERAL DIRECTIONS

For cutting the patches, you will need a master pattern of a 5″ square and a triangle. To make patterns, cut two 5″ squares from thin cardboard. Cut one cardboard square in half diagonally to make triangle pattern. If making a large patchwork piece or several pieces, cut a few patterns. As pattern edges become worn from marking, replace with a new one.

Press fabric and lay wrong side up. For layout of the squares, place edges along the grain of fabric. For layout of the triangles, place shorter edges along the grain; the diagonal will lie on the bias. Allow ¼″ seam allowance outside all edges; therefore, leave ½″ between patterns. Do not use selvages as pattern edges; trim them off. (Selvages are more tightly woven than the fabric body and can cause buckling.) Eight patch squares fit across the fabric width. Yardage requirements were based on turning triangle pattern if there was more than one row. Using light-colored pencil on dark fabrics and dark pencil on light fabrics, trace around each pattern according to the amount listed in individual directions. Cut out fabric pieces ¼″ outside marked lines.

After cutting patches, group them according to shape and color. To piece the patches together, hold them firmly in place with right sides together. Machine- or hand-stitch along marked outlines to join pieces according to individual directions. Along bias edges, stitch carefully to avoid stretching the fabric or stay-stitch edges beforehand. Stitch triangles into square patches first; then stitch squares together following piecing directions. To avoid bunching of fabric, excess seam allowances may be trimmed at corners.

After piecing, press seam allowances to one side, preferably toward the darker fabric so it will not show through on the front. Finish according to individual directions.

Star Hanging

MATERIALS: White fabric, 4¼ yds.; blue fabric, ¾ yd.; red fabric, 1 yd. Wooden dowel, 1″ diameter, 52″ long. Two nails.

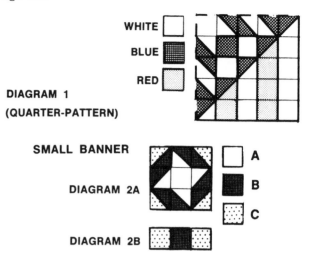

WHITE
BLUE
RED

DIAGRAM 1
(QUARTER-PATTERN)

SMALL BANNER

DIAGRAM 2A

A
B
C

DIAGRAM 2B

Patchwork: Read General Directions. Cut the following pieces for the star patchwork: From white, four rectangles each 5½″ wide and 20½″ long; four rectangles each 5½″ wide and 10½″ long; 12 squares; 32 triangles. From red, four rectangles each 5½″ wide and 15½″ long; four squares; eight triangles. From blue, four squares and 44 triangles. Following quarter pattern of Diagram 1, stitch each quarter together. Stitch pieced and solid squares into strips, then stitch strips together. Make one quarter as diagrammed, then reverse and repeat for the second quarter; reverse and repeat the first half for the second half. When you have pieced each quarter, sew the four together, forming star in center.

Edging: From red fabric, make four strips each 1½″ wide and 51½″ long, piecing to get the length. Fold each narrow end under ¾″ and press. Fold strips in half lengthwise with wrong sides together and press. On right side of patchwork, place raw edges of folded strip even with raw edge of patchwork, keeping each end of strip ¼″ in from each patchwork corner. Stitch together, making ¼″ seams. Repeat on other three sides.

Hanging Straps: Cut six strips along the lengthwise grain of white fabric, each 7″ wide and 11½″ long. For each strip, fold in half crosswise with right sides facing. Stitch together along lengthwise raw edges, making ¼″ seams. Turn right side out; press flat with seam lying in center of one side. Fold each strap in half crosswise with seam lying inside. Place each strap along top edge of patchwork corresponding to the white patches in the banner (see illustration). Pin to patchwork front on top of edging strip, keeping all raw edges even. Stitch across top edge through all thicknesses, making ¼″ seams.

Backing: From remaining white yardage, cut two pieces each 25½″ wide and 50½″ long; stitch together lengthwise with $\frac{1}{4}''$ seams to make a $50\frac{1}{2}''$ square. Place backing over star patchwork with right sides together and edging strips and straps still lying toward the center. All raw edges will be even. Stitch around the edges with $\frac{1}{4}''$ seams, leaving an 8" opening in center of one side. Turn right side out. At opening, fold raw edge under $\frac{1}{4}''$ and slip-stitch closed.

To Hang: Run dowel through the straps. Place two nails $50\frac{1}{4}''$ apart; rest ends of dowel on nails.

Small Banners

Instructions are for making one banner using any color combination; for successive banners, change color combinations as pictured.

MATERIALS: Color A fabric, $\frac{1}{2}$ yd.; Color B fabric, $\frac{5}{8}$ yd.; Color C fabric, $\frac{1}{2}$ yd. White fabric for backing, $\frac{7}{8}$ yd. Wooden dowel or dowels as desired.

Patchwork: Cut the following pieces for the patchwork: Color A, three squares and 12 triangles; Color B, two squares and 24 triangles; Color C, four squares and 12 triangles. Following Diagram 2A for star pattern, stitch pieced and solid squares into strips; then stitch strips together to form star pattern; make three patchworks of Diagram 2A. Following Diagram 2B, stitch three squares into a strip; make two strips of Diagram 2B. Stitch the star patchworks together with one dividing strip between each.

Edging: From Color B, cut two strips for the sides, each $1\frac{1}{2}''$ wide, and $56\frac{1}{2}''$ long, piecing to get the length, and two strips for the ends, each $1\frac{1}{2}''$ wide and $16\frac{1}{2}''$ long. Fold edgings and stitch to patchwork following directions given for Star Hanging.

Hanging Straps: Along lengthwise grain of Color C fabric, cut two strips each 7" wide and $11\frac{1}{2}''$ long. Seam strips as directed for Star Hanging. Place each strap at top edge of patchwork corresponding to patch of same color (see illustration). Pin to patchwork front on top of edging strip, keeping all raw edges even. Stitch across top edge, making $\frac{1}{4}''$ seam.

Backing: From white, cut two pieces each $15\frac{1}{2}''$ wide and 28" long. Stitch together crosswise with $\frac{1}{4}''$ seams to make a piece $55\frac{1}{2}''$ long. Sew backing to patchwork as directed for Star Hanging.

To Hang: Run dowel through the straps. Patchwork banners can be hung as shown or as desired. ☆

Bowknots Banner

shown on page 186

SIZE: $74\frac{1}{2}''$ square.

EQUIPMENT: Pencil. Ruler. Scissors. Thin, stiff cardboard.

MATERIALS: Closely woven cotton (or cotton blend) fabric 45" wide: black, $2\frac{1}{2}$ yds., white, $5\frac{1}{4}$ yds. (includes lining). Black and white sewing thread. Lightweight batting or other filler, such as flannel or a summer blanket.

DIRECTIONS

Read General Directions for Quilting (see Contents). Banner is made up of 1225 square and rectangular patches, plus border. Both piecing and quilting can be done on the sewing machine.

Patterns: Make patch patterns from cardboard as follows: Pattern A, 1" square. B, 1" × $1\frac{1}{2}''$. C, 1" × 2". D, 1" × 3". E, 1" × 4". F, $1\frac{1}{2}''$ square. G, $1\frac{1}{2}''$ × 2". H, $1\frac{1}{2}''$ × 3" I, $1\frac{1}{2}''$ × 4". J, 2" square. K, 2" × 3". L, 2" × 4". M, 3" square. N, 3" × 4". O, 4" square.

Patches: Marking patterns on wrong side of fabric and adding $\frac{1}{4}''$ seam allowance all around, cut patch pieces as follows: From black and white fab-rics, cut 72 (each) of B, 72 of C, 72 of D, 32 of F, 64 of G, 64 of H, 16 of I, 32 of J, 64 of K, 16 of L, 32 of M, and 16 of N. From white fabric, cut 45 of A, 12 of E, and 4 of O. From black fabric, cut 36 of A and 24 of E.

Assembling: Following Piecing Diagram, join patch pieces into 16 horizontal rows of 19 patches each. Sew rows together for one-quarter of banner. Make three more quarter blocks in the same manner. Make a small center block of five white and four black A patches, following checkerboard pattern shown in the heavy lines in lower left corner of diagram.

Group the four quarter blocks around the center block, aligning the "C" corner of each quarter block with a corner of the center block. Sew blocks together for main body of banner. Piece should measure 69" square, plus outside seam allowance.

Lining: From white fabric, cut two pieces $37\frac{3}{4}''$ × $74\frac{1}{2}''$. Sew together on long sides with $\frac{1}{2}''$ seams for piece $74\frac{1}{2}''$ square; press seam open. Cut a layer of lightweight filler the same size.

B	B	B	F	F	G	G	H	H	I	H	H	G	G	F	F	B	B	B
B	B	B	F	F	G	G	H	H	I	H	H	G	G	F	F	B	B	B
C	C	C	G	G	J	J	K	K	L	L	K	K	J	J	G	G	C	C
C	C	C	G	G	J	J	K	K	L	L	K	K	J	J	G	G	C	C
D	D	D	H	H	K	K	M	M	N	M	M	K	K	H	H	D	D	D
D	D	D	H	H	K	K	M	M	N	M	M	K	K	H	H	D	D	D
E	E	E	I	I	L	L	N	N	O	N	N	L	L	I	I	E	E	E
D	D	D	H	H	K	K	M	M	N	M	M	K	K	H	H	D	D	D
D	D	D	H	H	K	K	M	M	N	M	M	K	K	H	H	D	D	D
C	C	C	G	G	J	J	K	K	L	L	K	K	J	J	G	G	C	C
C	C	C	G	G	J	J	K	K	L	L	K	K	J	J	G	G	C	C
B	B	B	F	F	G	G	H	H	I	H	H	G	G	F	F	B	B	B
B	B	B	F	F	G	G	H	H	I	H	H	G	G	F	F	B	B	B
A	A	A	B	B	C	C	D	D	E	D	D	C	C	B	B	A	A	A
A	A	A	B	B	C	C	D	D	E	D	D	C	C	B	B	A	A	A
A	A	A	B	B	C	C	D	D	E	D	D	C	C	B	B	A	A	A

BOWKNOTS BANNER PIECING DIAGRAM

Quilting: Following General Directions for Quilting, pin and baste banner, filler, and lining together, centering layers so that lining and filler extend 2¾″ beyond banner all around. Starting in center and working around and outward, quilt on each white patch, close to seams.

Border: From black fabric, cut eight strips 3½″ × 75½″. Sew a strip to each side of banner (through all three layers) with ¼″ seams, centering so an equal amount extends at each end of each strip. Miter corners of black border (see Contents for directions).

For hanging loops, cut seven pieces 2½″ × 9″ from black fabric. Fold each piece in half lengthwise and stich long edges together with ¼″ seams. Turn pieces to right side; press. Fold pieces in half crosswise and baste along one side of banner (top), spacing evenly, with right sides together and matching raw edges.

Sew remaining black border strips around edge of border with ½″ seams, catching in hanging loops. Turn strips to back of banner, turn in edges ¼″; slip-stitch to lining. Press edges. ☆

170

Free-Form Hanging

shown on page 186

SIZE: 59″ × 51″.

EQUIPMENT: Pencil. Ruler. Scissors. Paper for patterns. Tracing wheel or dry ball-point pen. Dressmaker's (carbon) tracing paper. Tailor's chalk, dark and light. Sewing and quilting needles. Quilting frame (optional).

MATERIALS: Closely woven cotton fabric 45″ wide: black, 1 yd.; off-white, 3 yds.; dark brown, $1\frac{2}{3}$ yds.; medium brown, $\frac{1}{2}$ yd. Polyester or cotton batting. Matching sewing threads.

DIRECTIONS

Read General Directions for Quilting and How to Appliqué (see Contents). Enlarge patterns for appliqués on paper ruled in 1″ squares. Cut large appliqué from black fabric and small appliqué from medium brown; prepare as indicated in How to Appliqué.

Cut two background pieces 44″ × 52″ from off-white fabric. Sew the two appliqués to the right side of one background piece, placing black piece $5\frac{1}{2}$″ from bottom edge and brown piece $5\frac{1}{4}$″ from top edge; see illustration.

Quilting: With tailor's chalk, mark quilting lines on appliqués, starting at outside edge and following outline of each piece for design: On brown appliqué, mark two groups of concentric shapes as shown in illustration; on black appliqué, there are five groups of concentric shapes. Next, mark white background as shown, again using shapes of appliqués for design; draw first line around both appliqués, enclosing them; then continue drawing lines outward to edge; draw lines in center of background connecting appliqués with a series of radiating lines as shown. Width between lines on our hanging varies from $2\frac{1}{2}$″ to $\frac{1}{4}$″. Draw your lines

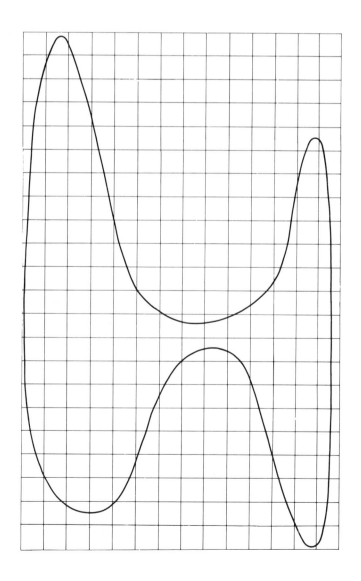

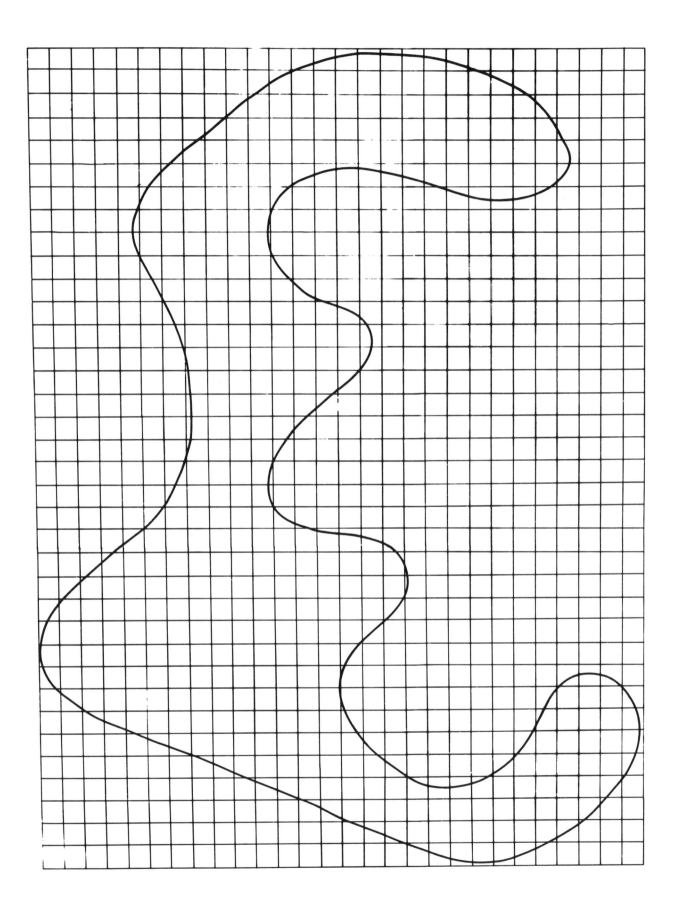

172

in a free-flowing manner, using illustration only as a general guide.

Cut batting 59″ × 51″. Following General Directions for Quilting, pin and baste the appliquéd background, batting, and second white piece together, centering fabric layers so that batting extends 3½″ all around. Starting in center and working around and outward, quilt on all marked lines, using white thread on appliqués and black thread on background.

Border: From dark brown fabric, cut eight strips 5″ wide, four 60″ long, four 52″ long. Sew a shorter strip to top and bottom of hanging (through all three layers) with ½″ seams, centering panel so that an equal amount extends at ends of each strip. Sew a longer strip to each side of hanging in same manner. Miter corners of border (see Contents for directions).

For hanging loops, cut five strips 2½″ × 10½″ from dark brown fabric. Fold each strip in half lengthwise and stitch long edges together with ¼″ seams. Turn strips to right side; press. Fold strips in half crosswise and baste along top edge of hanging, spacing evenly across, with right sides together and matching raw edges.

Sew remaining brown border strips around edge of border with ½″ seams, catching in hanging loops. Turn border strips to back of hanging; turn in edges ¼″, slip-stitch to lining. Press edges. ☆

Corduroy Tree and Fabric Trims

shown on page 188

Fabric Trims

EQUIPMENT: Paper for patterns. Tracing paper. Ruler. Pencil. Scissors. Straight pins.

MATERIALS: Scraps of printed cotton fabrics as desired. Sewing thread to match. Cotton or polyester batting for stuffing. Scraps of trims such as fake fur and woven braid. Scraps of narrow red bias tape. Small amount of red and blue embroidery floss.

GENERAL DIRECTIONS

Trace actual-size ornament patterns (on pages 174 and 176). Make a separate pattern for each part of candleholder.

For each ornament, pin pattern on doubled fabric and cut two pieces, adding ¼″ seam allowance all around. With right sides facing, stitch front and back together with ¼″ seams, leaving a small opening for turning and stuffing. Trim excess fabric; clip into seam allowance at curves. Turn to right side; push out corners with point of scissors. Stuff with batting, pushing it into corners. Turn edges of opening in and slip-stitch closed.

Stocking: Sew as directed, leaving top open. Turn right side out. Turn ¼″ at top to inside; press and stuff. Cut a 1″ × 4¼″ strip of fur; with right sides facing, stitch narrow ends together, making ¼″ seams. Turn to right side and sew around top.

Candy Cane: Pin cane pattern on bias of striped fabric and assemble following General Directions.

Reindeer: Before assembling, machine embroider antlers in narrow, close zigzag stitching. Embroider eye and nose in French knots, mouth in outline stitch, using three strands of floss (see Contents for Stitch Details). Place a 2¼″ strip of woven braid across middle of body. Assemble following General Directions.

Candleholder: Cut two pieces for each of the three parts of ornament. Sew and stuff each part separately following General Directions. Cut a 2½″ piece of bias tape; insert ends at crosslines into holder before completely stitching it closed. Sew flame to candle and candle to holder as shown.

Star: Assemble following General Directions.

Corduroy Tree

SIZE: Approximately 39″ × 34″.

EQUIPMENT: Paper for pattern. Tracing paper. Ruler. Pencil. Scissors. Dressmaker's tracing (carbon) paper. Tracing wheel. Straight pins.

MATERIALS: Green pinwale corduroy, 36″ wide, 1¼ yds. Scrap of brown cotton fabric, 7½″ × 6½″. Polyester batting. Green bias binding tape. 6 yds. Green and brown sewing thread.

DIRECTIONS

Enlarge tree pattern (on page 175) by copying on paper ruled in 2″ squares: fine lines indicate machine quilting design. Trace tree pattern with quilting lines. Cut entire tree out of muslin for lining. Cut tree trunk and tree apart along line on pattern.

With dressmaker's carbon and tracing wheel, on right sides of fabrics trace tree pattern on corduroy and tree trunk on brown fabric, including all the lines to be quilted. Cut out, adding ¼″ seam allowance all around each piece.

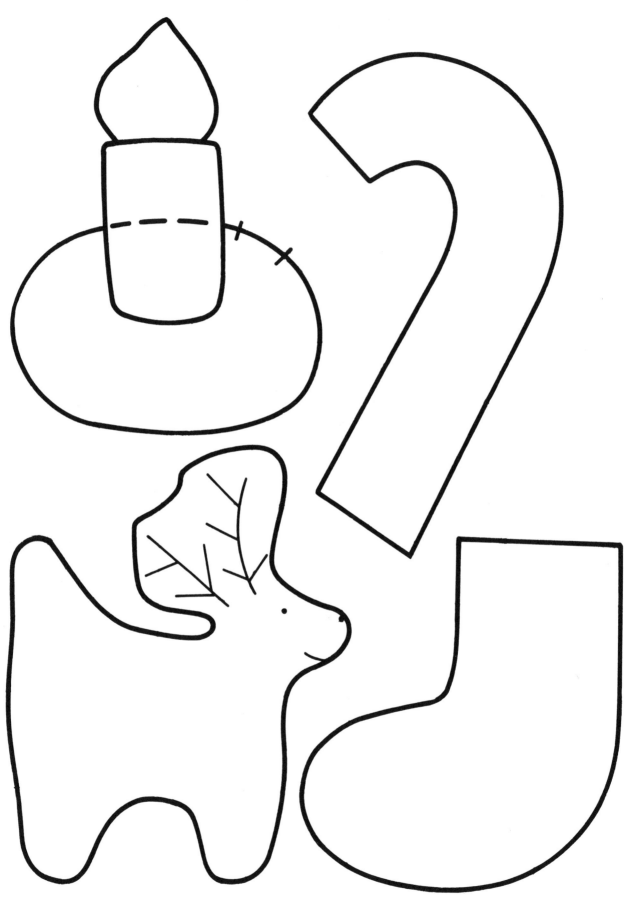

PATTERNS FOR CORDUROY TREE ORNAMENTS

To Quilt Tree: With right sides facing, stitch tree and trunk together with $\frac{1}{4}''$ seam; clip into seam allowance and press seam open.

With right sides facing, stitch bias tape all around tree and trunk. Cut a piece of batting the size and shape of muslin lining. Place lining on working surface and cover with batting. Place tree on top of batting, right side up. Smooth out wrinkles; pin and carefully baste all three layers together. Starting from inside of tree and working outward, machine-stitch quilting design on tree and tree trunk with matching thread. Do not cross a line of stitching and do not backtrack. To secure ends of quilting stitches, bring needle thread ends to back of work (lining side) and knot with bobbin thread ends close to fabric; trim thread ends. Trim excess batting, as necessary. Turn bias tape over to lining side and slip-stitch to lining. ☆

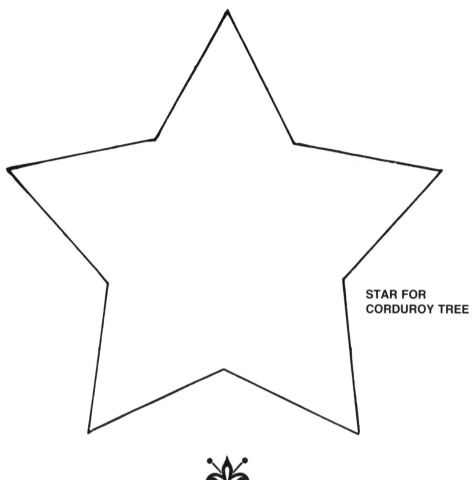

**STAR FOR
CORDUROY TREE**

Calico Patchwork Banner,
Pot Holders, and Hot Mat

shown on page 189

EQUIPMENT: Ruler. Pencil. Paper. Compass. Tape measure. Straight pins. Zigzag sewing machine. Sewing needle. ***For Joy Banner:*** Dressmaker's tracing (carbon) paper and tracing wheel.

MATERIALS: See individual directions.

Round Pot Holder

SIZE: 7″ diameter.

MATERIALS: Small amounts of muslin and red, blue, and yellow calico. Matching sewing threads. Red, single-fold bias binding tape, 27″. Small piece of batting.

DIRECTIONS

Use compass to draw circular patterns with the following diameters: A-7½″; B-7″; C-5½″; D-4″. Label and cut out patterns.

Trace patterns onto fabric as follows: A on red, B on muslin, C on blue, D on yellow; cut out. Pin yellow circle on blue, blue on red, so three circles are concentric. Using matching threads and close zigzag stitch, satin-stitch around edge of yellow circle, then around edge of blue circle.

Cut 3″ length of bias tape. Fold in half lengthwise and stitch together. Fold in half to form loop. Pin to front of fabric circle with loop facing toward center and cut edges even with raw edges of red calico. With right sides facing, pin remaining bias tape to outer edge of circle, keeping raw edges of tape and fabric even. Stitch together with ¼″ seams catching in loop ends.

Use pattern B to cut one layer of batting. Place batting on wrong side of fabric circle; place muslin on top of batting; pin to hold. Turn bias tape to muslin side; pin. Machine-stitch evenly over inner edge of bias tape through all thicknesses.

176

On front of pot holder, straight-stitch through all thicknesses along outside edge of each zigzag circle.

Square Pot Holder

SIZE: 6″ square.

MATERIALS: Three prints and one solid fabric, each 3½″ square; small scrap of another print. Muslin, 6½″ square. Coordinating color single-fold bias binding tape, 28″. Matching sewing thread. Batting, 6″ square. Tiny amount of stuffing.

DIRECTIONS

Make ¼″ seams throughout. With right sides facing, seam together two squares along one edge. Repeat with other two squares. With right sides facing, seam together pairs of squares along one lengthwise edge.

Using a nickel as pattern, trace circle onto small fabric scrap; cut out. Pin circle onto solid-colored square slightly off center and ⅜″ in from the seam allowance, with a bit of stuffing between. Using close zigzag stitch, satin-stitch to square around edge.

Cut off 3″ length of bias tape; reserve. With right sides facing, pin remaining tape around outer edges of square, keeping raw edges of tape and fabric even. Stitch together with ¼″ seams.

Place batting on wrong side of square; place muslin on batting. Pin together to hold layers. Straight-stitch around four sides of each small square ¼″ in from seamlines; do not carry stitching over from one square to another. Straight-stitch across solid-color square and diagonally opposite print square, diagonally in both directions; do not stitch over circle. Begin and end stitching within stitched corners of square outlines.

Turn bias tape to muslin side. Slip-stitch tape to muslin. Fold 3″ length of binding in half lengthwise; stitch together. Fold in half to make loop; turn in raw ends. Slip-stitch loop ends to back at one corner.

Biscuit Hot Mat

SIZE: 8½″ square.

MATERIALS: Print fabric for backing, 10″ square. Five assorted fabrics cut into 16 3″ squares. Muslin, cut into 16 2¼″ squares. Matching sewing thread. Polyester stuffing.

DIRECTIONS

Make each biscuit puff as follows: With wrong sides facing, pin 3″ fabric square to 2¼″ muslin square at corners. At center of each of three sides of square, fold excess fabric between corners into a pleat and pin to muslin with raw edges even. Insert stuffing through fourth side until well filled; pleat fourth side and pin. Baste together close to edges.

With right sides facing, sew a row of four puffs together, one at a time, with ¼″ seams; sew another row together. Seam two rows together along lengthwise edge; add two more rows in same manner to complete square.

Center puff square onto backing square with wrong sides together; pin to hold. Fold raw edges of backing fabric over ¼″; then fold over ½″, covering stitching at the edges of the puffs; slip-stitch all around.

Joy Banner

SIZE: 22″ × 18″.

MATERIALS: Green cotton fabric, 18½″ × 14½″. Red calico, ⅓ yd. Blue calico, 6″ × 9″. Yellow calico, 4″ × 7″. Small scraps of red polka-dot fabric, red corduroy, dark green cotton, and beige kettlecloth. Muslin, 22″ × 18″. Green, red, and gold sewing thread. Batting, two pieces each 22″ × 18″. Bit of stuffing.

DIRECTIONS

Enlarge pattern by copying onto paper ruled in 1″ squares; solid lines are cutting lines; dash lines indicate overlapped pieces; dotted lines indicate additional stitching. Make a separate pattern for each appliqué piece. Using pattern, cut appliqué pieces: cut leaves from dark green cotton, berries and exclamation point from red polka dot fabric, candle from beige kettlecloth, candlestick from red corduroy, flame, Y, and large circle from red calico, O and middle circle from green calico, J and small circle from yellow calico.

On the green cotton background fabric, trace complete pattern using dressmaker's carbon and tracing wheel. Using close zigzag stitch and matching or contrasting threads, appliqué each piece in turn onto green fabric. For the candle, appliqué large circle first, then middle circle, and small circle last. Appliqué candle flame, stuffing slightly as you work. Next appliqué the candlestick, stuffing in the same manner; for "wax dripping," fill in area at right of top edge with rows of machine stitching. Appliqué candle holder using zigzag stitching and continue to form loop; appliqué holly leaf. Zigzag appliqué all other pieces in place.

For the border, cut these pieces from red calico: four 3″ squares, two strips each 3″ × 14½″, and two strips each 3″ × 18½″. Make ¼″ seams throughout. To make upper and lower borders, sew one edge of one square onto each end of each 14½″ piece, with right sides together. To make side borders, sew one edge of each 18½″ length onto the 18½″ edges of the green background. At top and bottom of green background, sew on one lengthwise edge of upper and lower calico border pieces with right sides facing and raw edges even. Press seam open.

On wrong side of banner, center both layers of batting with muslin on bottom. Baste through all thicknesses around edges and lengthwise and crosswise through the center. Fold excess calico over to back over muslin, turning raw edges of calico under ¼"; pin or baste to hold.

Following dotted lines on pattern and using gold thread, machine-stitch details through all thicknesses. Using green thread, straight-stitch all around outer zigzag circle, letters, leaves, berries, and candle holder. Using matching thread, stitch around inner appliqué circles, flame, and candle. Stitch around green background ¼" in from the seamline. Using red thread, stitch ¼" in from seamlines and edges around each part of the calico border. On outer edges, be sure that stitching catches turned-under edge on muslin side. Remove basting threads. ☆

Dream House Hanging

shown on page 189

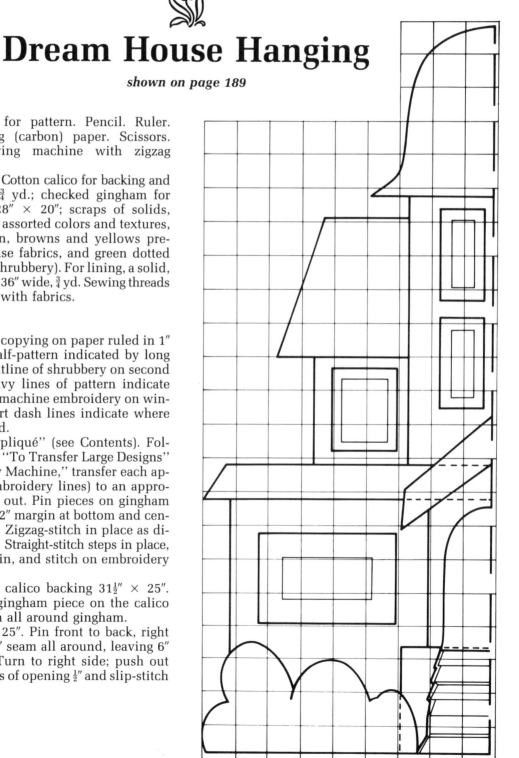

SIZE: 30½" × 24".

EQUIPMENT: Paper for pattern. Pencil. Ruler. Dressmaker's tracing (carbon) paper. Scissors. Straight pins. Sewing machine with zigzag attachment.

MATERIALS: Fabric: Cotton calico for backing and "frame," 36" wide, ¾ yd.; checked gingham for background, piece 28" × 20"; scraps of solids, stripes, and prints in assorted colors and textures, as desired (as shown, browns and yellows predominate in the house fabrics, and green dotted swiss is used for the shrubbery). For lining, a solid, heavier-weight fabric, 36" wide, ¾ yd. Sewing threads to match or contrast with fabrics.

DIRECTIONS

Enlarge pattern by copying on paper ruled in 1" squares; complete half-pattern indicated by long dash line, altering outline of shrubbery on second side, if desired. Heavy lines of pattern indicate appliqués, fine lines machine embroidery on windows and steps; short dash lines indicate where pieces are overlapped.

Read "How to Appliqué" (see Contents). Following directions for "To Transfer Large Designs" and "To Appliqué by Machine," transfer each appliqué (including embroidery lines) to an appropriate fabric and cut out. Pin pieces on gingham background, leaving 2" margin at bottom and centering between sides. Zigzag-stitch in place as directed, omitting steps. Straight-stitch steps in place, trimming away margin, and stitch on embroidery lines.

To Assemble: Cut calico backing 31½" × 25". Center and pin the gingham piece on the calico backing; zigzag-stitch all around gingham.

Cut lining 31½" × 25". Pin front to back, right sides facing. Stitch ½" seam all around, leaving 6" opening at bottom. Turn to right side; push out corners. Turn in edges of opening ½" and slip-stitch opening closed. ☆

Trapunto Wreath

shown on page 217

EQUIPMENT: Paper for pattern. Ruler. Hard-lead pencil. Black felt-tipped ink marker. Masking tape. Regular scissors. Sharp, pointed embroidery scissors. Knitting needle (for stuffing). Razor blade. Medium-size sable brush. Sewing machine. Sewing needle. Iron.

MATERIALS: Unbleached muslin, 24″ × 48″. White lining fabric, 24″ square. Fiberfill for stuffing. White sewing thread. Pastel sticks: red, pink, orange, dark blue, purple, light and dark green, light and dark yellow, brown. Crystal clear acrylic spray. Lavender grosgrain ribbon 2½″ wide, 2½ yds.

DIRECTIONS

To Prepare Design: Enlarge pattern by copying on paper ruled in 1″ squares. Darken outlines of pattern design with ink marker to make them clearly visible through the muslin.

Press muslin; cut in half crosswise. Reserve one piece for backing. Tape wreath pattern on working

180

surface; cover with one of the pieces of muslin, keeping it flat and taut by taping it to pattern at corners. With sharp, hard-lead pencil, trace design, including outer and inner circles, very lightly on muslin.

At this point, machine-stitch along dash lines on bananas only. Baste muslin and lining together, with marked-design side up. Cut out $\frac{1}{4}''$ beyond outer circle for seam allowance.

To Stitch Design: Machine-stitch along all outlines of design, using eight stitches to the inch. Do not cross a line of stitching, and do not backtrack. When stitching is completed, bring needle thread ends to wrong side of work (lining side) and knot with bobbin thread ends close to fabric to secure beginning and end of stitching. Trim thread ends.

To Puff Design: Place work lining side up. With embroidery scissors, cut slits in center of each outlined fruit and leaf. Be very careful not to cut through the muslin or the stitching. Using knitting needle, poke small amount of stuffing through the slits, pushing it into corners and angles of design. Do not overstuff; too much stuffing will create puckering and will distort the design. Check front of wreath each time after filling an area to make sure stuffing is evenly distributed. By hand, whip slits closed after stuffing each area.

To Assemble: Cut the muslin for backing into a circle the same size as puffed wreath. Pin circles together with right sides facing. Stitch along the inner circle seamline. Cut away the center fabric to within $\frac{1}{4}''$ of circular seam; clip into seam allowance all around circle.

Gather backing and push through center hole, so that puffed part of wreath is up. Stitch $\frac{1}{4}''$ from edge on both front and back of wreath; press $\frac{1}{4}''$ seam allowance to wrong side on both front and back. Slip-stitch front and back together, leaving a 5'' opening for stuffing. Stuff wreath until plump, but do not overstuff. Slip-stitch closed.

To Color Fruit and Leaves: With razor blade, shave side of pastel stick to make a powder. Dip brush in pastel powder and rub off excess powder on a piece of paper. Each time, before starting to color wreath, test color on a scrap of muslin. With a back-and-forth motion, work pastel powder into fabric. Repeat until you get color of desired intensity. Shade so that one area of fruit is darker in color. Wash and dry brush thoroughly between each color use. Color apple and cherries red; lemons, pale yellow; oranges, orange; plums, purple; bananas, dark yellow with streaks of brown; grapes, dark blue with some purple shading; peaches, orange with some red and pink. For limes, mix light green with yellow. Color pears dark yellow; mix dark yellow and some brown to shade one side. Color leaves light and dark green. For grape leaves, mix dark blue and dark green. When coloring is completed, spray wreath lightly with acrylic.

Tie a bow with grosgrain ribbon and sew to bottom of wreath. ☆

Lotus Blossom Jacket and Tote

shown on page 218

SIZES: Jacket, Misses Small-Medium-Large. Tote, 14'' square.

EQUIPMENT: Paper for patterns. Ruler. Hard-lead pencil. Dressmaker's tracing (carbon) paper. Scissors. Sharp, pointed embroidery scissors. Straight pins. Sewing needle. Small size knitting needle or tapestry needle (for stuffing). Sewing machine with zipper foot attachment. Iron.

MATERIALS: Unbleached muslin, 36'' wide, $\frac{5}{8}$ yd. Polyester fiberfill for stuffing. White buttonhole twist; matching blue sewing thread. ***For jacket:*** Blue cotton/polyester denim, 45'' wide, $2\frac{1}{2}$ yds. Blue printed cotton/polyester fabric for lining, same amount as for denim. Four wooden toggle buttons, each $1\frac{1}{4}''$. ***For tote:*** Blue cotton denim fabric, 45'' wide, $\frac{5}{8}$ yd. Blue printed cotton fabric to line and trim tote, 45'' wide, $\frac{3}{4}$ yd. Soft cable cord, $\frac{1}{4}''$ wide,

$2\frac{5}{8}$ yds. Two bamboo sticks or wooden dowels for tote handles, each $\frac{1}{2}''$ diameter $\times$ $8\frac{3}{4}''$.

GENERAL DIRECTIONS

To Prepare Design: Enlarge lotus pattern (on page 190) by copying on paper ruled in squares: For jacket back, enlarge on 1'' squares; for tote, enlarge on $\frac{3}{4}''$ squares; for jacket pockets, enlarge blossom only on $\frac{5}{8}''$ squares or use the pattern on the $\frac{3}{4}''$ squares for a slightly larger lotus blossom. Using carbon paper and hard-lead pencil, trace design onto a piece of muslin. Keeping fabrics smooth, baste muslin to wrong side of section to be worked.

To Stitch Design: Using white buttonhole twist thread only in the bobbin of sewing machine, stitch

(Continued on page 190)

Use up those odds and ends to make three sleepytime dolls in their own fabric world. Their sweet little faces are embroidered, and their simple pear-shaped bodies are dressed in buntings. Each can take turns riding in the machine-appliquéd balloon. "Grass" pockets are quilted. Hanging measures 26″ × 19½″. For Balloon Wall Hanging directions, see Contents.

182

This fantasy house is a happy blend of odd prints, machine-appliquéd on seersucker and then "framed" in calico. The picture measures 30″ × 24″.
For Dream House Hanging directions, see Contents.

Stellar results from the sewing machine! Quilted sun and
moon emerge from their muslin background with simple stitches

and padding. Pictures are $27\frac{1}{2}''$ square, framed. For Quilted
Suns and Moons Pictures and Pillows directions, see Contents.

(From Margaret Bower.)

Bowknots-in-patchwork banner motif is from an old weaving design. Black and white patches re-create the light-dark symmetry of the four-way pattern. For Bowknots Banner directions, see Contents.

Free-form appliqués inspire the contour of the quilting design, which curves in and around the appliqués in graceful waves. For Free-form Hanging directions, see Contents.

(Both hangings by Barbara McKie.)

Solid squares and half-squares combine to form a Milky Way pattern on six unique banners. All are made with the same basic shapes— a change in color combinations makes each one different. Each measures 56″ × 16″.

Wide strips in red and white and a star in blue and white combine to create a hanging, 51″ wide. The effective design is easy to make with 5″ squares, half-squares, and rectangles. For Bicentennial Patchwork directions, see Contents.

(Patchwork designed by Margaret Pennington. Commissioned by Kenbury Glass Works for national bicentennial promotion in department stores.)

Stitch a holiday tradition! Corduroy Christmas tree, 39″ long, is cleverly machine-quilted with tree-shaped motifs and decked with delightful scrap-fabric ornaments. Machine-appliquéd calico wall banner (opposite) has pieces padded for dimension. Sew a matching candle sconce pot holder, or patch a 6″ square. "Biscuit" quilted hot mat is a terrific way to use up scraps. For Corduroy Tree, Fabric Trims, calico Patchwork Banner, Pot Holders, and Hot Mat directions, see Contents.

(All designs from Cathy Ulasewicz.)

(*Continued from page 181*)
along outlines of design using 8 stitches to the inch. Do not cross a line of stitching and do not backtrack. When stitching is completed, bring bobbin thread ends to muslin side and knot close to fabric; trim threads.

To Puff Design: Read General Directions for Quilting (see Contents). Place work wrong side up. With embroidery scissors cut slits in center of each outlined section of lotus blossoms. For circle around lotus, cut slits every 2″. Be very careful not to cut through stitching or the denim. Using knitting needle or tapestry needle, poke small amount of stuffing through the slits, carefully pushing it into corners and curves of each outlined section of de-

sign. Do not overstuff; too much stuffing will create puckering and distort the design. Check front of design as you stuff to make sure stuffing is evenly distributed. By hand, whip slits closed after stuffing each area. Trim muslin to $\frac{1}{2}$″ around design.

Jacket

Using sharp colored pencil, draw lines across patterns on page 192, connecting grid lines. Enlarge small, medium, or large patterns by copying on paper ruled in 1″ squares. Omit collar pattern. Enlarge pocket on a separate piece of paper. Adjust patterns by lengthening or shortening jacket at waistline and by lengthening or shortening sleeves. Dash line on pattern for back piece indicates this is a half pattern; place this pattern on fold line of fabric. Lines ending with arrows should be on grain of fabric. Leaving $\frac{1}{4}''$ all around for seam allowances, cut out patterns from blue denim fabric and from lining fabric.

To work back design, cut 13" square of muslin. Center design (1" square size) on jacket back $4\frac{1}{8}''$ below seam allowance on neck edge. For pocket motifs, cut two muslin pieces $6\frac{1}{2}'' \times 5\frac{1}{2}''$. Position blossom design ($\frac{5}{8}''$ squares or $\frac{3}{4}''$ squares size) for pockets as shown. Stitch, stuff following General Directions. To line pockets after working trapunto, place denim and printed fabric together, right sides facing. Stitch around all sides, leaving a 2" opening at bottom. Turn to right side; slip-stitch opening closed. Pin pockets to jacket in position as shown on pattern. Topstitch around three sides of pockets.

To Construct Jacket: First work with pieces cut from blue denim. With right sides facing, seam front pieces to back piece at shoulders. In same manner, sew sleeve piece to armholes. Right sides facing, stitch up sides of jacket and sew long sides of sleeves together. Clip all curves; press.

To make button loops, cut 4 pieces of denim each $3\frac{1}{2}'' \times 1''$. Fold in half lengthwise, right sides facing. Stitch $\frac{1}{4}''$ seam, leaving ends unstitched. Turn to right side. Fold in half to form loop and tack ends together. Position loops on right side of jacket at right center front, raw edges even with edge of jacket. Place top loop 1" down from neck edge; space remaining three loops down front with $3\frac{1}{2}''$ between loops. Baste in place.

To line jacket, assemble lining pieces as for jacket. Pin lining to jacket, right sides facing, along neck edges, front edges, and bottom edges; match seams at shoulders and sides. Stitch, leaving 10" open at bottom. Clip seams around curves. Turn to right side; slip-stitch opening closed. Bring sleeves of lining through jacket sleeves. Trim seam allowance from lining at sleeve bottoms. Turn jacket

sleeve bottoms to inside along seam line; slip-stitch to lining. Topstitch around jacket edges. Position buttons to align with loops; sew in place.

Tote

From denim and printed fabrics, cut boxing strips, each $3\frac{1}{2}'' \times 45''$. From each fabric, cut two 15" squares. Cut two pieces of muslin each $10\frac{1}{2}''$ square. On the 15" square denim front and back sections, work the trapunto design as for jacket back; use the pattern made on $\frac{3}{4}''$ squares and center design on each square $2\frac{1}{2}''$ from top.

From print fabric, cut bias strips 2" wide. Sew together to make two lengths each 46". Cut two lengths of cording, each 46" long, and encase in wrong side of bias strips; stitch close to cord with zipper foot attachment. Pin piping to front and back sections with cord stitching placed $\frac{1}{2}''$ inside denim edges and piping facing to centers. Baste in place. Pin denim boxing strip to sides and bottom of front tote section, having right sides facing, piping between, and raw edges even. Stitch, making $\frac{1}{2}''$ seams. Pin back tote section around sides and bottom of boxing strip, right sides facing, piping between, and raw edges even. Stitch, making $\frac{1}{2}''$ seams. Turn tote to right side. Turn in top edge $\frac{1}{2}''$; trim piping, if necessary. Baste.

Handle Loops: Cut four strips from denim and four from print fabric, each $6\frac{1}{2}'' \times 2\frac{1}{4}''$. Place one denim and one print together, right sides facing; sew long sides with $\frac{1}{4}''$ seam, leaving ends unstitched. Turn to right side. Repeat procedure for other three loops. Fold each in half, print side out; stitch together across loops, 1" from folds. Baste two to front and back tote sections on inside, with each 3" in from piping.

Lining: Construct tote lining by sewing print boxing strip to front and back sections as for tote, excluding piping. Place lining in tote; turn in top edges $\frac{1}{2}''$; baste and stitch around all top edges, matching seams. Insert handles. ☆

Mandarin-Collared Vest

shown on page 218

SIZES: Misses Small-Medium-Large.

EQUIPMENT: Colored pencil. Pencil. Ruler. Scissors. Dressmaker's tracing (carbon) paper. Tracing wheel. Tailor's chalk. Straight pins. Sewing needle. Sewing machine. Iron.

MATERIALS: Blue cotton denim, 45" wide, 1 yd. Navy and white cotton ticking for lining, same amount as for denim. Polyester batting. Thread to match denim and lining fabrics.

DIRECTIONS

This vest is reversible, with vertical quilting along lines of ticking fabric. Using a colored pencil, draw lines across pattern, connecting grid lines. Enlarge small, medium, or large pattern by copying on paper ruled in 1" squares. Enlarge collar on a separate piece of paper; omit sleeve pattern. Use patterns to cut both vest top and linings. Dash line on vest pattern back indicates this is a half pattern: Place

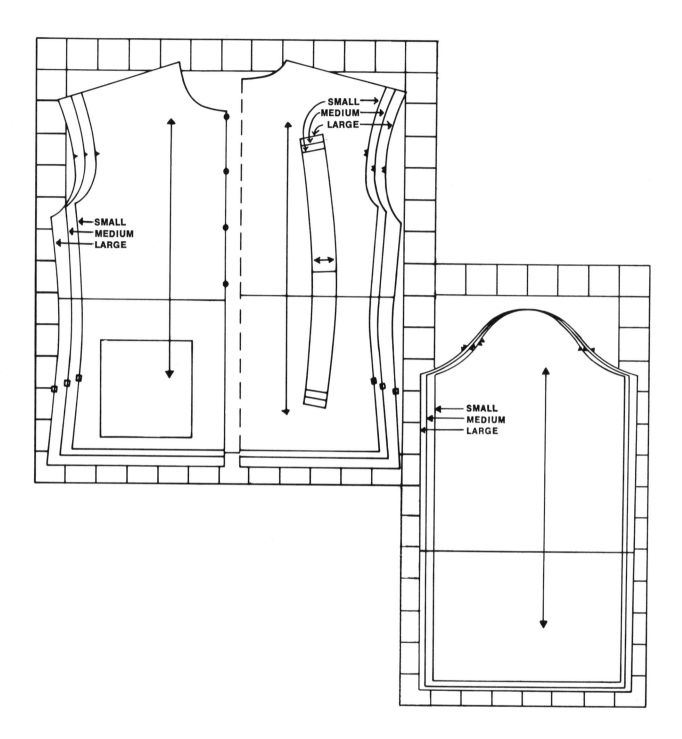

this pattern on fold-line of fabric; line ending with arrows should be along the grain of fabric (or along ticking lines of denim vest lining fabric). Leaving 1¼″ all around for shrinkage when quilting and for seam allowances, cut one back piece, a front left piece, a front right piece, and one collar from vest top fabric, lining fabric, and batting.

Place layer of batting between denim and ticking (right sides out) for each front and back. Baste the three thicknesses of each part together horizontally, vertically, and diagonally across to hold layers smoothly while quilting. Following vertical

stripes of ticking, stitch through all thicknesses with blue thread as follows: one line of stitching along each side of a blue stripe; skip next blue stripe; one line of stitching along each side of next blue stripe. Repeat pattern of stitching on each jacket piece to marked seam lines.

When quilting is complete, check pattern pieces on each quilted piece and remark seam lines as necessary to conform to patterns. Cut away batting around each piece to seam line to reduce bulk in seams. To stitch seams for reversible jacket, rip out any quilting stitching that extends over seam lines. Pin one front and back together, ticking sides facing. Stitch side and shoulder seam through both pieces of ticking, but only one piece of denim. Stitch all other seams in same manner. Fold under raw edges of unstitched denim seams, covering seam allowances of stitched seams and press; pin in place. Using matching thread, sew turned under denim seams by hand with slip-stitches.

Trim away outside edges of ticking $\frac{3}{8}''$ around armholes, bottom, and center fronts. Fold denim to ticking side to make hems; stitch.

Collar: If necessary, cut collar from denim and ticking fabric in two pieces, leaving $\frac{1}{4}''$ seam allowance all around. Right sides facing, seam two pieces together at center back. Place denim collar piece and ticking collar piece together, right sides facing. Leave long end shown on pattern nearest dash line of back pattern unsewn; stitch along seam lines

on other three sides. Clip corners; turn to right side. Turn under $\frac{1}{4}''$ along unstitched side of ticking fabric; press. With right sides facing and raw edges even, pin denim side of collar to denim side of vest at neck edge. Machine-sew along seam line. Clip curves; press seams toward collar. Pin ticking side of collar to ticking side of vest, with raw edge tucked in along pressed fold. Slip-stitch in place. Press.

Ties: From denim fabric, cut four strips each $2'' \times 10''$. Fold up edges of short sides $\frac{1}{4}''$, fold long edges in to meet each other, then fold lengthwise in half. Pin, press, then stitch $\frac{1}{4}''$ from all edges. At places indicated by circles on front pattern of vest, open seam between denim, batting, and ticking fabric and insert end of tie. Slip-stitch opening closed.

Finishing: Topstitch all edges of vest. ☆

Fan Belt

shown on page 219

SIZE: Fits 28″ waist (can be adjusted).

EQUIPMENT: Paper for pattern. Thin, stiff cardboard. Ruler. Scissors. Needle. Straight pins. Iron. Sewing machine. Dressmaker's tracing (carbon) paper. Tracing wheel. Pencil.

MATERIALS: White sateen and dark-colored velveteen, 36″ wide, ¼ yd. each. Small amounts of colored sateen (plain or small-figured prints) for appliqués. Sewing thread, to contrast with sateen and to match velveteen. Polyester batting. Two covered coat hooks and four eyes.

DIRECTIONS

Read General Directions for Quilting and How to Appliqué (see Contents). Enlarge pattern for belt by copying on paper ruled in 1″ squares; dash lines indicate overlapping of appliqués; dotted lines indicate quilting. *Note:* Belt is made to fit 28″ waist. To adjust size, make appropriate changes on pattern before cutting by adding or subtracting motifs. Mark belt pattern (including position of fan appliqués but omitting quilting lines) on right side

of white sateen, using dressmaker's carbon and tracing wheel. Do not cut out. Make two cardboard patterns, one for upper part of large fan and one for upper part of small fan. Using patterns, cut five large fans and seven small fans from colored sateen, adding ¼″ to turn under. Appliqué fans to marked belt shape, reserving one of the large fans for buckle.

Cut out belt, adding ¼″ all around for seam allowance. Using belt pattern, cut batting and velveteen, adding seam allowance and marking on wrong side of velveteen. Baste batting to wrong side of sateen belt. Baste velveteen belt to sateen belt, right sides facing; stitch on seam line leaving opening at one end between Xs on pattern. Turn right side out, tuck in edges of opening, and slip-stitch closed.

Mark quilting lines on sateen side of belt, marking straight lines on each fan and outlining small fans about ¼″ away; use dressmaker's carbon and tracing wheel. Thread sewing machine needle in a color to contrast with sateen; thread bobbin in

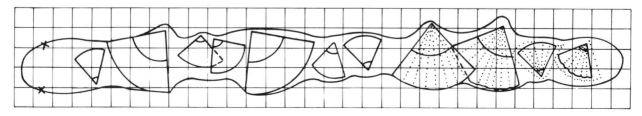

193

color to match velveteen. Sateen side up, stitch along all marked lines and around each fan; stitch $\frac{1}{8}''$ from edges of belt.

Buckle: Mark complete outline of large fan on white sateen; appliqué remaining upper fan in place. Cut batting and velveteen to match fan. Sew and quilt as for belt. Stitch two hooks on velveteen side of buckle and one eye at each end of belt on sateen side (fit belt around waist to determine correct positions). To make belt (but not buckle) reversible, sew an eye to each end of belt on velveteen side. ☆

Bird and Flower Bag

shown on page 219

SIZE: About 8″ × 10″.

EQUIPMENT: Paper for pattern. Pencil. Ruler. Scissors. Straight pins. Sewing needle. Dressmaker's tracing (carbon) paper. Tracing wheel.

MATERIALS: White sateen, 10″ × 12″. Small amounts of sateen in various colors. Fabric for backing, such as lightweight cotton or organdy, one piece 10″ × 12″. Velveteen to match or contrast with sateen, one piece 10″ × 12″. Fabric tubing for shoulder strap, 28″ long or desired length.

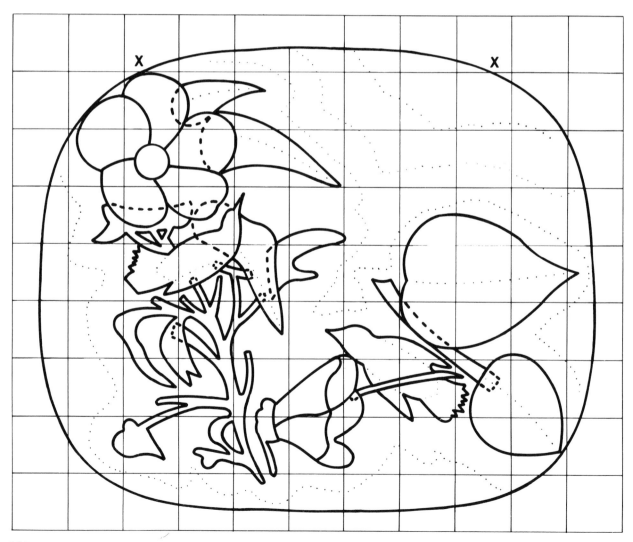

Lining fabric to match sateen, about $\frac{1}{3}$ yd. Sewing thread to match and to contrast with sateen. Matching zipper 6″.

Note: Purse was made from a fabric already printed with a design. Use our patterns, which approximate the printed motifs, or cut other motifs from a printed fabric and appliqué to purse. To quilt background, follow contours of overall design.

DIRECTIONS

Read General Directions for Quilting and How to Appliqué (see Contents). Enlarge purse pattern by copying on paper ruled in 1″ squares, including appliqués, indicated by solid lines (dash lines show overlapping) and quilting pattern, indicated by dotted lines. Using dressmaker's carbon and tracing wheel, mark purse pattern, including appliqués, on right side of white sateen; do not cut out. Cut appliqués from colored sateen and stitch in place. Cut out purse, adding $\frac{1}{2}$″ all around for seam allowance. Cut backing, batting, velveteen, and two lining pieces, same size as white purse piece. Pin sateen and backing pieces together with batting in between, edges even. Make a line of basting stitches

vertically, horizontally, and diagonally in two directions; baste all around edges on seam line. Using contrasting thread, quilt around all appliqués and on marked quilting lines.

Right sides facing, place sateen and velveteen pieces together. Place tubing between the two pieces, leaving ends extending outside at X marks on pattern. Stitch together all around, catching the ends of the tubing in $\frac{1}{2}$″ seam but making sure remainder of tubing is free for shoulder strap. Leave open between Xs on pattern. Clip into seam allowance at curves; turn right side out.

Right sides facing, stitch two lining pieces together, making $\frac{1}{2}$″ seams; leave opening at top between Xs and about 6″ open at bottom. Do not turn right side out. Insert outer purse in lining, matching top openings. Sew lining to outer purse along seam line of opening, stitching front lining piece to front of purse. Turn lining, slipping outer purse through bottom opening in lining. Slip-stitch lining opening closed and insert in outer purse. Insert zipper by hand, being careful not to go through outer layer of velveteen.   ☆

Leafy Luncheon Set

shown on page 220

SIZE: Place mats vary according to style; napkins are 17″ square.

EQUIPMENT: Paper for patterns. Tracing paper. Pencil. Ruler. Scissors. Straight pins. Sewing machine with zigzag attachment. Dressmaker's tracing (carbon) paper. Sewing needle. Dry ball-point pen. Iron.

MATERIALS: Cotton fabric: For place mats, calico in colors desired 45″ wide, $\frac{5}{8}$ yd. for each leaf; for napkins, solid colors to coordinate with place mats, piece 18″ square for each; contrasting calico scraps for appliqués. Polyester batting for padding place mats. Matching and contrasting sewing thread.

Place Mats

DIRECTIONS

Enlarge patterns for leaves and motifs by copying on paper ruled in 1″ squares. Heavy lines indicate cutting lines. Fine lines indicate zigzag stitching lines. Pin patterns on doubled fabric; cut out, adding $\frac{1}{4}$″ all around for seam allowance. Using dry ball-point pen and carbon paper, transfer

leaf vein lines to right side of one fabric piece. Using leaf pattern, cut a piece of batting $\frac{1}{8}$″ smaller all around. Place batting layer on wrong side of unmarked calico leaf; baste together.

With right sides facing, stitch around the two leaf pieces for place mat, making $\frac{1}{4}$″ seam; leave open around stem and 2″ on either side of stem for turning. Clip into seam allowance; turn leaf to right side. Push out points and curves of leaf with scissors' point. Turn in seam allowance around opening and slip-stitch closed. Press edges lightly.

On side of leaf with marked vein lines, pin all thicknesses together in unmarked areas, smoothing out leaf. With close zigzag stitch and contrasting thread, stitch along marked lines through all thicknesses. Use slightly wider zigzag stitch for center vein.

Napkins

DIRECTIONS

Turn $\frac{1}{4}$″ on all edges to wrong side, mitering corners (for directions, see Contents); press. Turn raw

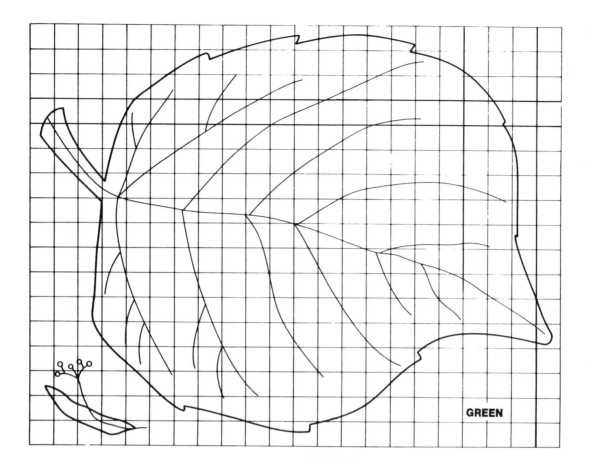

GREEN

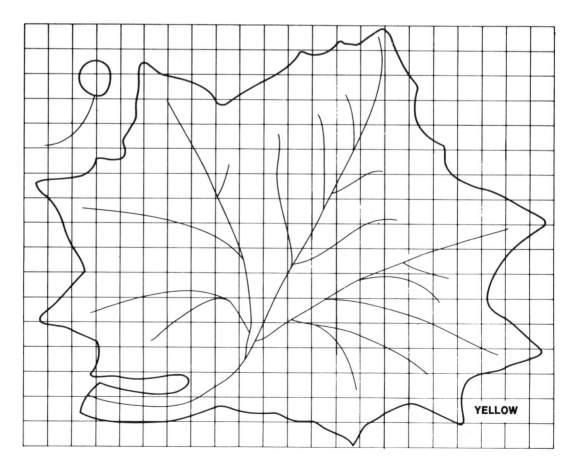

YELLOW

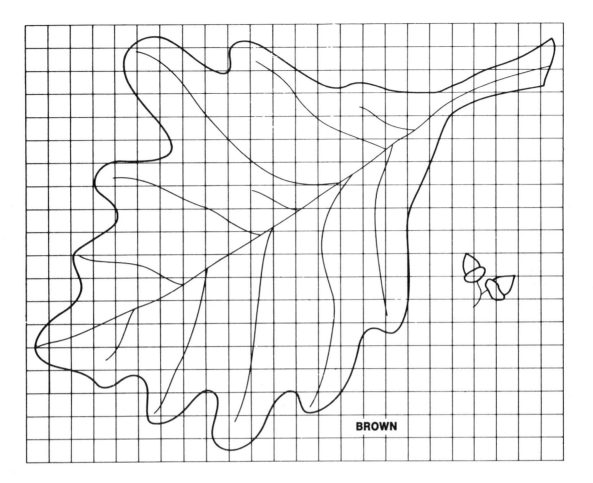

BROWN

edges of hem under ⅛"; press. Using medium-width zigzag stitch and matching thread, stitch hem along turned edge.

For napkin appliqué, trace enlarged motif. Using carbon paper and dry ball-point pen, mark and cut motifs from desired fabrics (choose colors that will contrast with the napkin color). Pin appliqué pieces near one corner of napkin; then mark stem for each, indicated by fine lines on patterns. Using close narrow zigzag stitch and matching thread, stitch along outlines of appliqué pieces and along lines marked for stems. ☆

Ruffled Clamshell Tea Cozy

shown on page 221

EQUIPMENT: Paper for patterns. Pencil. Ruler. Scissors. Straight pins. Sewing and quilting needles. Thin, stiff cardboard.

MATERIALS: Fabric for patches in five different small-print cottons 36" wide: four ⅛-yd. pieces; one ¼ yd. piece to include ruffle, Lining fabric, 36" wide ⅜ yd. Soft fabric for interlining, ⅜ yd. Batting. White thread.

DIRECTIONS

Enlarge pattern by copying on paper ruled in 1" squares; complete half-pattern indicated by dash lines. Make seven separate cardboard patch patterns, one for shell A and one each for partial shells B through G. Mark an X on right side of patterns B, D, E, and F (to reverse for other half of tea cozy). Mark patterns on wrong side of fabric with Xs face down. Add ¼" seam allowance all around patches A–E; for patches F and G, add ¼" on sides, 1" on bottom. Cut patches as follows: 24 of A, two of B, two of C, two of D, two of E, two of F, six of G. Reverse patterns B, D, E, and F with Xs face up and cut two more of each.

To Patch Front and Back: Sew patches together

197

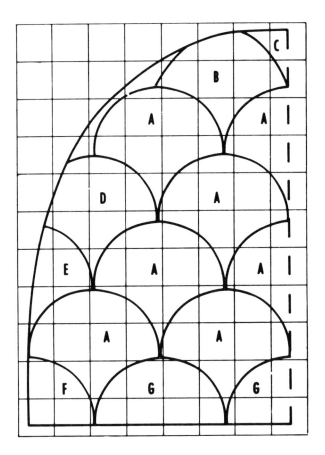

Row 1; four A in Row 2; one E, three A, one E in Row 3; one D, two A, one D in Row 4; and three A in Row 5. In Row 6, use one B, one C, and one B. Make front and back pieces the same. Clip curves and trim corners; press seams open. Lay patched piece flat, right side up. Place complete tea cozy pattern over patched piece, positioning symmetrically. Fill in remaining areas at both sides of Rows 5 and 6 with scraps of fabric, adding $\frac{1}{4}''$ seam allowance.

To Quilt: Cut batting and interlining same size as patched front. Pin and baste piece for front, batting, and interlining together. Quilt around each patch, $\frac{1}{8}''$ from seams on either side by taking small, even running stitches. Quilt back the same. Trim off edges of batting $\frac{1}{4}''$ around curve and 1" at bottom.

To Assemble: For ruffle, cut bias strips 4" wide and piece to make strip 58" long. Fold strip in half lengthwise and gather long raw edges. Baste ruffle to curved edge of quilted front piece, right sides together with raw edges out, and stitch with $\frac{1}{4}''$ seam. With right sides facing and ruffle inside, stitch front and back quilted pieces together $\frac{1}{4}''$ from edge (leave bottom open). Leave wrong side out.

For Lining: Cut two pieces of lining fabric, using tea cozy pattern, adding $\frac{1}{4}''$ for seam allowance around curve and 1" at bottom for hem. Stitch pieces together along curve, right sides facing. Leave wrong side out. Place outer tea cozy and lining together; stitch through all thicknesses, $\frac{1}{4}''$ from edges along curve, leaving last 2" free at beginning and end of curve. Turn outer piece over lining, so that wrong sides of both pieces are on inside of tea cozy. Turn up both lining and outer piece separately for 1" at bottom, so that hems are hidden inside tea cozy; slip-stitch closed along bottom edge. ☆

by hand with small running stitch, holding them with right sides together and stitching on marked seam line; fit one-half of top curve of one shell into curved point of another shell. Begin at bottom, following pattern, with one F, three G, one F in

Cottage Tea Cozy

shown on page 221

shown on page 221

EQUIPMENT: Paper for pattern. Pencil. Ruler. Scissors. Straight pins. Dressmaker's tracing (carbon) paper. Tracing wheel. Sewing and quilting needles. Tailor's chalk.

MATERIALS: Closely woven cotton fabric; yellow, 36" wide, $\frac{3}{4}$ yd.; gray, 6" × 14"; scraps of red, green, white, and calico for appliqués. Soft fabric for interlining, $\frac{3}{8}$ yd. Matching sewing thread. Batting. DMC pearl cotton, size 5: one ball each of black #310, green #907, yellow #973, and blue #798. Small amounts of embroidery floss: gold, red, white, and blue.

DIRECTIONS

Enlarge house pattern by copying on paper ruled in 1" squares; add 1" to bottom of pattern for hem. Dash lines indicate quilting lines. Using dressmaker's carbon and tracing wheel, mark outline only of house four times on wrong side of yellow fabric, leaving at least $\frac{1}{2}''$ between pieces. Cut out each of the house pieces, adding $\frac{1}{4}''$ for seam allowance.

To Appliqué Motif and Quilt Front: Mark position of appliqués on right side of one house. Do not cut out. Cut out appliqués for roof, door, shut-

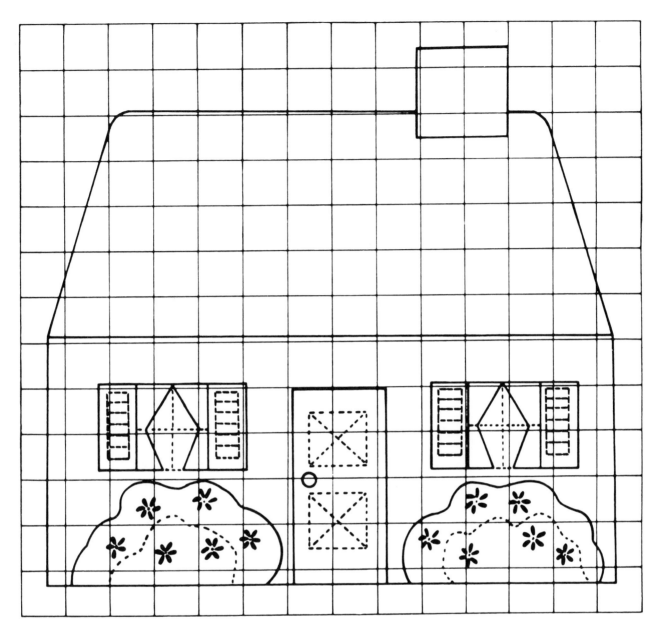

ters, curtains, and bushes in colors shown, adding $\frac{1}{4}''$ to turn under. Slip-stitch appliqués in place on marked house piece. Embroider flowers in embroidery floss with lazy daisy stitch petals and French knot centers; work doorknob in satin stitch (for Stitch Details, see Contents). Mark the horizontal quilting lines on house and roof $\frac{1}{2}''$ apart, using ruler and tailor's chalk. Mark vertical shingle lines on roof $1''$ apart, alternating placement on every other row. Transfer quilting lines of pattern to shutters, windows, door, and bushes, using dressmaker's carbon and tracing wheel. Using house pattern, cut batting and interlining. Pin and baste all together, with right sides of yellow fabric facing.

Quilt roof shingles with blue pearl cotton; house siding with yellow; shutters with green; around and inside bushes with green; window panes, outlines of door, and paneling with black. With right sides facing, stitch quilted house and one un-

quilted house together on all sides except bottom. Leave wrong side out.

To Make Lining: Cut house shape from interlining fabric and from batting, adding $\frac{1}{4}''$ seam allowance; add $1''$ hem on interlining. Mark $2''$ grid on interlining piece, using ruler and tailor's chalk. Pin and baste interlining piece and another yellow house piece together, with batting in between. Machine-stitch along grid lines. Stitch quilted interlining to third yellow house piece along three sides, with right sides of yellow fabric together; leave wrong side out. Assemble lining and outer piece as for Tabby Tea Cozy, page 200.

To Make Chimney: Mark pattern on right side of red fabric (front chimney); mark chimney shape again directly above to double pattern (back chimney). With ruler and tailor's chalk, mark quilting lines on front chimney only: four horizontal lines $\frac{1}{2}''$ apart; two vertical lines in first and third rows, one vertical line in second and fourth row. Cut out batting and interlining in double chimney-shaped pattern. Pin and baste batting and interlining beneath red fabric; quilt on marked lines with yellow pearl cotton. Mark parallel lines 1″ beyond both sides of chimney for added width. Cut out entire red piece, adding ¼″ all around for seam allowance. Fold in half lengthwise, right sides facing. Stitch lengthwise seam. Turn right side out and press so that seam is in center of back. Finish both ends by turning in raw edges and slip-stitching closed. Fold in half crosswise with ends of chimney overlapping front and back roof; slip-stitch in place. ☆

Tabby Tea Cozy

shown on page 221

EQUIPMENT: Paper for patterns. Pencil. Ruler. Scissors. Straight pins. Sewing and quilting needles. Dressmaker's tracing (carbon) paper. Tracing wheel.

MATERIALS: Lightweight cotton fabric such as broadcloth, 36″ wide, ⅔ yd. beige, scraps of royal blue. Soft fabric for interlining, ⅜ yd. Batting. DMC pearl cotton size 5: one ball each light orange #741, yellow #973, navy #336, maroon #815, gold #783. Beige sewing thread.

DIRECTIONS

Enlarge patterns for cat body and separate head by copying on paper ruled in 1″ squares; on head,

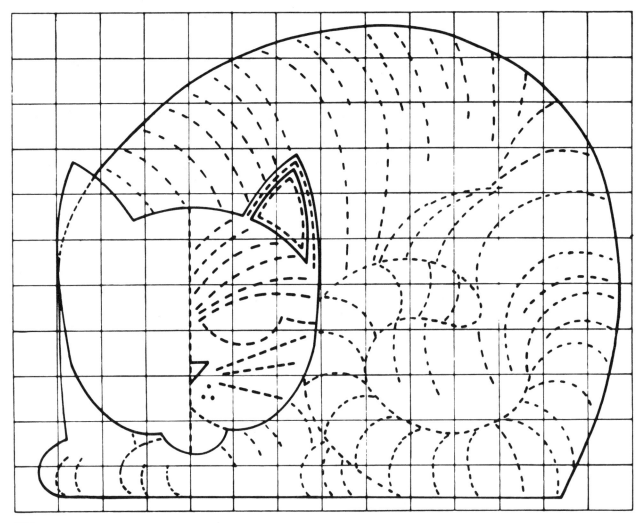

complete half-pattern details indicated by dash lines.

For Front: Transfer patterns onto beige fabric, marking on right side of fabric with dressmaker's carbon and tracing wheel; transfer dash line quilting design. Leave at least 1″ between the two patterns and 1″ along bottom of cat body for hem; do not cut out. Cut two inner ears of blue fabric, allowing ¼″ all around to turn under; slip-stitch appliqués to head.

To Quilt Front: Pin and baste marked beige fabric, batting, and interlining together. Quilt along dash lines with pearl cotton, making stitches about ⅛″–¼″ long. Make tiger-stripe lines yellow and orange, following illustration; outline ears in orange; make whiskers, mouth, paws, outline of tail and leg, and inside of ears maroon; make eyes navy. Embroider yellow French knots under nose; embroider nose in satin stitch with gold (see Contents for Stitch Details). Cut out the cat head and body, adding ¼″ all around for seam allowance, plus 1″ hem at bottom of body.

To Complete Outside: Cut one more head piece and one more body from beige fabric, marking on wrong side of fabric and adding ¼″ seam allowance all around, plus 1″ hem on body. With right sides

facing, stitch quilted and unquilted head pieces together, leaving 2″ unstitched. Turn head right side out; slip-stitch closed.

Sew quilted cat body to unquilted body along curve, right sides together; leave open all along bottom and leave piece wrong side out.

To Make Lining: Cut one cat body from interlining fabric and from batting and two from beige fabric, adding ¼″ seam allowance and 1″ hem. Mark 2″ grid on the interlining piece, using ruler and tailor's chalk. Pin and baste interlining piece and a beige body piece together, with batting in between. Machine-stitch along grid lines. Stitch quilted interlining to another cat body along curved edge, with right sides of beige fabric together; leave wrong side out.

To Assemble: Place lining and outer piece together so that unquilted side of outer piece faces quilted side of lining; pin and baste along curved edge, leaving last 2″ free at beginning and end of curve; stitch. Turn outer piece over lining, so that wrong sides of both pieces are on the inside of tea cozy. Turn up both lining and outer piece separately for 1″ at bottom, so that hems are hidden inside tea cozy; slip-stitch closed along bottom edge. Position cat's head and slip-stitch in place.   ☆

Dresden Place Mat

shown on page 221

SIZE: 14¾″ diameter.

EQUIPMENT: Paper for pattern. Pencil. Ruler. Compass. Scissors. Thin, stiff cardboard. Straight pins. Sewing needle. Sewing machine. Iron.

MATERIALS: Fabric for patched top: four different prints each with a different background color (we used white, red, yellow, and blue), 36″ wide, ¼ yd. each. For lining and interlining: tightly woven lightweight fabric 36″ wide, ½ yd. Pellon fleece, one 14½″ circle. Rickrack, 2 yds. Sewing thread to match fabrics.

DIRECTIONS

To Cut Wedge-Shaped Patches: Read General Directions for Quilting (see Contents). On tracing paper, complete half-pattern indicated by dash line. Cut pattern out of cardboard.

For patches, place cardboard pattern on wrong side of printed fabric; with pencil, trace around pattern outline. Cut out patch, adding ¼″ seam allowance beyond marked outline at side edges only. The marked lines on fabric will be seam lines. Cut four patches of each color.

To Make Patched Top: For interlining, cut out 15″ circle; cut 5″ circle from center. Patches are to be sewn on interlining, alternating the four colors. Place first patch on interlining with right side up and edges even. Pin and sew along one long side seam line. Place second patch on top of first patch, right sides together, matching stitched side seam line. Stitch through all thicknesses on matching seam line. Flop second patch over to right side; press. *With right sides facing, place next patch on top of previous patch, matching unstitched side seam lines. Stitch through all thicknesses along matching seam line. Flop this patch over to right side; press.* Repeat from * to * until all patches are used. At end, cut into interlining along raw edge of first patch. Pull side edges of first and last patches out through cut in interlining with right sides facing; sew these edges together. Insert back through opening. Stitch all around ¼″ in from outer edges to mark seam line.

To Assemble: Cut a 15″ circle for lining. Center and baste Pellon circle to lining. Baste rickrack around right side of patched top, with center of

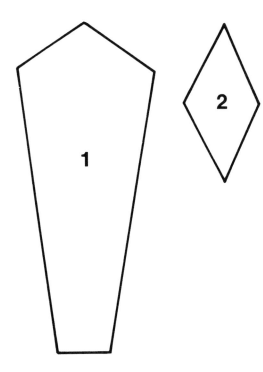

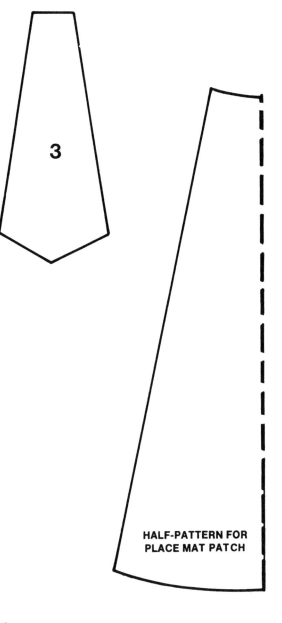

HALF-PATTERN FOR PLACE MAT PATCH

rickrack on seam line. With right sides facing, baste patched top to lining. Stitch together all around outer edge, making $\frac{1}{4}''$ seam. Turn right side out through center opening; press. To keep work flat, topstitch around center opening $\frac{3}{8}''$ in from raw edge through all thicknesses.

Cut $6\frac{1}{4}''$ circle from one remaining piece of print fabric; stitch $\frac{3}{8}''$ seam line all around. Stitch rickrack to $6\frac{1}{4}''$ circle, with center of rickrack along seam line. Turn edge of circle under $\frac{3}{8}''$ all around, leaving only tips of rickrack exposed; press. Baste circle over opening of patched top. Topstitch over rickrack, as close to edge of circle as possible, stitching through all layers. To quilt, stitch along seam line on right side between patches. Stitch through all layers. ☆

Backgammon Board

shown on page 222

SIZE: 19″ × 30″.

EQUIPMENT: Ruler. Pencil. Scissors. Thin, stiff cardboard. Tailor's chalk. Sewing machine.

MATERIALS: Closely woven cotton or cotton-blend fabrics, 36″ wide: $\frac{1}{4}$ yd. each green and blue; $\frac{1}{2}$ yd. white; $\frac{1}{8}$ yd. yellow; $\frac{1}{8}$ yd. each green and blue polka-dot fabric; $\frac{1}{2}$ yd. green printed fabric; $\frac{5}{8}$ yd. fabric for lining. Green singlefold bias tape, 3 yds. Polyester batting. White sewing thread. Purchased counters and dice.

DIRECTIONS

Piecing diagram is for one-quarter of board plus center strip and shows size and placement of each section. Solid lines indicate outlines of patches; broken lines indicate quilting.

Make cardboard patterns for patches as follows: Pattern A: Mark a rectangle 2″ × 6″; draw lines from center of one 2″ side to opposite corners. Pattern B: Half of A. Pattern C: Mark rectangle 3″ × 4″. Mark center point on each of the four sides.

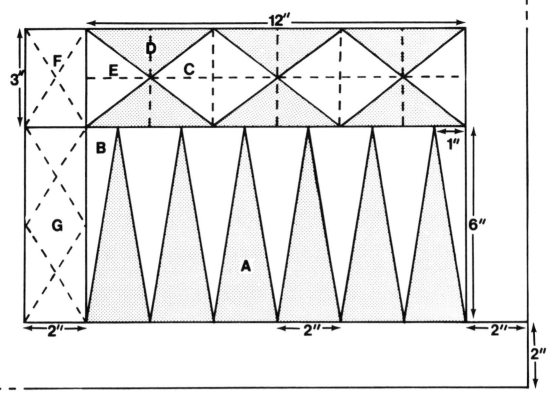

PIECING DIAGRAM FOR BACKGAMMON BOARD

Connect center points with four diagonal lines for diamond shape. Pattern D: Half of pattern C, cut on 4″ length. Pattern E: Half of pattern C, cut on 3″ width. Pattern F: 2″ × 3″. Pattern G: 2″ × 6″.

Mark around patterns on wrong side of fabrics. Adding ¼″ seam allowances all around, cut pieces as follows: Pattern A: 12 blue, 12 green, 20 white. Pattern B: 8 white. Pattern C: 4 yellow. Pattern D: 6 polka-dotted blue, 6 polka-dotted green. Pattern E: 4 yellow. Pattern F: 1 printed green. Pattern G: 2 yellow.

Following piecing diagram and photograph, assemble fabric pieces starting with four playing sections. Place pieces with right sides facing; stitch together ¼″ from raw edges, and press seam allowances open. Then assemble the two horizontal center strips and the center vertical strip in same manner. Join these assembled sections for main part of board. For border, cut four pieces 2½″ wide from printed green fabric, two 15½″ long and two 30½″ long. With right sides together and raw edges flush, stitch shorter pieces of border to ends of board, then longer pieces to sides, ¼″ from raw edges. Board should measure 30½″ × 19½″. Cut lining and batting same size.

Using ruler and tailor's chalk, mark quilting lines on board as shown by broken lines in piecing diagram. Pin and baste board, batting, and lining together. Using white thread and starting in center and working outward, quilt on all marked lines and along outline of each white triangle, close to all seams. Quilt along inner edge of border and ½″ from outer edge of board.

With right sides together, stitch single-fold bias tape around edges of completed board, stitching ¼″ from edges. Fold tape around edge of board and slip-stitch to back.   ☆

Patchwork Checkerboard

shown on page 222

SIZE: 17½″ square.
EQUIPMENT: Pencil. Ruler. Scissors. Tracing paper. Dressmaker's tracing paper. Hard-lead pencil.

Thin, stiff cardboard. Tailor's chalk. Zigzag sewing machine.
MATERIALS: Closely woven cotton or cotton-blend

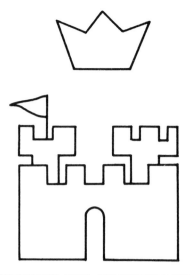

PATTERNS FOR CHECKERBOARD

fabric, 36″ wide, red and black, ½ yd. each. Scraps of printed red fabrics. Scraps of red and black felt. Black and red sewing thread. Polyester batting. Black double-fold bias tape, ½″ wide, 2 yds.

DIRECTIONS

From black fabric, cut four borders, 12″ × 2¾″; four corners, 2¾″ square; 32 center blocks, 1½″ square, adding ¼″ seam allowance around all sides of each piece. From varied red print fabrics, cut 32 center blocks 1½″ square; from red fabric, cut lining 17½″ square, adding 1¼″ seam allowance around all sides. Cut batting 17½″ square.

Alternating black and printed red squares, join them to make eight rows of eight blocks each; stitch blocks together with right sides facing, ¼″ from raw edges. Join rows together in same manner to make playing field as shown in photograph. Note that two corner squares of field are black and two are red.

Trace actual-size patterns on tracing paper. Transfer castle motif to four black 2¾″ squares, using dressmaker's tracing paper and pencil. Embroider castle, using small zigzag stitch and red thread; fill in flags on two blocks with red satin stitch.

With right sides facing, stitch two borders to opposite sides of playing field ¼″ from raw edges. Stitch embroidered corners with red flags to ends of one remaining border and corners with black flags to ends of other border. Stitch borders to playing field, with castle flags at outside edges. Press all seam allowances away from center of "board."

With tailor's chalk, mark diagonal lines in both directions over black blocks, going through corners. Place checker "board" wrong side up. Place batting on top, making sure it is smooth. Place lining on top of batting. Baste around all sides through all thickness, ¼″ from edges. Starting in center, stitch on marked diagonal lines and around edge of each black square, using black thread. Stitch along inner edges of black borders, close to playing field and continuing to outer edges. Bring threads to wrong side of "board" and knot.

With right sides together, stitch bias tape to edge of "board"; fold over to back, enclosing raw edges, and slip-stitch to lining.

Using bottle cap, or cardboard circle with 1½″ diameter, mark and cut out 24 red felt circles and 24 black felt circles. Cut 24 matching circles of batting. Transfer crown motif to 12 red circles and 12 black circles. Using zigzag stitch, embroider crown motif on red circles with black thread; embroider black circles with red thread. To make each checker, place a circle of batting between one embroidered circle and a matching plain circle; hold the three layers in place with basting stitches and stitch around the edges with zigzag stitch. Trim to edge of stitching if necessary. ☆

Baby Album Cover

shown on page 222

SIZE: For 11¾″ × 12¼″ photograph album.
EQUIPMENT: Scissors. Tape measure. Pencil. Dressmaker's tracing paper. Straight pins. Sewing needle. Large-eyed needle. Embroidery scissors. Zigzag sewing machine (optional).
MATERIALS: Paper for patterns. Heavy white cotton or cotton-blend fabric, 36″ wide, ⅜ yd. 25 fabric scraps for patches, each 2¾″ square. Fabric scraps for appliqués, including red for apple and green

for leaf. Bias seam tape, ½″ wide, 3 yds. Light weight white fabric for lining, 36″ wide, ⅜ yd. Quilt batting, one layer, 34″ × 13¾″. Sewing thread to match fabrics. Pearl cotton, size 3, one small skein each of yellow and blue, or colors desired.

DIRECTIONS

If the dimensions of album to be covered are different, measure height and width of album and adjust measurements before cutting fabric. From heavy white fabric, cut piece for back 13¾" × 18" (including back inside flap); piece for front inside flap, 13¾" × 5½"; and two strips for top and bottom borders of front cover, each 1½" × 11¾". From lining fabric, cut piece 13½" × 34¼".

Arrange patches in desired order to form a square with five rows of five patches each. Since four patches along right edge will be appliquéd with the word "BABY," keep colors of these appliqués in mind. Other appliqués can be arranged as desired. With right sides facing, stitch patches to-

matching thread and close zigzag stitch, stitch around each traced outline. Using embroidery scissors, trim away excess fabric close to stitching; be careful when cutting around letters not to cut into patchwork. Complete flower by adding contrasting center and stitching in place. Using contrasting thread, complete butterfly and balloon with zigzag stitching along broken lines.

To appliqué patches by hand, cut traced patterns from scraps, adding ¼" around all edges. To turn under edges of "holes" in letters "A" and "B," make slits in center of "holes" and clip into excess

gether ¼" from raw edges to make a row of five patches. Repeat for four other rows; stitch five rows together in same manner.

Enlarge appliqué patterns by copying on paper ruled in 1" squares; broken lines indicate embroidery lines. Using dressmaker's tracing paper, trace outlines of appliqués onto right sides of fabric scraps in various colors; trace apple on red fabric, leaf on green fabric.

To appliqué patches with zigzag sewing machine, baste each scrap, tracing side up, onto center of desired patch. Following photograph, place each letter of "BABY" on a patch along right edge. Place other appliqués on desired squares. Using

fabric. Turn edges under ¼" and baste all around. Slip-stitch appliqués in place.

With right sides facing and making ¼" seams, stitch strips of white fabric for top and bottom borders of front cover in place along upper and lower edges of patchwork square. In same manner, stitch piece for front inside flap along right edge of patchwork square; then stitch piece for back along left edge of patchwork square. Press all seams away from center.

Place album cover wrong side up. Place batting on top, making sure it is smooth. Place lining on top of batting. Baste all layers together. Stitch around all sides through all thicknesses, ¼" from edges.

Cut two 13¾″ lengths of bias tape. With right sides together, stitch strips along right and left edges of album cover, ¼″ from edges. Cut two 34¼″ lengths of tape; with right sides facing, stitch one strip to upper and one strip to lower edge of cover, ¼″ from each edge. Press bias tape outward, covering raw edges.

With right side up, fold each side edge of cover 4″ toward center, so right sides are facing. Stitch upper and lower edges together just inside stitching line of bias tape. Trim folded corners diagonally and turn right side out. Turn bias tape along upper and lower edges to inside and slip-stitch in place between the two flaps.

Thread large-eyed needle with two strands of one color of pearl cotton. Tuft cover at each corner of each patch. To tuft, push threaded needle from right side of album cover through fabric, batting and lining to back, leaving thread end on right side. Push needle back up again to right side, about ¼″ away from first stitch. Tie yarn in firm double knot. Clip ends to desired length, at least ½″. Make tufts, alternating colors of pearl cotton as desired. Slip cover onto album. ☆

Patchwork Star Vest

shown on page 223

EQUIPMENT: Pencil. Ruler. Scissors. Lightweight cardboard. Straight pins. Sewing and embroidery needles. Sewing machine.

MATERIALS: Patterns for vest (McCall's Pattern 5838 could be used for man's vest, or Pattern 5634 for misses' vest). Fabric scraps in a variety of colors and textures, such as satin, taffeta, velvet and brocade, in solid colors and patterns. One yd. lightweight fabric for lining, 44″ wide. Six-strand embroidery floss to match lining fabric. Six button molds, ½″ diameter. Four hooks and eyes.

DIRECTIONS

Patchwork can be a "crazy quilt" of squares, rectangles, triangles, and other shapes, or can be made mostly of squares, as in vest shown.

Patchwork is made in sections from which pattern pieces can be cut. To make patchwork, lay out scraps of fabric on a large, flat surface and arrange adjoining colors and textures for a pleasing effect, in either a random pattern or a geometric design. Cut scraps in desired shapes, allowing ¼″ seam allowance on all sides, so they can be stitched together into sections of the required size.

Vest shown has eight-pointed patchwork star worked into front sections of vest. Star is made of diamond-shaped patches, brown velvet on one side, brown satin on the other. To duplicate star, trace actual-size diamond pattern shown in Diagram 1 onto cardboard; add ¼″ seam allowance and cut out. Cut four complete diamonds for each side of front, plus a matching strip cut to dimensions shown

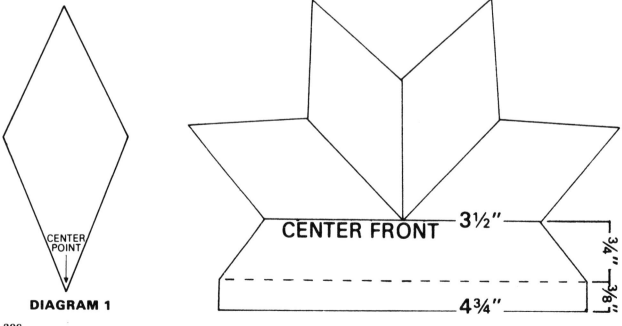

CENTER POINT

DIAGRAM 1

CENTER FRONT — 3½″ —

4¾″

¾″

³⁄₈″

in Diagram 2 (plus $\frac{1}{4}''$ seam allowance on all sides). Stitch pieces together by hand or machine as shown in diagram and place half-stars in patchwork layouts for front sections of vest, fitting contrasting patches between points. Stitch patchwork pieces for each section of vest together; press seams flat. With center front line of star matching center front line of pattern, pin and cut front sections of vest; then cut back sections. Stitch together following pattern directions. Trim front edge $\frac{3}{4}''$ on left side for men or right side for women. Machine-stitch $\frac{1}{2}''$ in from raw edges.

Four flower motifs are embroidered on front of vest shown. Any motif desired could be used, placed symmetrically or scattered at random over entire vest. Turn $\frac{5}{8}''$ seam allowance to wrong side around edges and armholes of vest, clipping $\frac{3}{8}''$ into seam allowances around curves; baste in place. Cut lining and assemble in same manner as vest. Machine-stitch $\frac{3}{4}''$ in from all raw edges and clip around curves. Turn edges under on stitching line and pin lining to vest, wrong sides together, with turned edges of lining meeting stitching line on vest. Slip-stitch lining to vest. Sew on four hooks and eyes or make "eyes" by hand in matching thread. Cover buttons following directions on package. Sew to vest $\frac{1}{2}''$ in from edge. ☆

Striped Patchwork Vest

shown on page 223

SIZE: Pattern is for a Misses' size 10; to make pattern larger or smaller, add $\frac{5}{8}''$ to, or subtract $\frac{5}{8}''$ from, each side seam for each one-size difference.

EQUIPMENT: Pencil. Ruler. Scissors. Paper for patterns. Pins. Sewing needle. Small crochet hook.

MATERIALS: Closely woven cotton or cotton-blend fabric, 45" wide, $\frac{1}{3}$ yd. each of nine printed fabrics in a related color scheme. Fabric for lining, 45" wide, $\frac{2}{3}$ yd. Polyester batting. Sewing thread. Small amount of yarn or crochet cotton. Three ball buttons.

DIRECTIONS

Enlarge patterns for front and back of vest by copying on paper ruled in 1" squares; complete half pattern indicated by broken line.

To make front of vest, cut center strip 2" × $21\frac{1}{4}''$. Cut 14 side strips, $1\frac{3}{4}'' × 21''$, cutting two each of seven different printed fabrics. Starting with center strip, place seven strips on each side of the center strip in a symmetrical arrangement of color and pattern. With right sides facing, stitch strips together $\frac{1}{4}''$ from raw edges on the 21" sides. Press all seam allowances open. Pin front pattern of vest to striped "fabric," placing center of pattern in center of middle strip. Cut out vest front in one piece, then cut through center of 2" strip to separate the front into two sides.

Join fabric for back of vest in same manner as for front, using seven $1\frac{3}{4}''$ strips on each side of the 2" center strip. Arrange strips in same color scheme as for front. Pin pattern for back of vest to striped "fabric," placing center of pattern in center of middle strip. Cut out back of vest in one piece.

Using paper pattern, cut lining for front in two pieces; cut lining for back in one piece. Cut two thin layers of batting a little larger than front; cut one thin layer of batting a little larger than back. Pin and baste batting to wrong sides of front and back. Pin and baste lining on top of batting, making sure raw edges of lining and striped "fabric" are even. To quilt, stitch on each strip next to seams. Trim batting to same size as each piece, then trim $\frac{1}{4}''$ in from each side and shoulder seam so batting will not be caught in seams.

With right sides facing, pin front and back sections of striped "fabric" together at shoulders and side seams, leaving lining fabric free. Stitch together $\frac{1}{4}''$ from raw edges; press seams open. At each seam, turn one raw edge of lining fabric under $\frac{1}{4}''$; overlap the remaining raw edge and slip-stitch in place. Stitch on finished seams to quilt.

From remaining printed fabric, cut bias strips $1\frac{1}{4}''$ wide for binding. Join bias strips to make binding approximately 4 yds. long. Stitch binding to all raw edges of vest with right sides together, stitching $\frac{1}{4}''$ from raw edges. Turn binding to inside of vest, leaving a $\frac{3}{8}''$ bound edge on the right side of the vest. Turn in raw edges of binding $\frac{1}{4}''$ and slip-stitch to lining.

Sew three ball buttons to front of vest, one at the top, and the remaining two spaced 3" apart. Crochet chain loops to other side of vest for fastening, using yarn or crochet cotton. ☆

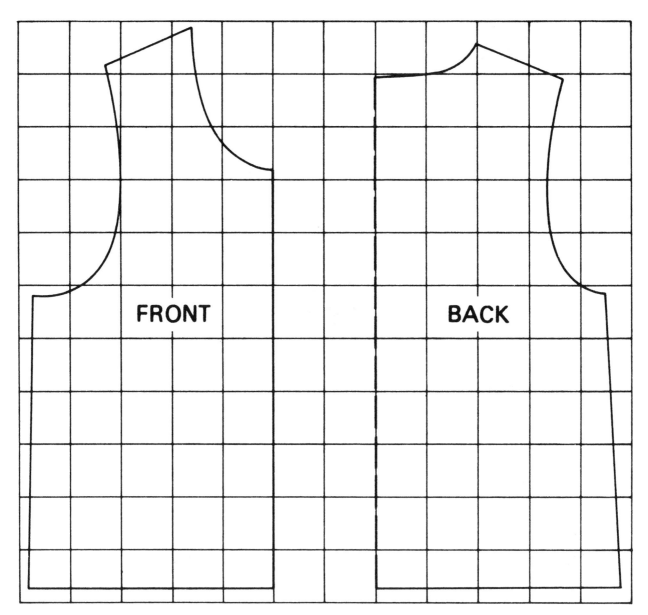

PATTERN FOR STRIPED PATCHWORK VEST

Needlepoint Eyeglass Case

shown on page 224

EQUIPMENT: Pencil. Ruler. Scissors. Tapestry needle. Masking tape. Straight pins. *For Blocking:* Brown wrapping paper. Soft wooden surface. Thumbtacks.

MATERIALS: Mono needlepoint canvas, 18 mesh-to-the-inch; 7½″ × 11″. DMC six-strand embroidery floss; ombre blue #67, 4 skeins; light blue #519, 6 skeins. Blue satin fabric, 8″ × 13½″. Matching

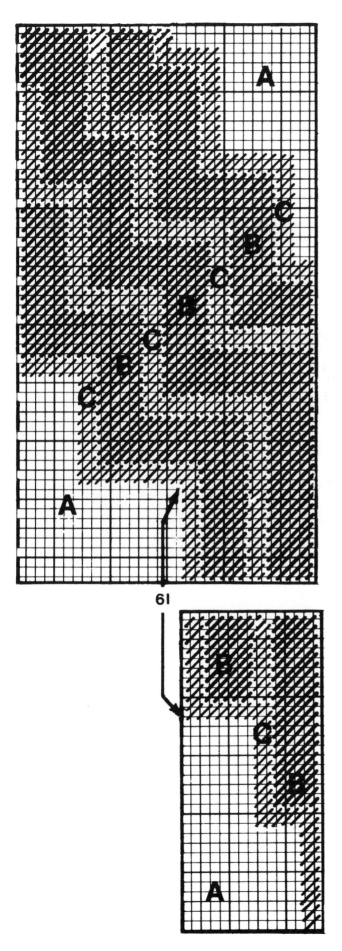

61

sewing thread. Pellon and cotton batting, $8'' \times 4\frac{1}{2}''$ piece of each.

DIRECTIONS

Mark size of design, $3\frac{1}{2}'' \times 7''$, on canvas, leaving 2" margins. Tape canvas edges to prevent raveling.

Read General Directions for Needlepoint (see Contents). Using the full six strands of floss in tapestry needle, follow chart, which is one-half of design. Work areas A in continental stitch using blue floss. Follow diagonal lines on charts in areas B and C for direction and length of stitches. Use ombre floss in B sections, working each stitch diagonally over 5 meshes. Use blue floss in C sections, working each stitch diagonally over 2 meshes. Starting at top right on marked area of canvas, follow charts working from top to bottom: Work 61 stitches between arrows in established pattern; finish bottom following smaller chart. Fill in remaining areas as A. Work other half of canvas in reverse. Block finished piece following General Directions for Needlepoint. Trim margins to $\frac{1}{2}''$.

To assemble eyeglass case, cut the $8'' \times 13\frac{1}{2}''$ satin fabric into three $8'' \times 4\frac{1}{2}''$ sections, two for lining and one for back.

For back, baste cotton batting to wrong side of one satin piece with Pellon in between. Right sides together, pin needlepoint canvas to back. Leaving top edge of case open, stitch other three sides with $\frac{1}{2}''$ seams. Trim seams; clip corners. Turn right side out; turn top edges in.

For twisted cord edge read How to Make a Twisted Cord (see Contents). Use full six strands of ombre floss doubled and make cord about 24" long. Starting with one end of twisted cord inside top corner of case, slip-stitch cord along top front edges of case, flush to needlepoint design; continue stitching to seams on other three sides, concealing end inside case when complete.

For lining, pin remaining two satin pieces together, right sides facing. Stitch around three sides with $\frac{1}{2}''$ seams, leaving one $4\frac{1}{2}''$ side open. Insert lining into case, folding top edges in. Slip-stitch to case on inside with front lining flush against cord edge. ☆

NEEDLEPOINT CASE

Four-Way Bag

shown on page 224

EQUIPMENT: Paper for patterns. Pencil. Ruler. Scissors. Straight pins. Sewing machine. Sewing needle. Dressmaker's tracing (carbon) paper. Tracing wheel.

MATERIALS: Satin fabric 45″–48″ wide, $\frac{1}{2}$ yd. Two acrylic bag handles $1\frac{1}{4}″ \times 8″$. Muslin 36″ wide, $\frac{1}{3}$ yd. Matching sewing thread. Batting.

DIRECTIONS

Enlarge pattern by copying on paper ruled in 1″ squares; complete half-pattern indicated by long dash lines. From satin fabric, cut four $9\frac{1}{2}″ \times 10\frac{1}{2}″$ bag panels ($\frac{1}{2}″$ seam allowance is included). With carbon between pattern and the right side of satin fabric, transfer the design onto two panels, using tracing wheel.

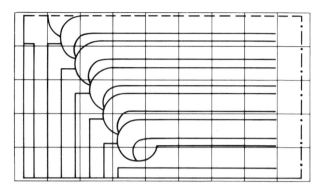

From muslin, cut two bag panels, $9\frac{1}{2}″ \times 10\frac{1}{2}″$. Cut two thin layers of batting the same size and place between the muslin and wrong side of satin front and back bag pieces. Baste the three layers of each together. Machine-stitch quilting design on both bag panels.

To Assemble Bag: With right sides of satin panels (front and back) together, machine-stitch along the dot-dash line. Trim seam and press. Do not turn.

With right sides of bag together, stitch side seams starting from the top to within $1\frac{1}{2}″$ from the bottom. Push the bottom seam up to meet the end of the side seam; center the bottom seam so that there is $\frac{3}{4}″$ on each side of the seam. This produces a $1\frac{1}{2}″$ bottom and side gusset.

Pin these folds and stitch each one from fold in to the side seam line, turn and stitch back to fold. Repeat for other side. Press. Turn bag right side out.

For inside pocket, cut a $6″ \times 5″$ rectangle from satin fabric. Turn the fabric under $\frac{1}{4}″$ along one 6″ edge; fold the edge over another $\frac{1}{4}″$ and press. Stitch folded edge. On right side of one satin lining panel, center pocket so that stitched edge is parallel to and 2″ below one $10\frac{1}{2}″$ edge. With pocket raw edges turned under $\frac{1}{4}″$, topstitch pocket to lining; leave already stitched edge open.

Sew the two lining pieces together in the same manner as the bag. Do not turn inside out. Press seams.

To Make Handle Cases: Cut four strips from satin, each $6″ \times 5″$. For each case, stitch two pieces together along 5″ sides only, right sides facing. Leave the other edges open. Turn to right side; press.

Fold each handle case in half so that the raw edges meet. Center handle case between dots on the outside of the bag with raw edges meeting the top of the bag. Stitch. Repeat on the other side for the second handle case.

Insert bag into lining with right sides together. Matching seams, pin at top edge. Make sure handle cases are lying between lining and outside fabric before sewing. Stitch lining to front and back of bag along the top edge, leaving a $4\frac{1}{2}″$ opening at one side between the ends of the front and back handle cases. Trim seams; turn bag right side out and press. Slip-stitch opening closed.

To Make Strap: Cut one strip of satin measuring $3\frac{1}{2}″ \times 45″$. With right sides together, fold the strip in half lengthwise. Making $\frac{1}{4}″$ seams, stitch open edges together, leaving a 4″ opening in the middle of the long side. Trim, clip corners, turn right side out and press. Slip-stitch opening closed.

Slide handles through cases. Thread each end of strap through the front and back handle holes, making strap ends equal. Tie ends of strap together with a square knot for a shoulder bag length or a bow for a handbag. ☆

Art Deco Bag

shown on page 224

EQUIPMENT: Paper for patterns. Pencil. Ruler. Scissors. Straight pins. Sewing needle. Dressmak-er's tracing (carbon) paper. Tracing wheel. Sewing machine with zipper foot attachment.

MATERIALS: Satin fabric 45″–48″ wide, 1 yd. Two acrylic bag handles 1½″ × 10″. Matching sewing thread. Batting. Muslin 36″ wide, ⅜ yd. Cable cord ⅜″ thick, 104″ long.

DIRECTIONS

Enlarge pattern by copying on paper ruled in 1″ squares; complete half-pattern indicated by long dash line.

Adding ½″ for seam allowance, from satin fabric folded double, cut two bag pieces, placing dot-dash line of pattern on fold. With carbon between quilting pattern and right side of one satin bag piece, trace the design onto both back and front of bag, using tracing wheel.

From folded muslin, cut one bag pattern same as satin. Cut a thin layer of batting the size of muslin and place it between the muslin and wrong side of satin bag with design on it. Baste the three layers together. Machine-stitch quilting design on bag and across center of bag along dot-dash line.

Fold bag in half, right sides together, matching edges along handle cases and sides. Stitch side seams only, starting from the top down to 3″ from the bottom fold. Push the bottom fold up to meet the end of the side seam; center the fold so that there is 1½″ on each side of the seam. This produces a 3″ bottom and side gusset.

Pin folds and sew each one from fold in to the side seam line. Turn and stitch back to fold. Repeat for other side. Trim seams and press. Turn the bag right side out.

Sew satin lining same as bag. Do not turn right side out.

To make handle casings, cut four facing strips: follow dash line on pattern for bottom cutting line and add ½″ seam allowance to top and sides of handle extension on pattern. With right sides together, sew facings to bag extensions at sides only; make ½″ seams and leave ½″ at top unstitched. Turn, clipping into bottom corners if necessary so that facing lies flat.

Place quilted satin bag inside lining, right sides together. Stitch lining to bag across casing tops, leaving facings free. Trim seams. Pushing these stitched layers out of the way, stitch across facings at top, trim seams. Now stitch bag and lining to-

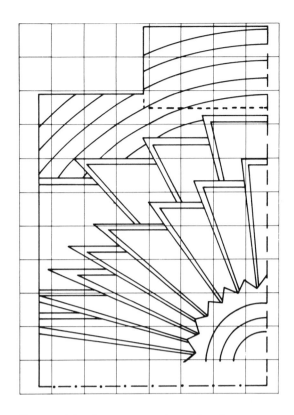

gether at sides between casings, leaving an opening of 6¼″ on one side. Turn bag to right side, clipping where necessary so seams lie flat. Slip-stitch opening closed.

To make straps, cut 2″-wide bias strips of satin fabric, piecing if necessary to measure 53″ long. With right sides together and edges even, fold the bias strip over the cord, starting with one end ¼″ beyond the cord center. With zipper foot, stitch across enclosed cord at this end, ¼″ from fabric edge; continue stitching fabric down long edge close to cord. Trim seam. To turn right side out, draw enclosed cord out of tubing as you push the fabric strip up to cover other cord half. Cut excess cord. Slide handles through cases. Thread cord strap through holes; abut cord ends, stitch together.

Cut a 1¼″ × 2″ tab from satin fabric to be placed over strap ends. With raw edges turned under, wrap tab around strap joining so that ends overlap slightly. Slip-stitch in place. ☆

Patchwork Totes

shown on page 225

SIZES: 5½″, 11″, 16½″ long.

EQUIPMENT: Pencil. Ruler. Paper for patterns (preferably graph paper). Scissors. Thin, stiff card-

board. All-purpose glue. Compass. Sewing needle. Sewing machine.

MATERIALS: Closely woven cotton fabric 36″ wide

(½ yd. or less of each color for each bag): red, bright green, olive, red-and-green print on white ground. (*Note:* Other shades of green were used as well; vary greens as desired.) Muslin 36″ wide, ½ yd. or less for each bag. Batting. Zipper, red or green in size to fit. Matching sewing thread.

DIRECTIONS

Patterns: Each bag is made up of one or more pieced blocks; see Piecing Diagram for one block, 5½″ square. To make patterns for patch pieces, draw a portion of Piecing Diagram on graph paper as follows: Draw a 5½″ square. In lower left corner, mark a point on each side 1″ from corner; connect points marked for pattern A. Mark four more points every ⅞″ along each of the two sides, as shown. Connect the points marked. On right side, mark three points at ⅝″, then a point at ⅜″, as shown; draw lines from these points straight across square to opposite side. Erase working lines no longer needed, indicated by dash lines, leaving lines for patterns B, C, D, E, F, G, H and I. (*Note:* Make full pattern for H; the overlapping corners are part of the design.) For Pattern J, draw a 1″ square. Label all patterns. Glue complete pattern to cardboard; let dry. Cut out individual patterns along lines drawn.

Patch Pieces: To cut out patch pieces, lay patterns on wrong side of fabric, placing right angle of A and parallel sides of all other patterns on straight of goods; mark around pattern with a sharp pencil. Cut out pieces ¼″ away from marked lines, which will be stitching lines. For each block, cut four pieces each with patterns A through I; cut one with pattern J. Cut A pieces from red fabric; cut F and H from bright green; cut G and I from olive; cut B, C, D, E, J from print.

Piecing the Block: Cut muslin piece 6″ square. Draw two corner-to-corner diagonal lines, crossing in center. Place J piece right side up in center of muslin with corner touching lines drawn; do not turn under seam allowance, but leave piece flat. Pin and baste in place. Place an I piece over J piece, right sides together and matching 1″ edges. Stitch along ¼″ seam line of I, through all three thicknesses. Turn I over to right side and press lightly. Stitch remaining three I pieces to remaining sides of J in same manner. Stitch the four E pieces in place, covering seam allowance along two sides of two adjacent pieces; turn and press. Continue adding pieces, working around in sequence (H pieces will overlap slightly as shown) until block is completed. Pieced block should measure 6″ square (5½″ plus ¼″ seam allowance remaining on all sides).

Making the Bag: To join blocks for bag piece, place two blocks together with right sides facing and stitch along one side with ¼″ seam. Press seam

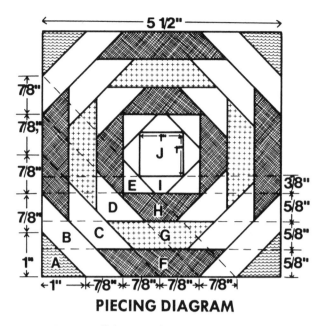

PIECING DIAGRAM

open. For small bag, make only one block for bag piece. For medium bag, make four blocks and join them in two rows of two blocks each; join rows for bag piece. For large bag, make nine blocks and join them in three rows of three blocks each; join rows for bag piece.

Cut layer of batting and a red lining piece, both the same size as bag piece. Place bag piece and lining together, wrong sides facing; insert batting between. Baste pieces together, ¼″ from edges all around.

Fold bag piece in half, right side inward. Join long edges on basting line at both ends, leaving open space between for zipper. Fold seam allowances of open space flat on each side and baste in place. Following package directions, stitch zipper in place, to make a tube.

To close ends of tube for each bag, cut four circles from red fabric and two circles from batting, using compass: 2½″ diameter for small bag, 3¾″ diameter for medium bag, and 5½″ diameter for large bag. For each end, place two circles together, wrong sides facing, and insert batting between. Baste together, then zigzag-stitch all around edges, to finish. With zipper almost closed and lining of bag facing out, stitch a circle in place at each end of tube. Unzip bag, turn right side out, and zip closed.

Handles: Cut two green strips for each bag: 1¼″ × 6″ for small bag, 1¾″ × 12″ for medium bag, and 2″ × 20″ for large bag. Fold each strip in half lengthwise, right side inward, and stitch ¼″ from long edges. Turn strip right side out and press. Attach strips to top of bag, one on each side of zipper, by folding in a corner of each end to make a triangular point; slip-stitch pointed end to bag, along points of red patches at end. ☆

Patchwork Pot Holders

shown on page 226

EQUIPMENT: Paper for patterns. Pencil. Ruler. Scissors. Thin, stiff cardboard. Sewing needle. Straight pins.

MATERIALS: Preshrunk pieces of tightly woven cotton fabric in solid colors and small prints as shown or as desired. White and matching sewing thread. Outing flannel for padding. White plastic ring 1″ diameter for each.

DIRECTIONS

Read General Directions for Quilting and How To Appliqué (see Contents). Enlarge patterns for designs by copying on paper ruled in 1″ squares; complete quarter-patterns indicated by long dash lines. The fine dash lines indicate quilting lines. Make a separate cardboard pattern for each part of design. Cut patches according to General Directions for Quilting, marking on wrong side of fabric and adding ¼″ seam allowance all around.

Following patterns, sew all the pieces together to complete pot holder tops. For back, cut one complete pot holder shape of matching or contrasting solid-color fabric, adding ¼″ all around for seam allowance. For each pot holder, cut two thicknesses of flannel the shape of pot holder but ⅜″ smaller all around. Baste both layers of flannel to top to hold in place. Place the top and back together with right sides facing; sew together along edges, making ¼″ seams and leaving an opening large enough to turn. Turn to right side; turn edges of opening in ¼″; sew closed.

Each pot holder is quilted through all thicknesses with white sewing thread. Quilt along all fine dash lines (see pattern) and along some seams. Remove basting stitches. Sew ring to back near edge of pot holder.

Pattern A: Cut 5¼″ square for piece 1 of white; cut pieces 2 of white; cut piece 3 of orange; cut pieces 4 of five different printed fabrics; cut pieces 5 of gold color. Sew the pieces of the fan shape together; pin in place on piece 1; turn under edges of points and sew in place. Sew pieces 2 in place. Cut ¾″-wide bias strips of solid-color fabric and sew together with ¼″ seams to make one strip long enough to fit all around pot holder. With right sides facing and making ⅛″ seam, sew one edge all around pot holder top. Turn binding to back. Turn raw edge under ⅛″ and slip-stitch to fabric, mitering corners (see Contents for directions).

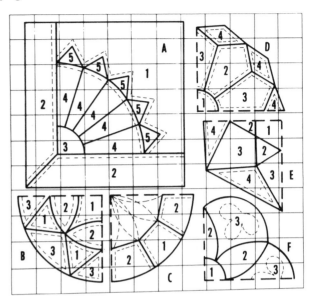

Pattern B: Cut pieces 1 of orange; cut pieces 2 of yellow; cut pieces 3 of white. For ruffled edge, cut a strip of orange on the bias about 45″ long, 1½″ wide. With right sides facing, sew ends together, making ¼″ seam. Turn to right side. Fold in half lengthwise; press. Gather raw edge to fit circumference of pot holder. Before sewing top and back together, baste ruffle around top with right sides facing and raw edges out. When sewing top and back together, make sure ruffle is on inside.

Pattern C: Cut piece 1 of red; cut pieces 2 of red-and-white checked gingham; cut piece 3 of white. Sew together and quilt by machine, using red thread for center design, white for other quilting. Make ruffled edge as for Pattern B.

Pattern D: Cut piece 1 of bright pink; cut piece 2 of dark green; cut pieces 3 of pink print; cut pieces 4 of white.

Pattern E: Cut piece 1 of blue; cut pieces 2 of orange; cut pieces 3 of blue-yellow print; cut pieces 4 of yellow.

Pattern F: Cut piece 1 of orange; cut pieces 2 of yellow; cut pieces 3 of aqua. Quilt through all thicknesses only along seams. Stitch along short dash lines through top fabric only and draw thread up tightly for puckered effect. ☆

Appliance Covers

shown on page 227

SIZES: Soup, 13″ × 9½″. Bread, 9″ × 12″. Flour, 14″ × 18″. Milk, 8″ × 17″.

EQUIPMENT: Colored pencil. Pencil. Ruler. Paper for pattern. Thin, stiff cardboard. Scissors. Dressmaker's tracing (carbon) paper. Tailor's chalk. Iron. Sewing needle. Sewing machine with zigzag attachment. Compass.

MATERIALS: Soft cotton or cotton-blend fabric 45″ wide: Soup: red, yellow, ¼ yd. each; gray, ⅝ yd. Milk: white, 1 yd.; blue, green, ¼ yd. each. Flour: yellow, ¾ yd.; orange, 1 yd. Bread: white, ¾ yd.; red, ⅛ yd. Batting. Thread to match.

GENERAL DIRECTIONS

Trace actual-size patterns for letter appliques. See Contents for How to Appliqué. Following appliqué directions and individual directions, cut pieces from fabric and batting; dimensions given include seam allowances.

Machine-appliqué letters and other pieces as directed to one (outer) main piece, using sewing thread to match appliqués. Baste batting to wrong side of outer piece. Place outer and inner pieces together, right sides facing, and stitch around edges with ½″ seams, leaving a 4″ opening for turning where necessary. Grade seams, trimming batting close to stitching. Turn piece to right side through opening; slip-stitch opening closed. Using thread to match background, topstitch through all layers around letters and where directed, working from center of piece out to edges. Assemble Cover as directed; slip-stitch butted edges together.

"Bread" Toaster Cover

Cut two pieces from white fabric and one piece from batting, each 19″ × 23″. Cut two sets of letters, BREAD, from red fabric. Place one white (outer) piece with long edges horizontal. Appliqué one set of letters 3½″ from nearest long edge, centered between sides. Turn piece around so that opposite long edge is nearest and appliqué second set of letters in same manner.

Baste batting to wrong side of outer piece. Place both white pieces together, right sides facing, and stitch around edges, leaving opening. Trim seams, turn, close opening. Topstitch around letters and all around edges. Fold piece in half, appliquéd side inward and bottom edges matching; slip-stitch each side together. Turn to right side. Fold in half, now with the two side seams centered. Fold down top of facing side seam for 3″, forming a triangle; slip-stitch lower edges of triangle in place. Repeat for other side of Cover.

"Soup" Can Opener Cover

From gray fabric, cut piece 27¾″ × 11¾″; using compass, cut two round pieces 9″ in diameter. From red and yellow fabric, cut one piece 5½″ × 27¾″ and one set of letters, SOUP, from each. From batting cut piece 10¾″ × 27″ and round piece 8″ in diameter.

To make can label, place red and yellow pieces together, right sides facing, and stitch on one long edge. Trim seam; press open. Place piece with long edges horizontal and appliqué SOUP to each section, 1″ from seam and centered between sides; place red on yellow and yellow on red. Turn edges of label under ¼″ all around; press.

To make side of can, place rectangular gray piece flat, wrong side up. Center rectangular batting over gray piece; turn fabric edges over batting, sides first, then top and bottom, mitering corners (see Contents for directions); baste in place. Pin can label right side up over batting and fabric edges, centering so there is a ⅜″ gray margin at top and bottom and a ⅛″ margin at sides. Topstitch along seam joining red and yellow section, around letters and around edges of label. With inner side facing out, slip-stitch side edges together to form a tube.

To make top of can, baste batting to wrong side of a gray circle. Right sides facing, stitch gray pieces together, leaving opening. Trim seam, turn, close opening. With compass, mark circles in center of top 3½″ and 6½″ in diameter. Topstitch on lines. Slip-stitch top to side around upper edge. Turn Cover to right side.

"Flour" Mixer Cover

From yellow fabric, cut two pieces 19½″ × 22″ and two sets of letters, FLOUR. From orange fabric, cut two pieces 19½″ × 22″, two pieces 8″ × 12½″, and four strips 1½″ × 22″. Cut two pieces batting 19½″ × 22″. Fold each 8″ × 12½″ orange piece in half twice and round off unfolded corner, for long oval.

Place each yellow (outer) piece with 22″ edges at top and bottom; appliqué the following to each: an orange strip 1½″ from bottom edge and a strip 3½″ from top edge; an orange oval centered lengthwise between the strips; the letters FLOUR centered lengthwise on the oval. Baste batting to yellow pieces. Sew yellow pieces together, right sides facing, along one side. Sew orange pieces together in same manner. Place orange and yellow pieces together, right sides facing, and stitch together at top and bottom, leaving ½″ free at each end. Trim seams. Turn to right side. Topstitch around letters,

(Continued on page 233)

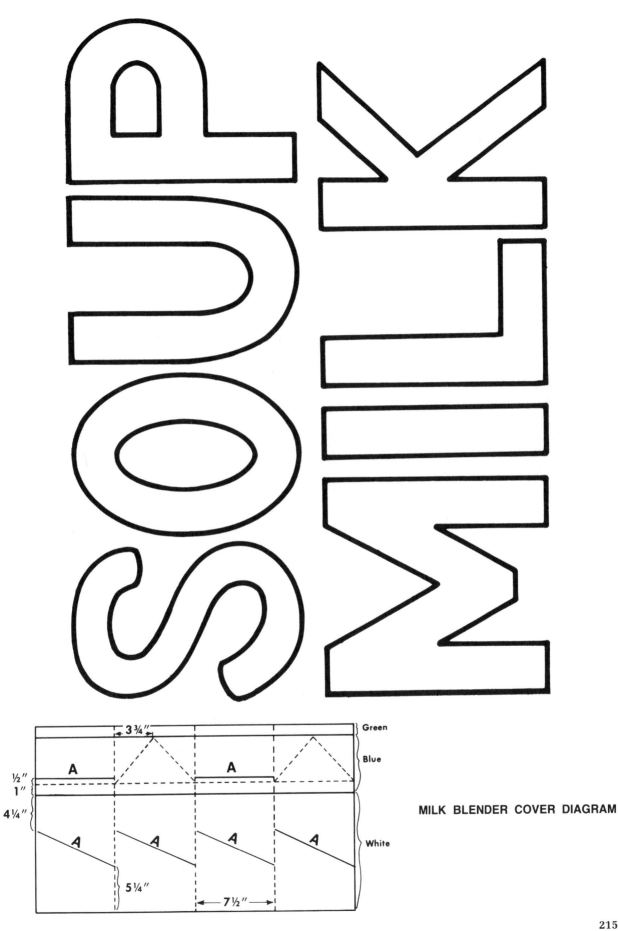

SOUP
MILK

MILK BLENDER COVER DIAGRAM

Green
Blue
White

3 ¾ ″
A   A
½ ″
1 ″
4 ¼ ″
A   A   A   A
5 ¼ ″
7 ½ ″

216

"SCULPT"
A FABRIC
WREATH

Delicate fruits and leaves in
trapunto quilting, puffed and gently shaded,
form an elegant wreath.
For Trapunto Wreath directions, see Contents.

Trapunto lotus blossoms on jacket and tote
really stand out. Just stitch and stuff. Machine-quilt lines
on reversible vest the easy way—follow inside ticking
fabric lines. For Lotus Blossom Jacket & Tote
and Mandarin-Collared Vest directions, see Contents.

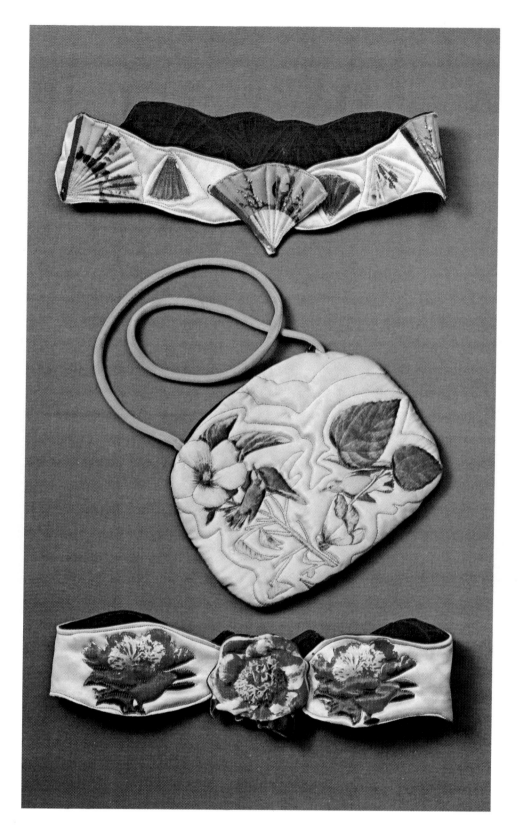

Make these soft and satiny accessories with appliqués or printed fabric, then quilt. We give directions and patterns for Fan Belt. Make Peony Belt in the same way, but cut motifs from a flowery print. Bird and Flower Bag is made either way. For Fan Belt and Bird and Flower Bag directions, see Contents.

(Designed by Susan Zucker.)

Tree leaves are "pressed" forever in calico, with machine stitching for bright country charm. Place mats are padded with batting. Each color-cued napkin has a one-corner motif of the fruit of the tree.
For Leafy Luncheon Set directions, see Contents.

(Luncheon Set by Cathy Ulasewicz.)

Tea cozies are just the thing for keeping tea (or coffee) piping hot. Make Ruffled, Cottage, or Tabby Tea Cozies with the simplest machine and hand sewing. Pretty place mats for any table are in the traditional Dresden Plate quilt pattern. Stitch tiny floral prints together into a kaleidoscope of colors.
For Ruffled Clamshell, Cottage, and Tabby Tea Cozies and Dresden Place Mat directions, see Contents.

Portable games for adults and a fun gift for baby all use patch-work in clever ways. Backgammon and checker-boards made of fabric are easy to pack up and take along to a faraway beach or a nearby back yard. Both projects are easy to quilt because all the stitching is done in straight lines.

The patchwork-covered baby album is a cinch to make and a one-of-a-kind gift for proud new parents. Colorful scraps will do nicely both for patches and appliqués—and you can make the present more personal by substituting a name and some special motifs. For Backgammon Board, Patchwork Checker-board, and Baby Album Cover directions, see Contents.

Vests are top-layer fashion—for the man in your life, too. If he's the romantic type, make him a luxurious vest to wear at home or for holiday parties. Patchwork can be a "crazy quilt" of festive fabrics or made mostly from squares, as shown.

Invest a little time in making a vest that's different from any other in the world! How? By creating your own material from strips of fabric you simply stitch together and quilt. The vest is then cut from this quilted patchwork—and because you did it all, the result is really unique. For Patchwork Star Vest and Striped Patchwork Vest directions, see Contents.

Shades of blue are worked on 18-mesh-to-the-inch canvas for a needlepoint eyeglass case, made in DMC six-strand floss with a twisted cord frame. Four-Way Bag is machine stitched, with wide self-ribbon and clear handles for versatility. 9″ wide. Machine-quilted bag can be carried as clutch or as shoulder bag. For Needlepoint Eyeglass Case, Four-Way Bag, and Art Deco Bag directions, see Contents.

Three patchwork totes that
fit inside each other for storage
or as separate compartments
are great for those on the go.
They are soft and flexible
to pack easily in small spaces,
each zips closed to keep things in
their place, and all three are easy to make.
Red and green are perfect for
a holiday theme, but any colors would
look super. Bags are made from
pieced cotton fabric and then
padded and lined. For Patchwork Totes
directions, see Contents.

(Designed by Margaret Pennington.)

Patterns in patchwork are stitched into bright little
pot holders. Start quilting with these easy projects,
then go on to make a quilt in the same patterns.
For Patchwork Pot Holders directions, see Contents.

Inspiration from the pantry! Our colorful "soft sculptures" are appliance cover-ups! *Milk*: for blender; *Flour*: for mixer; *Soup*: for can opener; *Bread*: for toaster. Sew them up "puffy" with a soft layer of batting. Great bazaar idea! For Appliance Covers directions, see Contents.

Trapunto quilting creates a softly "sculpted" effect in this unusual pillow. The face design is machine-stitched through two layers of fabric—sheer off-white on top, darker underneath for shadows—and then is given dimension with puff padding. Size of pillow is approximately 18″ across. For Face Pillow directions, see Contents.

(By Elsa Brown.)

Pillow portraits, straight from the pages of Louisa May Alcott's endearing classic, are appliquéd, then "framed" in the softest lace. Make just one—or all—of the four (but start with your little girl's favorite!), then stitch a gingham "title page" to complete the pillow set. Each dress is carefully detailed, and the names are stitched on in simple hand embroidery. Portrait pillows are 18″ × 18″, without lace. The title page pillow is 21″ × 14″. For Little Women Pillows directions, see Contents.

These patchwork fashions are white, bright, and just right for summer! The vest has patch pockets that are quick and easy to piece with white and bright stripes. Pair it with a 15½" quilted clutch bag.

The button-up jacket has an attention-getting cross variation of the log cabin on the back. The shoulder bag is pieced in a traditional pineapple design. For Patchwork Fashions directions, see Contents.

(Designed by Margaret Pennington.)

Jolly Santa came down the chimney and decided to stay on—as a mantel screen! Big, bold pieces of felt are machine-appliquéd to a sheath of red; wood stretchers, 28″ × 12″, are used to form the three-panel screen. For Santa Screen directions, see Contents.

(Continued from page 214)

ovals, and strips and at top and bottom edges, leaving ends free as before. Turn piece to orange side. Pin side edges of orange piece back ½"; stitch side edges of yellow piece together. Trim. Unpin orange edges, fold under, and slip-stitch together. Slip-stitch top edges together. Placing piece flat, fold in top corners for 3" toward center; slip-stitch in place along top edge. Turn Cover to right side.

"Milk" Blender Cover

From white fabric, cut piece 12½" × 31" and piece 18½" × 31". From blue fabric, cut piece 6" × 31". From green fabric, cut piece 2" × 31" and six sets of letters, MILK. Cut batting piece 18½" × 31".

To assemble outer piece, sew smaller white piece to blue piece on long edges, then green piece to other long edge of blue piece. Outer piece should measure 18½" × 31", same as larger white (inner) piece.

Lay outer piece flat, right side up and with long edges at top and bottom. Using ruler and tailor's chalk, lightly mark ½" seam allowance at sides, then mark off the 30" area between seam lines into four sections 7½" wide; see vertical dash lines on Diagram. Mark another line 1" above the seam joining white and blue piece, as shown. Mark a triangle above this line in second and fourth marked sections. Mark six A lines as shown.

Appliqué the word MILK to each A line with bottom of letters resting on line. Baste batting to wrong side of outer piece. Place inner and outer pieces with right sides together; stitch along top and bottom edges, leaving ½" free at each end. Trim seams and turn piece to right side. Topstitch on marked (dash) lines, around letters, and along top and bottom edges, leaving ends free as before. Fold piece along horizontal topstitching on blue sections and stitch through all layers close to fold, making a ridge; unfold.

Turn piece to inner side. Pin side edges of inner piece back ½"; stitch side edges of outer piece together. Trim. Unpin inner edges, fold under, and slip-stitch together. Slip-stitch top edges of cover together. Placing piece flat, fold in top corners until they meet at center; slip-stitch in place along top edge. Turn Cover to right side. At top, slip-stitch green side edges together. ☆

Face Pillow

shown on page 228

SIZE: Approximately 18" across.

EQUIPMENT: Tracing paper for pattern. Pencil. Ruler. Dressmaker's carbon paper in a light color. Tracing wheel or sharp, hard pencil. Sewing needle. Knitting needle or other suitable instrument for poking stuffing into small areas. Sharp, pointed embroidery scissors.

MATERIALS: Fabric: Off-white sheer fabric (you should be able to see your hand through it), such as organdy, polyester-cotton voile, or a polyester curtain fabric, two pieces each about 20" × 24"; black, dark brown, or dark gray loosely woven lightweight fabric, such as voile, one piece about 20" × 24"; white opaque fabric, such as cotton, one piece 20" × 24"; unbleached muslin for inner pillow, two pieces 20" × 24". Mercerized sewing thread in beige. Fiberfill for stuffing.

DIRECTIONS

Enlarge pattern by copying on tracing paper ruled in 2" squares. Darken outlines to make them clearly visible on other side of tracing paper. Place paper pattern, centered, face down on wrong side of dark fabric with carbon paper in between. Using tracing wheel or sharp, hard pencil, transfer pattern outlines, including outer (seam) line, to fabric.

Pin dark fabric, marked side up, to wrong side of one sheer fabric piece; make sure raw edges of both pieces are even. Baste together, with basting radiating outward from center. Using beige thread in both bobbin and needle of machine, stitch along all outlines of design using long machine stitch. Check bobbin and needle thread tension, since bobbin side will be right side of pillow. To allow for greater maneuverability, use darning stitch if machine provides for it. When stitching is completed, remove basting. Bring bobbin thread ends to wrong side of work and knot with needle thread ends close to fabric to secure beginning and end of stitching. Trim thread ends.

To stuff, place work with dark fabric uppermost. Slit dark fabric only in center of areas to be stuffed. Stuff eyelids, pupils, mouth, and neck detail firmly, using knitting needle to poke small amounts of stuffing through the slits. Stuff remaining areas loosely in same manner (except for areas between hair and seam line, which remain unstuffed). Check front of pillow occasionally to make sure stuffing is evenly distributed. In loosely stuffed areas and around features a dark shadow will form when the dark fabric backing shows through. When stuffing is completed, sew slits closed.

To assemble pillow, place stuffed side of pillow right side up on flat surface. Place remaining sheer fabric piece on top, and then opaque fabric on top of that; make sure raw edges are even. Pin, baste, and stitch all layers together along seam line; leave 8″ opening at bottom of pillow. Trim seam to $\frac{1}{2}$″; turn to right side.

To make inner pillow, transfer seam line of pattern to center of one muslin piece. Stitch the two muslin pieces together along seam line, leaving 4″ opening. Trim seam to $\frac{1}{2}$″, and turn pillow right side out. Stuff inner pillow until plump, but not overstuffed. Fold edges of opening $\frac{1}{2}$″ to inside; slip-stitch closed. Insert inner pillow in outer pillow. Slip-stitch outer pillow closed.

Note: If desired, small areas may be stuffed as follows: Thread a large-eye blunt needle (such as a bodkin needle) with heavy, fluffy white yarn. Poke a hole with the needle through the dark fabric at one end of area to be stuffed. Draw the needle between the lines of stitching and between the two fabric layers. Bring needle out at other end of area. Trim yarn ends close to fabric. Stuff remaining large areas as directed. ☆

Little Women Pillows

shown on page 229

SIZE: Portrait of pillows, 18″ square. Little Women pillow, 21″ × 14″.

EQUIPMENT: Pencil. Ruler. Yardstick. Paper for patterns. Scissors. Dressmaker's tracing (carbon) paper. Tailor's chalk. Dry ball-point pen. Sewing, embroidery, and quilting needles. Quilting frame (optional). Sewing machine. Embroidery hoop (optional). Small dessert plate.

MATERIALS: Closely woven cotton fabric 45″ wide in coordinating colors: green gingham, $\frac{1}{2}$ yd. for Little Women pillow; floral print, $1\frac{1}{2}$ yds. for Portrait pillows; chocolate brown, $2\frac{1}{2}$ yds. for all pillows. Scraps of printed, striped, checked, and solid fabrics for appliqués (including 18″ square of each main dress fabric). Ecru Cluny lace 3″ wide, $10\frac{1}{2}$ yds. Six-strand embroidery floss in blue, brown, and dark shades of dress and hair colors for outlining. Sewing thread to match fabrics. Batting. Polyester fiberfill.

GENERAL DIRECTIONS

Using sharp pencil, draw lines across patterns, connecting grid lines. Enlarge patterns by copying on paper ruled in 2″ squares for Little Women pillow and 4″ squares for Portrait pillows. Heavy lines on pattern indicate appliqués, fine lines embroidery, and dotted lines quilting.

For pillow fronts, cut one 15″ × 22″ rectangle from green gingham for Little Women pillow and four 19″ squares from floral print for Portrait pillows. Transfer patterns to right side of pillow fronts. Transfer individual appliqué pieces from patterns to fabrics to match quilt and cut out; make border appliqués for Portrait pillows, using pattern for Little Women pillow but changing the length of the sides to 18″.

Using dressmaker's carbon and dry ball-point pen, transfer individual appliqué pieces to fabrics following illustration. Referring to How to Appliqué (see Contents), cut out pieces. Preparing pieces for hand appliqué one by one as you work, pin, baste, and slip-stitch pieces in place; begin by centering border appliqués on pillow fronts so that $\frac{1}{2}$″ of background fabric extends beyond border for seam allowance. Replace patterns and transfer fine and dotted lines to pillow fronts.

Using three strands of floss in needle, embroider fine lines in brown, except Meg's dress and Beth's blue eyes. Using darker shade of each color, outline hair and costumes in outline stitch and embroider fine lines of Meg's dress.

Quilting: Read General Directions for Quilting (see Contents). Using yardstick and tailor's chalk, mark cross-hatched quilting lines on background, drawing parallel diagonal lines $\frac{3}{4}''$ apart, sloping to the right across entire area; repeat, sloping lines to the left. For each pillow, cut a same-size piece of muslin and batting and baste to wrong side. Starting at center and working outward in all directions, quilt along all marked quilting lines and around appliqués close to the seams. From brown fabric, cut one $15'' \times 22''$ rectangle and four $19''$ squares for pillow backs. Pair pillow backs with same-size pillow fronts and stitch together with right sides facing and edges even, and making $\frac{1}{2}''$ seams; round corners and leave $4''$ opening for turning. Turn and stuff with fiberfill. Turn in open edges and slip-stitch closed. Cut lace into five $75''$ strips. Pin lace to pillow edges as shown, taking small tucks at corners to add fullness. Overlap lace ends where they meet, trim off excess; turn raw edges $\frac{1}{4}''$ to wrong side; slip-stitch. Slip-stitch lace to pillow edges all around. ☆

236

Patchwork Fashions

shown on pages 230–231

EQUIPMENT: Pencil. Ruler. Graph paper. Thin, stiff cardboard. All-purpose glue. Straight pins. Sewing needle. Sewing machine.

MATERIALS: Unbleached muslin 45″ wide: See individual directions for amounts. Polished cotton, red, blue, purple, yellow, green, olive: small amounts for each project. Batting. Fiberfill for stuffing. Sewing thread to match muslin.

GENERAL DIRECTIONS

The patchwork for each item is a variation of the "log cabin" pattern. (Exception: The Shoulder Bag is worked in "pineapple" pattern.) Patchwork and quilting are done simultaneously in one or several blocks for each item, using the same general method throughout.

Make patterns for patch pieces: For each item, see diagram, which represents one block. Following dimensions shown, mark actual-size outline of block on graph paper, using ruler and sharp pencil. Beginning at outer edge of block with longest strip and working toward center, mark strips and squares as shown on diagram, making each strip 1¼″ wide. When all are marked, label shaded parts with letter shown. Glue graph paper design to cardboard; let dry. Cut on marked lines for individual patterns.

Cut out patch pieces; press fabrics smooth. Place patterns with the grain, on wrong side of fabric, leaving at least ½″ between pieces; mark around pattern with sharp pencil held at an outward angle. Place lettered patterns on polished cotton, following Color Key; Place unlettered patterns on muslin. Cut out each piece ¼″ beyond marked lines, for seam allowance.

Block: For each block, cut two pieces of muslin and one of batting, all ½″ wider and longer than dimensions given on diagram. On one muslin piece, mark two corner-to-corner diagonal lines, crossing in center, unless otherwise directed. Place batting between muslin pieces, with marked side facing up, and baste layers together.

Sew strips and squares to prepared block, starting in center and working in circular fashion out to edges. Place center square, right side up, on marked muslin, matching corners of square to marked lines; do not turn under seam allowance. Baste in place ¼″ from edges. Place smallest adjacent piece right side down over center piece, matching raw edges on adjacent side. On this side, machine-stitch through all thicknesses on marked seamline of second piece. Turn second piece to right side and press lightly in place. Place another adjacent piece (same size or next largest) right side down over first two pieces, matching raw edges on adjacent side; stitch, turn, and press as before.

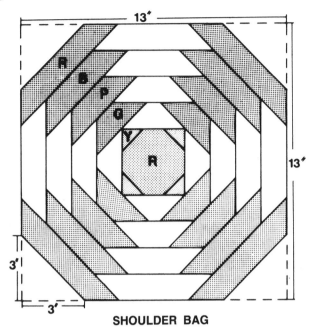

SHOULDER BAG

Continue adding pieces in this manner, always overlapping one piece with another, until all are used and muslin block is covered; raw edges of outer pieces and block should match. To finish block, machine-baste all around ⅛″ from edges. Complete item as directed.

Shoulder Bag

SIZE: 13″ square.
MATERIAL: Muslin, ¾ yd.

DIRECTIONS

Read General Directions. To work "pineapple" patchwork, use the same stitch, fold, and press method as for "log cabin" patchwork. Make patterns, following diagram: Mark a 13″ square on graph paper. Mark four horizontal lines 1¼″ apart and parallel to bottom edge. Repeat on other three sides. On each edge of block, mark a point 3″ from each corner. Cut a 1¼″-wide strip from cardboard, about 8″ long. Use strip to mark diagonals as shown, starting in corners at marked points. For Y triangles in center, mark points 1″ from corners. Shade diagonal pieces as shown, erasing overlapped lines, and label. Make cardboard patterns (discard corner pieces) and cut out patch pieces for one block, following General Directions. Prepare muslin block (13½″ square), then sew on pieces: Begin in center with R octagon (centering each diagonal edge on a diagonal guideline), then add Y triangles, the four smallest muslin pieces, the four G pieces, etc., until all pieces are used. Cut away corners of block to match raw edges of R strips. Finish edges.

Using block as pattern, cut three pieces from muslin. Place one muslin piece over block, right sides facing, and stitch around ¼" from edges, leaving 4" opening for turning. Turn to right side, fold in raw edges and slip-stitch opening closed, for front of bag. For back of bag, baste batting to wrong side of a muslin piece; trim to shape. With right sides facing, pin remaining muslin piece to padded muslin piece and stitch as for front of bag, turning and closing. Slip-stitch back of bag to front along five edges, forming a pouch.

For strap, cut two 36" × 2½" strips from red fabric. Pin and baste layer of batting to wrong side of one piece. With right sides facing, pin and stitch straps together all around, leaving opening for turning. Turn to right side, fold raw edges to inside, and slip-stitch opening closed. Insert each end of strap 1" into bag at sides; stitch securely in place.

Clutch Bag

SIZE: 7¾" × 15½".
MATERIALS: Muslin, 1⅓ yds. Velcro fastener, 15½".

DIRECTIONS

Read General Directions. Make patterns and cut patch pieces for one block, as directed. Prepare muslin block (16" square), then sew on pieces: Begin in center with R square, then add Y strips, shortest muslin strips, G strips, next muslin strips, etc., until all pieces are added. Finish edges.

Cut three pieces from muslin and one from batting, all 16" square. Place one muslin piece over block, right sides facing, and stitch around ¼" from edges, leaving 4" opening for turning. Turn to right side, fold in raw edges, and slip-stitch opening closed, for outer bag piece. For inner bag piece,

baste batting to wrong side of a muslin piece. With right sides facing, pin remaining muslin piece to padded muslin piece and stitch as for outside of bag, turning and closing. Place inner and outer bag pieces together, muslin sides facing, and slip-stitch around all four edges. Place bag piece so that red strips are at top and bottom, then turn piece to muslin side. Slip-stitch Velcro fasteners across top and bottom, behind red strips. Fold piece in half, fastening top edges; slip-stitch sides together, to form pouch.

Vest

MATERIALS: McCall's pattern 6876, View A (minus sleeves) or other, similar pattern. Muslin, twice the yardage noted on pattern. Lining fabric, ¾ yd., less than yardage noted on pattern.

DIRECTIONS

For patchwork pockets, read General Directions. Cut ¼-yd. piece from muslin. Make patterns following diagram: Draw block 6⅞" square on graph paper, then mark strips ⅝" wide. Cut patch pieces for two identical blocks, as directed. Prepare two muslin blocks (each 7⅜" square), then sew on pieces: For each, begin in center with muslin square; add Y square, then Y strip; continue around in clockwise direction until all pieces are added. Finish edges of the blocks. For linings, cut two pieces 7⅜" square. With right sides facing and making ¼" seams, stitch a lining piece to each block, leaving opening at bottom G edge for turning. Turn to right side, fold in raw edges, and slip-stitch opening closed, for pocket. Set pockets aside.

For vest, cut remaining length of muslin in half crosswise.

To quilt fabric, use tailor's chalk to mark lines 1" apart on right side of one piece of muslin, running from selvage to selvage. Place marked muslin

COLOR KEY
R—RED
B—BLUE
P—PURPLE
G—GREEN
Y—YELLOW

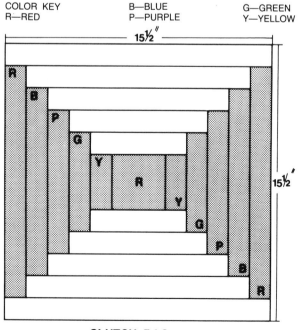

CLUTCH BAG

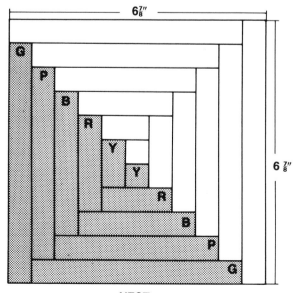

VEST

on work surface, wrong side up; place batting over muslin, then position plain muslin fabric over batting; pin and baste together all around edges and diagonally to prevent shifting. Machine-stitch along each marked line with matching thread; backstitch at beginning and end of each row.

Using purchased pattern, cut out pieces for View A from quilted fabric and lining, omitting sleeves and pockets; do not follow cutting layout of pattern, but place vest pieces lengthwise along quilting lines; do not double fabric, but cut out each piece singly, reversing pattern as needed.

Assemble vest, following steps 1 through 4 in purchased pattern directions; substitute patchwork pockets for regular pockets, positioning as shown in illustration. Omit step 5. Sew lining pieces together, following Step 6 and omitting any reference to sleeves. Machine-stitch $\frac{5}{8}''$ away from edge of each armhole on lining. Clip into stitching and press to wrong side. Fold raw edges of quilted armholes $\frac{5}{8}''$ to inside, making $\frac{1}{4}''$ clips as necessary. When sewing lining into vest, slip-stitch pressed edge of lining to quilted fabric, covering raw edges. Complete vest, following pattern.

Jacket

MATERIALS: McCall's pattern 6854, View A, or other, similar pattern. Muslin, twice the yardage noted on pattern, plus $\frac{3}{4}$ yd. Lining fabric, yardage noted on pattern. Shoulder pads. Hook and eye or button for closure.

DIRECTIONS

For patchwork inset, read General Directions. Cut $\frac{1}{2}$-yd. piece from muslin. To make patterns, follow diagram. Draw block $6\frac{1}{4}'' \times 6\frac{7}{8}''$ on paper, mark strips $\frac{5}{8}''$ wide. (**Note:** If making jacket in size 6 or 8, draw block $5'' \times 5\frac{1}{2}''$ square and mark strips $\frac{1}{2}''$ wide.) Cut patch pieces for four identical blocks, as directed. Prepare four muslin blocks (each $7\frac{3}{8}'' \times 6\frac{3}{4}''$), omitting diagonal guidelines; mark vertical and horizontal lines, crossing in center, as guides. Sew on pieces: For each block, begin just above center with muslin square, aligning bottom seamline (not raw edge) of piece with horizontal guideline and centering piece widthwise. Add Y square, then shortest horizontal muslin strip, then shortest vertical muslin strip. Continue around in coun-

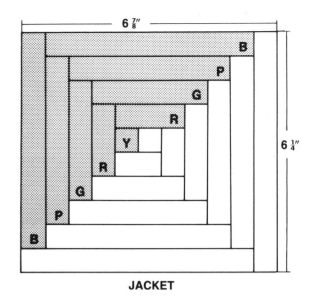

JACKET

terclockwise direction until all pieces are added. Finish edges of the four blocks.

To assemble inset, lay out the blocks as shown in illustration, placing longer edges vertically. Cut joining strips from yellow fabric, two $1\frac{1}{8}'' \times 6\frac{3}{4}''$ and one $1\frac{1}{8}'' \times 14\frac{7}{8}''$ (measurements include seam allowance). Sew a short strip between blocks in each vertical row, then sew long strip between vertical rows, making $\frac{1}{4}''$ seams. Inset should measure $13\frac{5}{8}''$ wide $\times$ $14\frac{7}{8}''$ long.

For jacket, cut remaining length of muslin in half crosswise. Place one piece with selvages at sides. Mark a line across piece 7'' above and parallel to bottom raw edge. Mark a rectangle $12\frac{5}{8}''$ wide $\times$ $13\frac{7}{8}''$ long centered on line, then extend top line of rectangle out to selvages: Cut fabric apart along marked lines; discard marked rectangle. With right sides facing and making $\frac{1}{4}''$ seams, sew sections on either side of discarded rectangle to pieced inset; sew upper and lower sections back in place. Press seams open.

Quilt fabric as directed for Vest, marking lines on piece with inset. Cut away batting and second muslin layer directly beneath inset, if desired.

Pin purchased patterns in place, centering back pattern over inset; do not follow cutting layout of pattern, but keep quilted fabric in single layer, cutting out each piece separately; reverse patterns as needed. Complete jacket, following pattern directions. ☆

Santa Screen

shown on page 232

EQUIPMENT: Paper for pattern. Pencil. Ruler. Tracing paper. Dressmaker's tracing (carbon) paper. Dry ball-point pen or hard-lead pencil. Reg-

ular and pinking shears. Straight pins. Sewing machine. Sewing needle.

MATERIALS: Felt: red 72'' wide, $1\frac{1}{8}$ yds.; white 36''

wide, ¾ yd.; bright green, 5″ × 16″; pink, 9″ × 13″; chartreuse and black, each 9″ × 12″. Sewing thread to match felt. Three pairs of wooden canvas stretchers, each 28″ × 12″.

DIRECTIONS

Enlarge pattern by copying on paper ruled in 2″ squares. Make separate tracing of each part of pattern (heavy outlined areas); dash lines indicate where pieces are overlapped; finer lines indicate stitching lines. Double vertical lines marked with Xs are stitching lines to divide panel. Make face pattern a little larger than area shown.

Using traced patterns, cut beard-moustache piece, hatband-pompon piece, and two eyebrows of white felt. Cut face of pink felt. Cut hat of bright green felt. Cut leaves of chartreuse felt. Cut nose and berries of red felt. Cut eyes of black felt.

With dressmaker's carbon and pen or hard-lead pencil, transfer all stitching lines to beard, hat, and leaves as indicated.

For background, cut two pieces of red felt each 29¾″ × 38⅝″ with pinking shears. Lay one red piece out on flat surface and pin the Santa pieces in place, hat flush with top edge and beard sides about 1½″ from side edges. Baste in place.

On machine, stitch along edges of each piece 1/16″ in from cut edges. Stitch along all marked stitching lines. Pin the two red felt pieces together with stitched Santa on top. Stitch across top and down each side ¼″ from edges. Stitch down vertical double lines on each side as indicated by Xs.

To make paneled screen, assemble stretchers into three frames 28″ × 12″; insert a stretcher frame into each section. Fold excess fabric at bottom over frame and baste, so frames may be removed. ☆

Basic How To's

How to Enlarge a Pattern

Count the number of boxes on the pattern that go across and the number that go down. On a large piece of paper, draw the same number of boxes across and down, but make the boxes the size given in the directions. For example, if the directions say, "Enlarge pattern on paper ruled in 1″ squares," make the sides of each box equal to 1″.

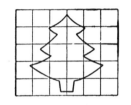

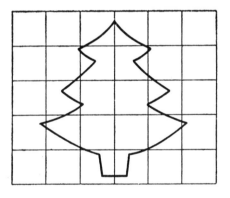

Start with the first row of boxes on the pattern. On our pattern here, there are no design lines in the first box, and none in the second. But in the third box, there is a curved line. The line goes from the bottom left corner up to a little more than halfway on the right side of the box. Draw a line that does the same thing on your piece of paper. Box by box, copy the design lines to look the same way on your paper that they do on the pattern.

How to Appliqué

Choose a fabric that is closely woven and firm enough so a clean edge results when the pieces are cut. Press fabric smooth. There are two methods of transferring appliqué patterns to fabric.

TO TRANSFER LARGE DESIGNS

Mark a pattern on paper for each appliqué piece; do not cut out. Place paper on right side of fabric, inserting dressmaker's tracing (carbon) paper between fabric and pattern. Go over lines of pattern with tracing wheel or a dry ball-point pen, to transfer design. Remove pattern and carbon. Mark a second outline $\frac{1}{4}$″ outside design outline. Appliqué as directed.

TO TRANSFER SMALL DESIGNS

For each motif, make a cardboard pattern: Trace design; do not cut out. Glue tracing paper to thin, stiff cardboard and let dry; cut along traced line. Place cardboard pattern on right side of fabric. Holding sharp, hard pencil at an outward angle (light-colored pencil on dark fabric and dark pencil on light fabric), mark around pattern. When marking several pieces on the same fabric, leave at least $\frac{1}{2}$″ between pieces. Mark a second outline $\frac{1}{4}$″ outside design outline. Appliqué as directed.

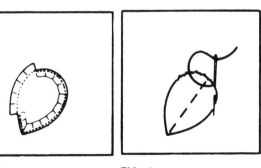

FIG. 1

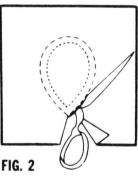

FIG. 2

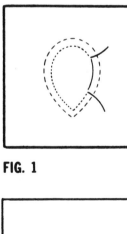

FIG. 3

FIG. 4

241

TO APPLIQUÉ BY HAND

Using matching thread and small stitches, machine-stitch all around design outline, as shown in *Fig. 1.* This makes edge easier to turn and neater in appearance. Cut out appliqué on the outside line, as in *Fig. 2.* For a smooth edge, clip into seam allowance at curved edges and corners, then turn seam allowance to back, just inside stitching as shown in *Fig. 3,* and press. (*Note:* You may prefer to place some pieces so they overlap the extended seam allowance of adjacent pieces; study overall design before turning under all seam allowances.) Pin and baste the appliqués on the background, the underneath pieces first, and slip-stitch in place with tiny stitches. See *Fig. 4.*

TO APPLIQUÉ BY MACHINE

Cut out appliqués on outside lines. Pin and baste appliqués in place; do not turn under excess fabric. Straight-stitch around appliqués on marked lines. Trim away excess fabric to $\frac{1}{8}''$ or less from straight stitching. Set sewing machine for close zigzag stitch as directed ($\frac{1}{4}''$ wide or less). Zigzag around appliqués, covering straight stitching and excess fabric.

How to Complete a Half Pattern

Trace the picture twice using two pieces of tracing paper. Turn one of the tracings over to the back. Tape the two pictures together with the dash lines touching.

Put another piece of tracing paper on top, and trace the whole picture.

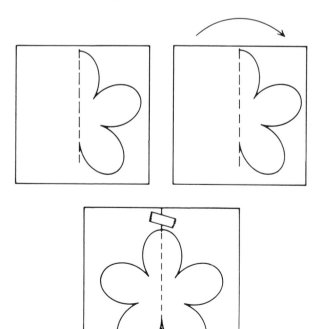

How to Make a Pompon

Cut two cardboard disks desired size of pompon; cut $\frac{1}{4}''$ hole in center of both. Thread needle with two strands of yarn. Place disks together; cover with yarn, working through holes. Slip scissors between disks; cut all strands at outside edge. Draw strand of yarn down between disks and wind several times very tightly around yarn; knot, leaving ends for attaching pompon. Remove cardboard disks and fluff out pompon.

How to Make a Tassel

Wind yarn around cardboard cut to size of tassel desired, winding it 20 or more times around, depending on thickness of yarn and plumpness of tassel required. Tie strands tightly together around top as shown, leaving at least 3″ ends on ties; clip other end of strands. Wrap piece of yarn tightly around strands a few times, about $\frac{1}{2}''$ or 1″ below top, then tie and knot. Trim the ends of the tassel to a uniform length.

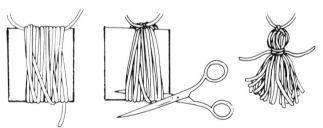

How to Make a Twisted Cord

Method requires two people. Tie one end of yarn around pencil. Loop yarn over center of second pencil, back to and around first, and back to second, making as many strands between pencils as needed for the thickness of cord; knot end to pencil. Length of yarn between pencils should be three times length of cord desired. Each person holds yarn just below pencil with one hand and twists pencil with other hand, keeping yarn taut. When yarn begins to kink, catch center over doorknob or back of chair. Bring pencils together for one person to hold, while other grasps center of yarn, sliding hand down and releasing at short intervals, letting yarn twist evenly to form cord.

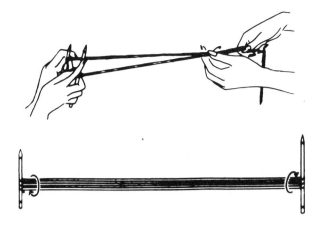

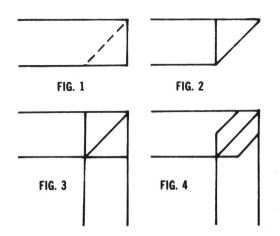

How to Make Mitered Corners

Place two strips together, one on top of the other, right sides facing. Fold end up so that end is flush with top edge (see Figs. 1 and 2); press. Unfold and stitch along fold $\frac{1}{4}''$ in from each edge. Open out strips (see Fig. 3) Trim seam; press open (see Fig. 4). Repeat with two remaining strips. Then miter the corners of each pair of strips together to form a "frame," or border, of fabric. Press $\frac{1}{4}''$ of both inner and outer edges to wrong side for hem; baste. Finish following individual instructions.

How To Draw a Star

Stars are a very popular motif in applique, patchwork and quilting designs, but how to create one if you can't find one to trace in the size you want is usually a puzzle. At the far right is a half-pattern of a five-pointed star in eight different sizes which we hope you'll find useful. Trace the half-pattern in the size you need and reverse it to make a complete pattern. If you need a larger size star, use the following method illustrated by the diagrams at the right.

DIAGRAM 1: Draw a circle of the same diameter as the diameter of the size star desired. Using a compass or dividers, find and mark five equidistant points A on the circumference of the circle. Draw connecting lines between the points to form a pentagon.

DIAGRAM 2: Using the same center-point of the circle, draw a smaller circle inside the first one, as shown in diagram. The distance between the inner circle and the outer circle determines the depth of the points of the star. Mark center-point on each side of the pentagon; these points are marked B in diagram. From each point B, draw a line through center of circle to the opposite point A.

DIAGRAM 3: To form the star, draw lines from points A on the pentagon to where the dividing lines intersect the inner circle. These points are marked C on the diagram.

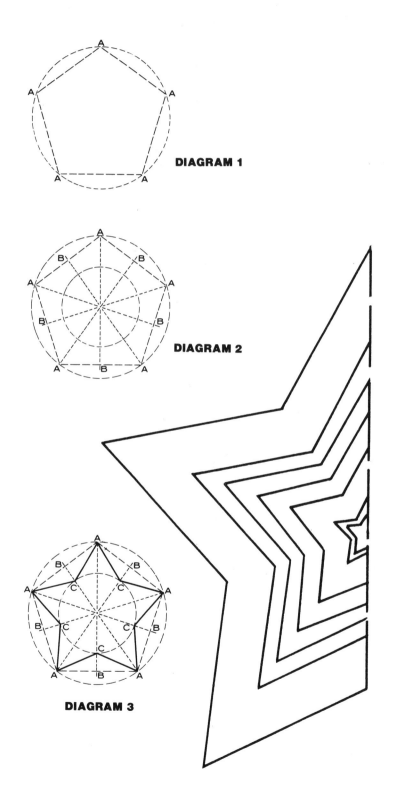

DIAGRAM 1

DIAGRAM 2

DIAGRAM 3

What Size Quilt?

39" x 75"	54" x 75"	60" x 80"	78" x 75"	76" x 80"	78" x 80"	72" x 84"

Size is the very first thing you must consider when you decide to make a quilt—or any bedcover. But bed and mattress sizes have become very confusing as larger and larger beds have become popular. So the first step is to accurately measure the mattress on the bed in question. Here is a list of so-called "standard" sizes, but even these vary depending upon individual mattress manufacturers, and a difference of one inch or more in either direction is not unusual. Except for the crib size, the comparative sizes are shown graphically above.

CRIB SIZE . . . . 27" x 48"	DUAL SIZE . . . . 78" x 75"
TWIN SIZE . . . . 39" x 75"	KING SIZE . . . . 76" x 80"
FULL SIZE . . . . 54" x 75"	DUAL KING . . . . 78" x 80"
QUEEN SIZE . . . . 60" x 80"	CALIFORNIA KING . . 72" x 84"

After determining the correct measurements of the mattress, you must decide just what type of quilt you want. A complete bedspread covers the pillows and reaches all the way to the floor on three sides, or at least far enough down to cover the top of a dust ruffle. So add twice the amount of overhang to the width of the mattress, plus seam allowances if necessary; to the length, add the amount of overhang at the foot and about 20" to cover the pillows. Then add 4" or 5" all around to make up for what will be taken up in quilting if the "quilt" is actually quilted.

A coverlet, used primarily for extra warmth at night, doesn't have to cover the pillows, but should have enough overhang on three sides to allow for what is taken up by anyone sleeping under it. So add the desired overhang, plus seam allowances if necessary, and quilting allowance all around if coverlet is to be quilted.

The usual size for throws, used for napping and such, is about 48" x 72". The same size is comfortable for automobile and stadium blankets. Always add seam allowance if seams are involved and quilting allowance if the cover is actually quilted.

The Finishing Touch

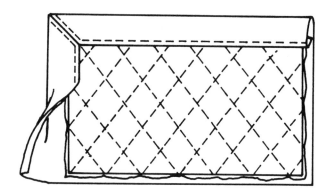

BINDING WITH THE BACKING:

The fabric used for the backing can also be used to bind the edges of the quilt and makes a very effective finish, especially if the backing is in a contrasting color. However, this method should be planned ahead so the backing can be cut large enough to allow for as wide a binding as desired; in most cases, the wider it is, the more effective it will be. (This does not apply to quilts which already have a border as part of the quilt top design.)

To finish a quilt in this manner, trim the extending backing to an even width on all sides. Turn the raw edges in 1/2" and press in place. Bring the backing around the edges to the top of the quilt and pin and then baste in a straight, even line. Stitching along the fold, slip-stitch the edge of the backing to the quilt top, or sew in place by machine. The same method can be used in reverse to cover the edges with the fabric used for the quilt top.

BINDING A REVERSIBLE QUILT:

The simplest method of finishing the edges of a quilt is frequently used, and gives a finished look to both sides. The first step is to make sure the quilt top and the backing are equally and evenly trimmed on all four sides of the quilt. Turn the edges of both in the same amount and press. Then simply stitch the edges together, either by hand or by machine. It's a good idea to stitch two rows around all four sides of the quilt for a secure finish. Or you may prefer to add some decorative stitching that will look well on both sides. Don't think this method of finishing is only for reversible quilts; it's fast, easy and effective for almost any type of quilt.

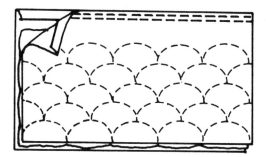

After the three layers of a quilt have been put together, the edges can be finished in several different ways. Here, four favorite methods.

APPLYING A BIAS BINDING:

Finishing a quilt with a bias binding is an easy and effective method and allows considerable choice from the standpoint of design. You can make your own bias binding from any fabric you choose, provided it's sturdy enough to withstand the wear the edges of a quilt will be subjected to. So the color and texture of the binding, as well as whether it's printed or plain, is up to you. Bias binding can also be purchased in a fairly wide range of colors and in several different widths. It's even possible to find it in attractive calico-type prints, although the choice here is somewhat limited.

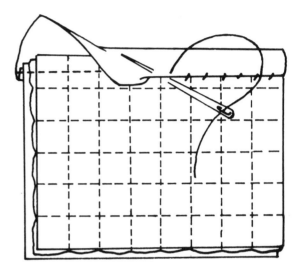

The binding can be applied from either the back or the front. To finish it with hand-stitching on the right side of the quilt, place it against the backing side with the right sides facing and the raw edges together. Baste in place and stitch 1/4" from the edges by hand or machine, using small running stitches either way. Wrap the binding around the edges onto the quilt top, turn under the remaining 1/4" raw edge, and stitch the turned edge to the quilt top, using a slip-stitch, overcasting, or small running stitches. The final stitching can also be done by machine.

BINDING A SCALLOPED EDGE:

The design of many quilts is based on circular motifs, such as the popular "Rob Peter to Pay Paul" pattern. A very attractive finish is achieved by simply outlining the outer row of half-circles with satin or zigzag stitching. The top and backing are then trimmed away together, close to the outer edge of the stitching, leaving a neatly scalloped edge.

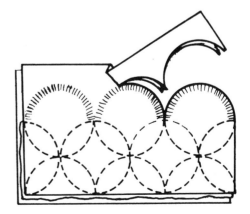

General Directions for
Needlepoint

To start a needlepoint piece, mark outline of design in center of canvas, leaving at least a 2″ margin around all sides. Bind all raw edges of canvas with masking tape. Find center of canvas by basting a line from center of one edge to the center of opposite edge, being careful to follow a row of spaces. Then baste another line from center of third edge to center of fourth edge. Basting threads will cross at center.

Designs are represented in chart form. Each square on chart represents one mesh on canvas. Each symbol on chart represents a different yarn color.

Cut yarn strands in 18″ lengths. When starting first strands, leave 1″ of yarn on back of canvas and cover it as the work proceeds; your first few stitches will anchor it in place. To end strand or begin a new one, run yarn under a few stitches on back of work; do not make knots. Keep yarn tension firm and even. Stitching tends to twist the working yarn; untwist from time to time, letting yarn, needle hang straight down to unwind. If a mistake is made, run needle under stitch and snip yarn with sharp scissors; do not reuse yarn.

Continental Stitch: Start at upper right corner and work across to left; turn work upside down for return row. Always work horizontal rows from right to left; see Details 1 and 2. Work vertical continental stitch from top to bottom; see Details 3 and 4.

Brick Stitch: This is a series of straight stitches taken over two or four canvas threads and laid in staggered rows like bricks. Work rows left to right, then right to left. The first row skips a space between each stitch, then this space is used by the second row of stitches. In this way the rows interlock.

Mosaic Stitch: This is a series of long and short stitches, worked on the diagonal. For short stitch, follow directions for Continental Stitch. Long stitch skips a space, making a stitch twice the length of short stitch. Interlock rows by placing short stitches under long stitches and long stitches under short stitches. In covering a specific area, such as square shown here, spaces around the edge are filled in with Continental Stitch.

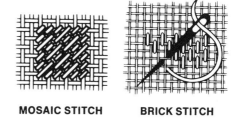

MOSAIC STITCH   **BRICK STITCH**

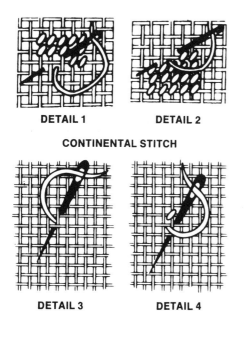

DETAIL 1   DETAIL 2

CONTINENTAL STITCH

DETAIL 3   DETAIL 4

Blocking: Cover a softwood surface with brown paper. Mark canvas outline and center lines on paper for guide, using T- or carpenter's square. Place needlepoint right side down over guide; if piece has raised stitches, block right side up. Match center markings on canvas with those on paper. Fasten canvas to wood with rustproof tacks spaced about $\frac{1}{2}$″ to $\frac{3}{4}$″ apart along edge of canvas; stretch canvas to match guide. Wet thoroughly with cold water; let dry. If piece is badly warped, block again. (*Note:* If yarn is not colorfast, dissolve salt in cold water. Block with salt water.)

To mount a needlepoint picture: After canvas has been blocked, stretch it over heavy cardboard or plywood cut the same size as worked portion of canvas. Use heavy cardboard for small pictures

(12″ or less); for larger pictures and panels, use ¼″ plywood. If cardboard is used, hold canvas in place with pins pushed through canvas into edge of cardboard. If canvas is mounted on plywood, use carpet tacks. Push pins or tacks only part way into edge; check needlepoint to make sure rows of stitches are straight. Carefully hammer in pins or tacks the rest of the way. Using a large-eyed needle and heavy thread, lace loose edges of canvas over back of cardboard or plywood to hold taut; lace across width, then length of picture.

HOW TO MAKE PILLOW

To Make Knife-Edge Pillow: After blocking needlepoint, trim canvas margins to ½″. Cut backing fabric same size as trimmed canvas. If cording is desired follow directions below to make fabric welting. With right sides facing, stitch back piece and needlepoint front together, making ½″ seams; leave opening in center of one side. Clip corners of canvas diagonally; seal canvas edges with glue. Whipstitch canvas margins to back of needlepoint; turn pillow right side out. Following directions below, make inner pillow; insert through opening. Add stuffing to corners if necessary. Turn raw edges ½″ to inside; slip-stitch.

To Make Welting: Welting, a fabric-covered cord used as an edging, is a tailored way to finish a pillow. (It is also called piping or cording.) Welting can be purchased ready-made in some upholstery supply stores or can be easily made. To make welting, measure the perimeter of pillow, then cut 1½″-wide bias strips from fabric to this length, piec-

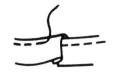

JOINING WELTING ENDS

ing strips and adding 1″ for seam allowance. Center welting cord along bias strip on the wrong side; fold strip over cord so that edges are aligned. Using zipper-foot attachment, maching-stitch along strip with needle as close to cord as possible.

To attach welting to pillow cover, begin in the middle of one side; pin welting to right side of cover so that raw edges of welting line up with raw edges of pillow cover; overlap ends 1″. Starting 2″ from beginning of welting, stitch all around to 2″ from end of welting. Snip out 1″ of cord from overlapping end. Turn under ½″ of extra fabric and, butting ends of cord, fit it over the start of welting (see diagram). Finish stitching welting to pillow cover.

To Make Inner Pillow: Cut two pieces of muslin the same shape as pillow, but measuring 2″ wider and longer than finished pillow size. (For very firmly stuffed pillow, cut muslin 3″ wider and longer than pillow size.) Stitch pieces together with right sides facing and making ½″ seams; leave 3″ opening in center of one side. Clip seams diagonally at corners; turn to right side. Stuff inner pillow until full. Turn raw edges of opening ½″ to inside; slip-stitch opening closed.

Stitch Details

BLANKET STITCH

CHAIN STITCH

OUTLINE STITCH

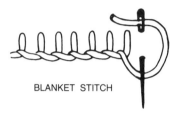

LAZY DAISY

BUTTONHOLE STITCH

FRENCH KNOT

SATIN STITCH

STRAIGHT STITCH

RUNNING STITCH

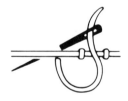

COUCHING

LAID STITCH

SPLIT STITCH

STAR STITCH

250

Glossary

ALBUM QUILT: A quilt composed of individual blocks made and signed by different people and then joined. Sometimes the quilt has a theme; more frequently, the designs and colors are left up to the individual contributors and so are unrelated. Usually presented as a token of esteem to a distinguished person.

AMISH QUILTING: A distinctive quilting style indigenous to the Amish people of Pennsylvania. Typically of pieced patchwork in a simple geometric pattern, and always in subtle, off-beat color combinations.

AUTOGRAPH QUILT: A quilt made up of individual blocks, each featuring one or more signatures written in India ink. Sometimes the signatures are embroidered over the ink.

BACKING: The material used for the bottom layer of a quilt. Usually made of lengths of plain or printed fabric stitched together to match the size of the quilt top.

BATTING: A fluffy polyester or cotton filler in sheet form used as padding between the top and backing of a quilt. Also called wadding or stuffing, it is usually pre-cut to quilt size and sold in cellophane bags, sometimes under the manufacturer's own trademarked name.

BLOCK: The design unit or pattern of a quilt, usually a square, rectangle or hexagon, repeated many times to form the quilt top. A block may be any size, containing any number of pieces; it may also be the entire quilt top if the design is large and non-repetitive.

BORDER: The outer margin that surrounds the major part of a quilt and serves as a frame. It may be made of plain, pieced or appliqued material and is often quilted in elaborate patterns.

COVERLET: A quilt large enough to cover the top of a bed without covering the pillows, and with less overhang than a full-size bedspread. Used primarily for extra warmth at night.

CRAZY QUILT: A quilt composed of irregularly-shaped scraps of fabric fitted together in random fashion like a puzzle; attached by stitching one to another or to a foundation block. The patches are usually of luxurious fabrics such as satin and velvet, and the joining seams are usually embellished with embroidery. Crazy quilting is actually a form of patchwork.

FOUNDATION BLOCK: A piece of muslin or other soft fabric that serves as the base or foundation for joining pieces or patches. Used in pressed quilts and crazy quilts.

FRIENDSHIP QUILT: Similar to the album quilt and the autograph quilt in purpose, the friendship quilt was usually presented to mark a special occasion or celebrate a marriage. Each block was made by a relative, neighbor or friend, who all met to set them together. Also presented to families moving away from a community, especially when "going West."

LATTICE STRIPS: Strips of solid-color fabric from two to four inches wide used to outline and join pieced blocks in a quilt. They form a grid which contrasts with the blocks; to prevent the grid from dominating the pattern, squares of another contrasting color are sometimes set into the intersections.

MARKING: The process of drawing a quilting design on the top or backing of a quilt before quilting it, or of tracing or transferring an embroidery design to fabric before stitching it. Also tracing around the outline of a template to produce a design.

MITER: The method of turning a 90° angle in a straight strip of fabric or binding at corner, or of joining two strips, with a 45° diagonal seam from the inner angle of the strip to the outer corner. The excess fabric under the seam is trimmed away and the seam allowance pressed flat. This is a desirable way to finish the four outside corners of a quilt.

MOLA: The quilt blocks and panels worked in reverse applique by the San Blas Indians and other natives of Central and South America.

PATCHWORK: The pieced-together fabric produced by stitching small pieces of material together, often in a geometric design of squares, rectangles, triangles, diamonds, hexagons or other shapes. The joinings can also be in a random pattern, as in crazy quilting. In a patchwork quilt, the small pieces of fabric are stitched together into blocks, which are then joined.

PIECE: Used as a verb, to stitch together pieces of fabric, usually to form a design block.

PRESSED QUILT: A quilt made by joining pieces or patches to a foundation block with running stitches. After the first piece, each subsequent piece is placed face down on the preceding piece; with right sides together, a seam is stitched through both patches and the foundation block. The new piece is turned to the right side and "pressed" down, ready for the next piece to be joined in the same manner.

PUTTING IN: A colloquial term meaning the attachment of a quilt to a quilting frame by securing the top and bottom edges to two muslin-covered poles. The portions of the quilt above and below the area being quilted are rolled on the poles.

QUILT: A bedcover, usually made of three layers called the top, padding and backing which are stitched together in a decorative design. Also a bedcover made of patchwork or applique which may or may not also be quilted.

QUILTING FRAME: A wooden stretcher made of four strips of wood which holds the quilt taut while it is being quilted by hand.

REVERSE APPLIQUE: An applique technique in which pieces of fabric are cut away instead of being added to form a design. Several layers of fabric, each a different color, are basted together. A design is cut *out* of the top layer, revealing the next layer of fabric. A smaller design is cut out of the second layer, revealing the third layer; and so on. The cut edges are turned under and hemmed.

SCRAP QUILT: A quilt made up of leftover scraps of fabric, regardless of color or pattern, and joined in random fashion. They utilize any scraps available and have an unplanned effect which is pleasing and entirely different than quilts with a very regular design.

SETTING TOGETHER: Sewing quilted, appliqued or patched blocks together to form the quilt top. This is done either by sewing the blocks to each other or to plain blocks or lattice strips that separate them and are part of the design.

TEMPLATE: An actual-size pattern of plastic, metal or cardboard used as a guide for cutting accurate, identically-sized fabric patches.

TIED QUILTING: A quick, easy method of attaching the three layers of a quilt together, also called tufting. The layers are joined by individual, double stitches, the loose ends of which are then tied together in a knot or a bow.

TRAPUNTO: A term sometimes used for corded quilting, in which two layers of fabric are stitched together by parallel rows of running stitch or backstitch that form channels. A cord is drawn through the channels and between the top and bottom layers, forming a design which stands out in high relief.

Index

Page numbers in **bold** indicate illustrations.